WITHDRAWN

The Narrative Secret
of Flannery O'Connor

The Narrative Secret
of Flannery O'Connor

The Trickster as Interpreter

Ruthann Knechel Johansen

THE UNIVERSITY OF ALABAMA PRESS

TUSCALOOSA AND LONDON

Copyright © 1994
The University of Alabama Press
Tuscaloosa, Alabama 35487-0380
All rights reserved
Manufactured in the United States of America

designed by Paula C. Dennis

∞

The paper on which this book is printed meets the minimum requirements
of American National Standard for Information Science-Permanence of
Paper for Printed Library Materials, ANSI Z39.48-1984.

Library of Congress Cataloging-in-Publication Data

Johansen, Ruthann Knechel, 1942–
The narrative secret of Flannery O'Connor : the trickster as
interpreter / Ruthann Knechel Johansen.
p.   cm.
Includes bibliographical references and index.
ISBN 0-8173-0717-6
1. O'Connor, Flannery—Technique.   2. Point of view (Literature)
3. Trickster in literature.   4. Narration (Rhetoric)   I. Title.
PS3565.C57Z717   1994
813'.54—dc20   93-30919

British Library Cataloguing-in-Publication Data available

to the Beloved

The hint half guessed, the gift half understood, is Incarnation.
—T. S. Eliot, "The Dry Salvages,"
Four Quartets

Contents

Acknowledgments

The seeds of this book, like Flannery O'Connor's seeds in the blood, were planted long before I began the project. Family, friends, and numerous mentors have nurtured these seeds, shaping the way I see and hear the world. Hoping they will know their importance to me, I gratefully acknowledge their examples and influence.

Several people deserve specific recognition because they have assisted in bringing this work to flower. Early in my studies, Merrill Skaggs encouraged me to read Flannery O'Connor. A reluctant reader at first, I now consider Professor Skaggs's suggestion a demonstration of her insight into Flannery O'Connor and into my imaginative proclivities. As adviser and friend she read early drafts critically, offering encouragement through her own knowledge, invaluable comment on style, and prudent correctives to excessive claims. John Warner's abiding goodwill toward the project and his knowledge of myth as well as literature have been especially helpful. The scholarly efforts of Giles Gunn to bring religion and literature studies to bear on each other have contributed conceptually to this study. Many students, colleagues, and friends have helped me refine these interpretations through our discussions. I am especially grateful to Sandra Winicur whose close reading of the manuscript helped sharpen the focus of this analysis. The meticulous care and patience with which Sherry Reichold and Cheryl Reed of the University of Notre Dame Faculty Steno Pool typed countless revisions into the computer have made preparation of the text pleasant. Finally, to my husband Robert and our children Erik and Sonia, who believed the project was still worth doing after it had been lying at rest for five years while we focused our attention on the survival and rehabilitation of our son and brother, I offer my deepest thanks. Their faith and hope through unexpected reverses remind me that the holy is manifest in our concrete lives and in each lived moment.

Permissions

For permission to quote from published works, acknowledgment is made to the following:

Excerpts from *Everything That Rises Must Converge* by Flannery O'Connor. Copyright © 1965 by the Estate of Mary Flannery O'Connor. Reprinted by permission of Farrar, Straus and Giroux, Inc.

Excerpts from *Mystery and Manners* by Flannery O'Connor. Copyright © 1969 by the Estate of Mary Flannery O'Connor. Reprinted by permission of Farrar, Straus and Giroux, Inc.

Excerpts from *The Violent Bear It Away* by Flannery O'Connor. Copyright © 1960 by Flannery O'Connor. Copyright renewed © 1988 by Regina O'Connor. Reprinted by permission of Farrar, Straus and Giroux, Inc.

Excerpts from "A Good Man Is Hard to Find," "The River," "The Life You Save May be Your Own," "A Late Encounter with the Enemy," and "A Stroke of Good Fortune" from *A Good Man Is Hard to Find and Other Stories,* copyright 1953 by Flannery O'Connor and renewed 1981 by Regina O'Connor, reprinted by permission of Harcourt Brace & Company.

Excerpts from "A Temple of the Holy Ghost," and "The Displaced Person" from *A Good Man Is Hard to Find and Other Stories,* copyright 1954 by Flannery O'Connor and renewed 1982 by Regina O'Connor, reprinted by permission of Harcourt Brace & Company.

Excerpts from "A Circle in the Fire" from *A Good Man Is Hard To Find and Other Stories,* copyright 1948 by Flannery O'Connor and renewed 1976 by Mrs. Edward F. O'Connor, reprinted by permission of Harcourt Brace & Company.

Excerpts from "Good Country People" from *A Good Man Is Hard to Find and Other Stories,* copyright 1955 by Flannery O'Connor and renewed 1983 by Regina O'Connor, reprinted by permission of Harcourt Brace & Company.

Excerpts from "The Artificial Nigger" from *A Good Man Is Hard to Find and Other Stories,* copyright 1955 by Flannery O'Connor and renewed 1983 by Regina O'Connor, reprinted by permission of Harcourt Brace & Company.

Excerpt from "The Dry Salvages" in *Four Quartets,* copyright 1943 by T. S. Eliot and renewed 1971 by Esme Valerie Eliot, reprinted by permission of Harcourt Brace & Company.

Excerpts from *The Great Code: The Bible and Literature,* copyright © 1982, 1981 by Northrop Frye, reprinted by permission of Harcourt Brace & Company.

Reprinted by permission of the publishers and the Trustees of Amherst College from *The Poems of Emily Dickinson,* Thomas H. Johnson, ed., Cambridge, Mass.: The Belknap Press of Harvard University Press, Copyright © 1951, 1955, 1979, 1983 by the President and Fellows of Harvard College.

Reprinted with permission of Macmillan Publishing Company from *Collected Poems of W. B. Yeats.* Copyright 1924 by Macmillan Publishing Company, renewed 1952 by Bertha Georgie Yeats.

Reprinted with permission of the University of California Press from Robert Pelton, *Trickster in West Africa: A Study of Mythic Irony and Sacred Delight.* Copyright © 1980 The Regents of the University of California.

Introduction

A wonderful enigma in American literature, Flannery
O'Connor has been variously labeled a regional, Christian, grotesque, gothic writer. Her fiction, which defies
labeling, continues to generate strong reactions since its
earliest publication. Despite an enthusiastic readership
and hundreds of critical books and essays published on
her works during the thirty years since her early death,
the surprise with which the decision to publish *Flannery
O'Connor: Collected Works* in the prestigious Library of
America was initially greeted bespeaks our uncertainty
about the stature of this American author who wrote
intensely in an abbreviated life. To seek explanation for
this uncertainty represents not simply an effort to understand one author but rather the culture and literary
environment that produced her, yet continues to find
her puzzling. Ironically O'Connor's major contribution
to American literature may be also a principal cause of
her ambiguous stature, a paradox she would have found
bittersweet.

One associates O'Connor with American writers whose
contributions have long been unquestioned. In her understanding of the darkness of the human heart and the
problem of evil, she belongs with Poe and Hawthorne.
Her psychological perceptivity and intricate structures
suggest Henry James, an indebtedness she was eager to
acknowledge. Although she was by her own confession a
believing Catholic uninterested in metaphysical speculation, her stories leave in the reader's mind metaphysical

riddles that recall the restless and daring spirit of Melville. Her humor and familiarity with confidence men remind one of Twain. Like Faulkner, she is a southerner whose stories are rooted in the South. Yet, though she resembles each of these writers in some way, she writes in her own unique voice.

Flannery O'Connor's religious faith and artistic vision were informed by sympathies more familiar to medieval saints and intellectuals than to twentieth-century readers. Portraying southern fundamentalists, she creates a troubled human community in a religious framework when most fiction of our century depicts the isolated, alienated hero in a religionless age. From these religious fanatics she weaves dramatic tales that, when they do not simply shock or baffle, illustrate the continuous need for what sociologists have identified in other cultures as some process of renewal within a community or what Christians call redemption. In an age that eschews the communal, the frantic search for sentimental connections makes apparent this need for restoration, which O'Connor believed she could present clearly only through extravagance. In their brutality and force, in their dependence on rituals and their demands for sacrifice, these tales of God-intoxicated southerners seem primitive. Yet they are inhabited by characters disturbingly and comically familiar to contemporary nihilist and devout alike. Despite their tenacious roots in a concrete southern environment, these tales ironically suggest a reality more comprehensive than their specific circumstances and more mysterious than many modern readers are accustomed to. O'Connor writes about a South that resides in all of us. Her works force us toward parts of our personal and collective histories we thought we had shed long ago.

O'Connor's importance is not simply that she brings many strands of America's literary and social heritage together in her narrowly focused works, but more significantly that her fiction exposes and judges the human spirit, which engages in a relentless quest for freedom while resisting it at every turn. Although we may ignore or deny common religious and mythological roots, O'Connor shows us those which have grounded both American longing and rebellion. Like the biblical narratives before them, O'Connor's tales tell us about bondage that comes from broken covenants. Simultaneously bold in their extravagances to make an unbelieving age "see" and subtle in their density—which arises from the artist's deft weaving of sounds and hues of other times and tales—O'Connor's stories confront us with the startling possibility that we may as easily be that which we abhor as

that which we affirm.[1] This possibility not only extends and complicates our sense of ourselves but also gives O'Connor's fiction its artistic
and religious power, a power that challenges traditional critical approaches and exceeds glib doctrinal interpretations.

As readers we may at one moment be irresistibly fascinated by such
power and at another defend ourselves against its hold on our imaginations. Invariably our interpretation reflects both tendencies: imaginatively attracted by the vitality of O'Connor's stories we move
paradoxically to reduce and grasp something we call their "meaning,"
most frequently expressed either in theological explanations or more
recently in postmodern revisions of O'Connor's beliefs. Flannery
O'Connor's letters reveal that during her lifetime she answered thousands of questions about her stories, her religious convictions, and the
relationship between the two. Criticism of her work through the 1970s
generally focused either on the theological significance of the religious themes embedded in the stories or on the identifying characteristics of her literary style that might link her to precursors such as
regional or gothic writers. Despite the growing number of sophisticated analyses of O'Connor's literary techniques outlined by Frederick
Crews,[2] the connections between those and her religious concerns
warrant more examination, as John R. May acknowledged in 1986.[3]
Recent books like Frederick Asals's *Flannery O'Connor: The Imagination
of Extremity* (1982), Louise Westling's *Sacred Groves and Ravaged Gardens*
(1985), Marshall Bruce Gentry's *Flannery O'Connor's Religion of the Grotesque* (1986), Edward Kessler's *Flannery O'Connor and the Language of
Apocalypse* (1986), building on Marion Montgomery's earlier insightful
criticism,[4] and Robert Brinkmeyer's *The Art and Vision of Flannery
O'Connor* (1989), illustrate the helpful shift from thematic content to
form.[5]

Clearly indebted to such studies as well as to Robert Coles's interpretation of the social significance of O'Connor's religion and art,[6] the
present study also reflects the concerns of the rich and diverse field of
narratology. Indeed, this book springs from my search for a way to
explore the means through which O'Connor's fiction produced in me
the experience of encounter or dialogue. Frustrated by the limits of
thematic interpretations and the parochialism of scholarship confined
within narrow disciplinary lines, I found myself sketching the design
or layout of O'Connor's stories. These sketches were not limited to
location or organization of events but included gestures and actions as
well. Only recently did I recognize what I must have understood intu-

itively as a child when at recess my friends and I scraped elaborate architectural plans for castles and communities into the playground gravel of my Civil War hospital-turned-elementary-school with carefully selected sticks: that we learn things perhaps first through our bodies. Through the sketches of her narrative landscapes, I reversed O'Connor's artistic journey from cartoonist to storyteller and in the process was claimed more and more firmly by the mysteries of her texts.

In two-dimensional form of lines and shapes, my sketches of individual story events revealed the following recurring characteristics: geography and architectural forms ground or dominate every story; borders, boundaries, and claims on territory preoccupy characters; circular patterns of action connect individual parts of stories, are repeated across stories, and sometimes reflect cyclic movements in nature; tendencies toward constriction and expansion in characters' attitudes or behavior create opposing pressures in the narratives; strange figures enter and leave the thresholds of the story world enigmatically; linguistic patterns of speech, resonances of ancient myths, biblical stories or religious beliefs, and characters' gestures and actions often mirror the shapes and condition of the physical terrain. These sketches provided a visual map of the landscape that includes more than geography or architecture as a backdrop for action. By extending my definition of landscape, they provided a bridge between the narrative structures of O'Connor's stories and the history of ideas. As I worked on these "maps" I became more and more convinced that there were elements of ritual activity embodied, not simply narrated, in O'Connor's fiction that threatened the reader. And I wanted to investigate these operations.

Increasingly such explorations led me to the disciplines of anthropology, folklore, linguistics, and narratology, which share some common interest in language and story structures. The works of Claude Lévi-Strauss, Roland Barthes, Gérard Genette, and J. Frank Kermode offered my imagination fruitful ways to investigate the resonances of other stories present in O'Connor's fiction.[7] During the early 1980s as I was writing preliminary drafts of this work, Paul Ricoeur published his magnificent three-volume *Time and Narrative;* Tzvetan Todorov continued to write about the relationship between literary structures and style and between symbolism and interpretation; and Susan Lanser perceptively explicated a poetics and philosophy of point of view in *The Narrative Act.*[8] In biblical studies during this same period, scholars like David Gunn, Adele Berlin, Meir Sternberg, and Mieke Bal were investigating the poetics and rhetoric of biblical narrative. Although I worked independently of such writers, I have found, upon reading their works, some of my own intuitions and approaches to narratives confirmed; others have been challenged or broadened further by their ideas. I mention them here to draw the outlines of an intellectual landscape in which this work of O'Connor criticism belongs.

Using some of the resources of narratology, previous Flannery O'Connor criticism, and reader response criticism, this present work, then, expands and deepens the collective critical effort in two ways: by appearing at first glance to complicate the analysis with an examination of narrative structures and by illustrating indirectly how previous criticism has anticipated such analysis and synthesis. The goal of complication is of course illumination of two central puzzling questions: Why does such a slim collection of fiction continue to arouse profoundly with praise or rebellion? Why do the stories haunt their readers and lead them back not only into the story environments again and again but also toward something elusive, "the gift half guessed."

Stories that evoke such reactions lead to more stories. This interpretation offers a storylike exploration, or a poetic gloss, of O'Connor's narrative landscape. I have wanted to offer a fresh reading rooted in O'Connor's stories themselves without a lot of detours into other critical texts; therefore, where my work touches on or differs from others' interpretations, I so indicate usually in the endnotes. As a Vermeer or Rembrandt painting yields insight into a world without "imposing a rigid schema upon it," so may this interpretation lead us to "a sudden sense of revelation, with poignant recognition."[9] By inviting readers to reconsider O'Connor's stories through their structures and actions, where the absence of the sacred seems so apparent in the characters' conscious conditions that hope in its presence is aroused in and projected from both the unconsciousness of the characters and the engaged mind and heart of the reader, I encourage an interplay among O'Connor's narrative structures, the human psyche, and the institutions and traditions of our collective history—particularly including ancient myths and legends. Such an approach is supported by the publication of *Mystery and Manners* (1957) and later *The Habit of Being* (1979), which disclosed O'Connor's preoccupation with making the Incarnation real for an unbelieving age. For the writer who believes "that our life is and will remain essentially mysterious . . . his kind of fiction will always be pushing its own limits outward toward the limits of mystery, because for this kind of writer, the meaning of a story does not begin except at a depth where adequate motivation and adequate psychology and the various determinations have been exhausted."[10]

The critic interested in the works of such writers turns irresistibly to the means—the narrative structures and techniques—through which the artist pushes at boundaries and defies or reshapes conventions on which traditional literary notions and religious institutions presumably rely. Asals's analysis of O'Connor's "imagination of extremity" moves in the direction of this investigation of the means through which she hoped to embody the Incarnation.[11] By examining her dependence on dualities, doubled characters, either/or choices, and incongruities, Asals makes abundantly clear her psychological-spiritual links to Judeo-Christian mythology rooted in and sustaining a dualistic world view. Coles traces similar linkages sociologically as well as metaphysically. This book, rather than reanalyzing O'Connor's theological-metaphysical indebtedness to Christian saints and thinkers, turns attention to the narrative forms through which O'Connor creates a shifting landscape.

Though tied to Christian history, symbol, and myth, her narrative landscape pushes beyond constricted religious notions or cultural particularities toward illumination where narration and incarnation intersect. Gentry's and Brinkmeyer's studies anticipate such intersection. By presenting the grotesqueries abounding in O'Connor's fiction not as aberrant or purely negative forces in life but rather as departures from the ideal to which they remain tied and by examining the operations of the grotesque within O'Connor's characters who often bring about their own revelatory experience, Gentry prepares us to explore the interaction between human consciousness and narrative structures. Through his application of Mikhail Bakhtin's ideas on dialogism and dialogic art, Brinkmeyer investigates O'Connor's faith and artistic purpose as they influence her story forms. He asserts that her narrators and the author engage in a kind of dialogue that erupts in the stories, which are put under pressure by the tension between fundamentalist and Catholic visions.[12]

O'Connor's intention to make real a historic event—itself presented in narratives and myth—through *her* narratives, in which spectacles and resonances reminiscent of earlier myths and parables appear, has insinuated this interpretive method rooted in structures. Cross-cultural study by anthropologists, linguists, mythologists, and biblical exegetes previously mentioned offer useful tools for examining the interplay between what Lévi-Strauss called the *sequence* (the chronological order and apparent content of a narrative) and the *schema* (the latent content) in mediating fundamental oppositions presented in myths and many narratives.[13] Victor Turner's work on the ritual process, on structures and anti-structures, and on the centrality of liminality in many narrative traditions has influenced my focus.[14] Genette's efforts to delineate more sharply among the terms *story*, *narrative*, and *narrating* and to refine concepts like point of view and focalization, as well as to welcome emendations to his theories from other narratologists have aided my explorations of O'Connor's intricate landscapes.[15] Ricoeur's discussion of the ways the linguistic devices of narrative and metaphor affect our locations, dislocations, and capacity for insight and transformation has also contributed to my investigation.[16] Finally, in the recent works of Henry Louis Gates, Jr., on literary theory and signification in the black tradition,[17] and in William J. Hynes's and William G. Doty's new work on tricksters, I have found confirmation of the trickster's important role in tale-telling and intertextuality.[18]

The following chapters then explore how an understanding of O'Connor's narrative landscape assists readers interested in moving closer to the mystery or secrecy of her stories in particular and narratives in general. Intertwining the word *secret* with the words *self* and *ethics*, O'Connor's stories reveal that the "deeper purpose of secrecy is not to cover up *what the ego wants* to hide, but to bring the ego into connection with the Self, where, in secret, it comes to learn of its ethical obligations."[19] Throughout O'Connor's narratives run figures, gestures, or actions that, as they seem to deceive or disorient us, also facilitate connection between the Self and the ethical by precipitating encounters between the unlikely and the upright, the unsuspecting and the skeptical, the unconscious and consciousness, the divine and the human. Although not an intentional device of O'Connor's this havoc-wreaking figure or movement in and among the stories resembles the archetypal trickster.[20]

The trickster has been described most frequently in anthropological and sociological studies of other cultures and in Carl Jung's work on psychological archetypes. Sometimes taking the physical form of an animal or human, able to change sex, to add and remove body parts, to pass between social groups and worlds, the trickster embodies change and illusion. As such he mediates or presides over all change and over social as well as imaginative exchanges. He functions in rituals of renewal for many so-called primitive societies and resides in the tales of many literatures. Varying in form from the demonic to the messianic, the trickster has appeared in the guises of the shaman, the fool, the knave, the picaro, and the prophet. Considered "among the most archaic of all mythical generators,"[21] the trickster is the *simia dei,* the ape of God.[22] Although he may not be readily recognized in all his disguises or in his most archaic forms in American literature, he is familiar as the cunning, shrewdly self-conscious confidence man who, even in mockery, appears to justify any self-aggrandizing venture. The trickster's change in form reflects other sociological changes, such as the rise of individualism, expansionism, materialism, and secularism. As these interests surpassed former sacred and communal values, the trickster moved farther and farther into the recesses of human consciousness. In the twentieth century, most human beings believe themselves to be enlightened beyond the influence of ancient myth or the disorderly antics of the trickster.

Without the trickster to assist interpretation, Flannery O'Connor's narratives, so reliant on religious myths and allusions, may seem confusing and disorderly or even blasphemous. The violence that pervades her work, abetted often by the most pious characters, offends rationalist twentieth-century sensibilities inclined to displace the propensity for violence in human beings onto causes or conditions and to disallow violence altogether in the sacred because it threatens the Christian canon. On the other hand, through tricksteresque activity, O'Connor's narratives push the reader to acknowledge and to readmit the disorderly and unseemly aspects of human and divine behavior into a vision of reality that, without both darkness and light, evil and goodness, the fall and redemption, is otherwise partial and prone to distortion from repressed and unmediated violence.

With relentless conviction, both artistic and religious, O'Connor unmasks the violence that exists at the heart of the sacred, illustrating how violence used sacrificially restores order to a community or society. Recasting the myths of Christian tradition in fictions that are themselves, like the trickster, agents of change, O'Connor turns the reader to the redemptive event of violence—God's sacrifice of Christ on behalf of human beings overcome by their own violence. Her narratives grotesquely depict the violent consequences both of ignoring religious rituals that protect a society from its own violence and of prostituting religion into an abstraction unneedful of sacrifice. O'Connor suggests that the failure of human beings to recognize their own violence plus their need for a scapegoat or surrogate victim cause them to perpetrate violence overtly or covertly against all creation as their imperial right.[23] In so doing they destroy the entire human community and distort reality.

The religious secret of O'Connor's narratives, revealed in shimmering environments where narration and incarnation meet, is that both good and evil, the ideal and its grotesque distortions, peace and violence, God and Satan, the human and the divine exist together as an original and sacred unity. All human institutions, systems, and conventions—which would separate the mysterious from the profane—are not simply efforts to protect human beings from the dread of freedom; they also yield an inevitably distorted picture of reality and threaten to sever human beings from the deepest sources of life. O'Connor's stories conclude that the only way to live fully and wholly is to acknowledge both the divine and human capacities for evil and the inescapable dependence on sacrifice to mitigate and to transform life's violence. Because this secret threatens the premises of much institutional religious belief in a secular society, O'Connor's works have seemed a riddle.

Flannery O'Connor's literary secret, through which she discloses the religious one, is that narratives which return human beings to original mythic events by recasting these events in contemporary fiction perform a ritual function as necessary in an individualistic, technological age as in a communitarian, primitive one. By shaping ancient myths into modern fiction, pervaded with rebellion and denial, the artist as trickster informs people of their common origins and of the mutual dependence among human beings and between the human and the divine. Using details from her region and of her own religious tradition, O'Connor not only reacquaints us with our lost nature and heritage; she also renews the myth that has been literalized through rationalism and scientific reductionism. Ambivalence about O'Connor's preoccupations, which generally have been interpreted as either conservative and largely irrelevant for sophisticated, post-Christian minds or metaphysically confusing, has obscured the significance of her literary contribution. Yet O'Connor herself made clear in a 1963 interview with C. Ross Mullins, Jr., that the fiction writer is always to some extent experimenting with secrets and riddles: "When you write fiction you both reveal and obscure the things you know best or feel most concerned about."[24]

Given O'Connor's clarity about the artistic and religious convictions with which she approached her fiction, this text investigates her works as a continuous experimentation to "repeat" the Incarnation. Using some of O'Connor's earliest stories, chapter 1 surveys the major structural elements and narrative devices O'Connor employs to create her fictional landscape. Chapters 2 and 3 treat the stories in her two collections both as independent works and as units. By examining how she refines and complicates her techniques throughout her works and assessing the significance of her preoccupation with her reader, we gain a deepening apprehension of the true condition of the modern human spirit. Focusing on the novels, chapter 4 analyzes how O'Connor's narrative techniques intersect, through inversion and repetition, with her metaphysical ideas, moving from a grotesque rendering of the annunciation early in her career with *Wise Blood* toward the later more apocalyptic *The Violent Bear It Away* and the subsequent stories of *Everything That Rises Must Converge*. The concluding chapter examines the creative spirit lying behind these works of fiction. The artist herself becomes the supreme trickster leading readers through narration toward strange encounters with the Incarnation continually breaking into and disrupting our univocal interpretation of ourselves and the world.

Through her narrative landscape, O'Connor exposes the canons of a smug, secular, positivistic culture shaped, even in rebellion and denial, by the Judeo-Christian myth. As the trickster activity in the narratives reinforms the canons of their rejected religious-mythological roots, it simultaneously enlarges the partial vision of any canon neglectful of its underside. O'Connor's fiction challenges the reader to accept truth, though absolute, as an elusive mystery often hidden in darkness, contradiction, and untruth. By resurrecting the trickster into the consciousness of the text and of the reader, O'Connor's stories illustrate how all literature and every act of interpretation may be a sacrificial repetition of an original and violent action to communicate between apparently separate parts,[25] the sacred and the profane, of one reality.

This kind of structural-poetic investigation of Flannery O'Connor's fiction holds potential significance for other literature study because finally it illustrates the double tendencies of human language through which transformations become possible. On the one hand, language erects boundaries, conventions, systems, institutions—in short, a cultural canon—to secure people from freedom or the threat of chaos. On the other hand, language can playfully subvert the canon regularly, to challenge it with freedom, by returning it to its wild, forgotten origins for renewal. The inability to understand the nature and interdependence of narration and incarnation turns both literature and religion into systems that protect one from rather than pull one toward freedom. As a mediator in all exchanges, as an agent who undermines to renew and restore order by turning it tumultuously from underneath, and as a weaver and reweaver of texts, the trickster subverts narrow boundaries, inflexible conventions, and arbitrary categories characteristic of any literary or religious canon. Ignoring the trickster yields reductionist literary theories and lifeless theological systems, not engagement and enactment of our own stories called forth by our history.

The Regionless Region
Shapes and Voices of the Landscape

Presence is never mute.
—Teilhard de Chardin

In order for interpretation to illumine rather than obscure an original text, it must be guided by the organizing principles of the work itself. Flannery O'Connor believed that proper study of a novel "should be contemplation of the mystery in the whole work and not of some proposition or paraphrase."[1] In so saying, O'Connor implied a conviction that every work of imaginative literature has a primal intuition, "some deeply felt, if not fully or even partially conscious, assumption about what . . . constitutes the ground of experience,"[2] that becomes the organizing principle of the work. In addition, O'Connor's statement here and elsewhere admonishes us about the dangers of interpretation, of climbing out of a story into its meaning.[3] Ambiguity about the mystery which O'Connor believes lies at the center of every work poses an impossible contrary to interpretation. Because, as Robert Young argues, "interpretation *is* repression," the *only* way to avoid it is to reformulate the question we ask of stories.[4]

Faced with this difficult contrary, we are more likely to let the primal intuition of a work expose itself and direct interpretation if we reformulate the question we ask of stories from "*what* does the story mean?" to "*how* does the story mean?" When we turn the question in this way, Roland Barthes reminds us that we are in the company of four patrons of poetics: Aristotle, Valéry, Jakobson, and Gérard Genette.[5] Changing the question from what to how frees us as readers "to perform all sorts of operations of linkage, both small and large, and at the same time to make constant discriminations among related but different words, statements, actions, characters, relations, and situations."[6] Such varied operations are essential in reading the works of O'Connor, for whom fiction was so very much an incarnational art, in order to carry out our interpretive task that is deepened and complicated by the convergence in O'Connor's fiction of sounds, images, figures, and motifs drawn from sources as diverse as biblical literature, Sophocles' drama, medieval ritual festivals, and of archetypal presences resembling native American or West African trickster tales.

O'Connor's heavy reliance on biblical themes, characters, and parables—indeed, the parabolic quality recognized frequently in her works themselves—pulls readers backward to forgotten or dimly remembered stories and impels us to enter contemplatively into a kind of conversation with the texts. Parables invite dialogue by placing one experience or one idea—even a tradition—beside another for comparison so that each may inform the other. O'Connor's stories are driven by such juxtapositions or comparisons as the individual struggling within or against a community, personal consciousness overtaken by unconscious forces, and abstract ideals manifested in grotesque physical forms. Frank Kermode explains that although parable means comparison or illustration or analogy in classical Greek, "in the Greek Bible it is equivalent to Hebrew *mashal,* which means 'riddle' or 'dark saying.'" This enlargement of the definition is illuminating when we consider O'Connor's parabolic narratives, for we may expect them to "proclaim a truth as a herald does, and at the same time conceal truth like an oracle."[7]

By believing that a good story should not be paraphrasable, O'Connor confirms that it is irreducible and needful of perpetual interpretation or dialogue because of its riddle-like nature or the truth that lies concealed from view at its center. In short, "the pleasurable play of fiction" in all narratives and in O'Connor's stories will usher us "into an inner zone of complex knowledge about human nature, divine intentions, and the strong but confusing threads that bind the two."[8] The artist whose interest lies in exploring this complex inner zone which the human and divine share will inevitably investigate the relationship between reality and imagination, between the visible and the invisible, between the Word and human language, and those investigations will "affect and enter the structure of the work of art."[9]

Flannery O'Connor firmly roots her narratives in the southern fundamentalist region, yet they reflect the post-Christian age that prefers
the movement of social forces to mystery and the typical to the grotesque. The central question then that we will examine in the following chapters is: How do the structures of O'Connor's narratives allow
her to transcend the limits of her particular time and space and lead
us as readers to a deeper mode of perception and experience? In her
essay "The Grotesque in Southern Fiction," O'Connor observed that
storytellers and readers alike desire to be lifted up by fiction. However,
as letters from some of her readers attest, ironically, storytellers and
readers do not always have the same destinations in mind for their
uplift. Thus, by investigating the means O'Connor used to construct
her narratives, we will discover how, through her anagogical vision,
she embodied in her stories this longing for the redemptive act, the
cost of which we have forgotten or not calculated.[10]

Clues for this investigation arise from O'Connor's process of creation—particularly her use of the grotesque in the service of anagogical vision—and from the structures and narrative techniques,
apparent in all her stories, which hint that her fiction in provocative
ways repeats earlier narratives. Through comparison of O'Connor's
narrative form and techniques with those of biblical narratives or
trickster tales of which we find evidence in her stories, for example, we
may discover continuity and connections that potentially recall us to a
place we have lost—to Middle Earth—where imagination and mystery
are mutually informing.[11]

A structural study that is primarily exegetical—to bring the "dead
language" of a text back to life—and only secondarily interpretive
insinuates itself within these narratives because they and their author
are preoccupied with bringing an apparently dead event, the Incarnation, to life in fiction. Since the eighteenth century the mysteries
of life have gradually fallen to rationalism, science, and materialism.
O'Connor wrote for an audience shaped by this evolving cultural belief system and whose religious feeling, she was convinced, "[had]
become, if not atrophied, at least vaporous and sentimental."[12]
Although themselves influenced by this cultural belief system, O'Connor's narratives defy it by simultaneously exposing it for its narrowness and distortion through the use of the grotesque and providing
the structure through which the mysterious, the unruly, the ambiguous, the radically disturbing action or event—the anti-structure—can
play at hide-and-seek.

O'Connor undertakes this double challenge by manipulating space, time, character, and language in story structures that guide us between what might be called the manifest and the resonant levels of the narratives. In this enterprise, so freighted by her incarnational purposes, O'Connor treats language not simply as a linguistic system of signification through which people convey communication but as a metaphoric system involving "several 'types' of language acts" (*paroles*),[13] which may be either verbal or nonverbal. Therefore, the verbal construction of place, the visions and the gestures of O'Connor's characters, the movement of the story facilitated by words and actions bear as much significance as the words the characters speak; they are simply different *paroles* that sometimes harmoniously and sometimes dissonantly influence the manifest level of the narrative structure and hint at resonances or deeper structures that "lie implicitly or unconsciously beneath, around, or alongside of the text."[14]

Through her skillful management of these various language acts, O'Connor not only treats language itself metaphorically, pointing us toward the experience of bringing an informing Word (the resonance) to life in words (the manifest). She also signals her reliance on indirect communication to bring about the intersection of these two levels of her stories. We can better understand O'Connor's literary methods by thinking about the goals and nature of indirect communication, which Søren Kierkegaard described at length and which became the goal of this artist interested in showing things, not saying them.[15] In direct communication the communicator's goal is to transfer some objective truth to a receiver who hears it without misunderstanding. By contrast, the goal of indirect communication is to deliver the receiver to himself wherein he experiences the truth that is subjectivity.[16]

O'Connor's concern with *showing* truth turned her to the artistic configuration of human life through which she might deliver readers to themselves. In order to accomplish this configuration, she created narratives in which words that pass between communicators and receivers—in this case, characters within the texts as well as between characters, narrators, and readers—must fulfill a double function. Elaborating on the process involved in indirect communication, James D. Whitehill explains that "words that pass between communicator and receiver in an indirect communication are placed under a double demand: first they must be so shaped that their appropriation, in the mode of a direct communication, is frustrated and hindered at every turn; second, they must act in concert so as to activate reflection—not upon the communicator, the nature of objective truths, the delicacy and grace of the style, the possibilities of writing a historicocritical article for a professional journal exposing the world significance of the communication—rather to activate reflection upon oneself in one's own primitivity and freedom."[17]

Through all the verbal and nonverbal language devices, the goal of indirect communication in O'Connor's narratives is to configure human life in a way that "escapes the receiver's attempts to make it fixed, secure, ordered, understood, and tolerable, while simultaneously seducing him into rapt attention. This essential elusiveness is achieved . . . [through] language [that] may be convoluted to the point of exasperation . . . [and through] masks, incognito, mystification, seduction, irony, humor, asides, and disgressions."[18] The artist who seeks to meet her audience (receivers) where they are and simultaneously seduce them into "rapt attention" where outer reality engages their subjectivity, even pushing them toward mystery, must create narrative structures that have the effect of erupting around, within, and beyond them.

O'Connor creates such structures, which repeatedly bring the term *spectacle* to mind, in part by relying on visual imagery and by disturbing and convoluting direct communications. As presentations of the spectacular, her works often seem like dramas, or more precisely, dramatic occasions or ritual reenactments of events that may move us to another dimension or place. In the explication of several O'Connor stories, Louise Westling interprets such dramatic occasions as evidence of O'Connor's ability to write "intense and classically crafted fiction."[19] Not only do her techniques operate within individual narratives, but also these narrative structures have the composite effect of performing a *quasi* ritual function for an age obsessed with direct communications and suspicious of or oblivious to indirect ones. Therefore, by examining O'Connor's works individually and collectively over time, we will be looking for the ways these narrative *paroles* are altered or refined—perhaps by time, intention, and response—and how they also lead readers "into confrontations with new possibilities that lie ever deeper in [their] primitivity and . . . are imbedded in the human condition."[20]

The specific narrative *paroles* that sustain the indirect communication of O'Connor's narratives include: (1) the spatial and temporal elements with which she locates her stories; (2) the use of characters who cast multiple reflections as spectators and metaphoric spectacles;

(3) the linguistic devices she adopts, including speech activity and narrative voice; and (4) the signs of the trickster. Together these devices contribute to the construction and manipulation of the story structures, which themselves, as we will see, form a kind of anti-structure built on the faith that words disclose the Word for readers to encounter.

Space and Time

Flannery O'Connor's use of spatial elements in particular has been noted previously by Frederick Asals and Louise Westling. Asals concludes that the visual imagery of the sun, moon, and sky is central to O'Connor's whole symbolic pattern.[21] Confirming Asals's observations, Westling argues that "the land, the trees, the sky, and the relentless eye of the sun are so powerfully charged in her fiction that they become some of its most powerful characters." Of even greater significance to this investigation of O'Connor's use of spatial elements, however, is Westling's conclusion that in several places O'Connor inverts "traditional patterns of landscape imagery in myth and literature."[22] Although Westling attempts to show how such inversions of mythic patterns create problems, which she compellingly investigates as O'Connor's presentation of women, I see these inversions contributing to a potentially larger artistic purpose. Inversions of all sorts characterize trickster activity, leaving those affected disoriented and needful of reorientation.

Paradoxically, most of O'Connor's stories, particularly the early ones like "Wildcat" and "The Turkey," convey a strong sense of place despite the absence of a geopolitical region or specific time in which the narrative events occur. For example, in "Wildcat" we know only that we are pressed on all sides by the movements of some hunters into and out of the woods. When a blind, old, would-be hunter is left behind by the hunting party, he moves between remembered woods in the interior spaces of his mind and the architectural space of his bedroom, which could be located anywhere. Similarly, Ruller's turkey chase in "The Turkey" occurs in a woods and along the brush rows of a field; only the topography anchors most of the story until at the end he returns to an unnamed geopolitical space, his hometown. O'Connor's "A Temple of the Holy Ghost" depends more heavily on architectural than geopolitical space—the home in which Temple One and Temple Two visit for the weekend, the carnival tent, and Mt. St. Scholastica—and alludes to Mayville as the home of Sister Perpetua, a teacher at Mt. St. Scholastica. Here, as with the other two stories, one recognizes that these small spatial markers are incidental to a more mysterious realm O'Connor suggests in order to "venture to the 'place'" where she might meet her readers.

In these three stories, we discover how deftly O'Connor uses space, weaving it with character and linguistic devices to shape the narrative structures that cling to our minds. Immediately we recognize, even if dimly, that each of these stories is constructed in three parts; each part, though tied to a particular outer space, moves the reader gradually inward toward some unexpected confrontation. Such confrontations could include an individual with his community, a character's conscious life with unconscious forces, the present with the past through memory, or the natural with the supernatural. They are unexpected because the human ego tries to defend against them. In "Wildcat," hearing the preparations of younger men for a wildcat hunt from which he is excluded in the opening section of the story, blind old Gabriel turns, in the second part, to his memory both to heighten and to relieve his frustrated desire for adventure. Left behind, he relives in memory a wildcat attack on Hezuh and thus fuels his own excitement and dread. In the final section of the story he is haunted by a terror that becomes so palpable to Gabriel and readers alike that the imagined wildcat attack seems no longer remote in space—the woods outside Gabriel's home. Rather, Gabriel's memory and emotion have weakened the ego's defense, and the dreaded attack has been incarnated as present and actual in his and the reader's minds.

The similar theme of pursuit and chase develops in the three parts of "The Turkey." The story opens as Ruller stalks an unseen interloper. After one paragraph the story turns unexpectedly, in the second part, into an actual turkey chase, with Ruller now as trespasser. He winds in and out around trees, through fencerow underbrush, pushing the spatial boundaries of the woods as well as the boundaries of his memory and imagination. Desperate for victory over this evasive turkey, Ruller's inner dialogue with his grandmother's religious admonitions and his need for recognition in the family propel him forward in rebellion and lead him in frustration to accuse God of deceit. When Ruller finally subdues the turkey, he heads out of the woods toward town righteously justified and therefore unprepared for his final humiliation and loss, which occur in the third part at the hands of some intervening friends.

Again in "A Temple of the Holy Ghost," O'Connor constructs a three-part narrative. The first dramatic center develops in the home where two girls, Temple One and Temple Two, come from Mt. St. Scholastica for a weekend visit and where Catholic Christianity encounters Protestant fundamentalist Christianity. The second part moves the two guests and Wendell and Cory beyond their humorous liturgical exchanges on the porch of the architectural space in which these two "temples" are guests to the fair where they confront the bizarre incarnation of the hermaphrodite in the less substantial space of the carnival tent. That encounter, reported to the girl child late at night back in her home and embellished in her imagination, prepares her and the reader for an even more mysterious encounter in the final section of the story when, on the road home from Mt. St. Scholastica, the girl child beholds the vision of the sun "like an elevated Host drenched in blood."[23]

The organizing structures of over half of O'Connor's narratives are thus influenced by the space or place in which they occur—in or near the woods or rural wilderness or the city that contains a labyrinthian wildness about it. Usually the entire action of the story does not take place in the woods, but at least the pivotal event or that "gesture of a character that is unlike any other in the story" happens there.[24] The already mentioned stories plus "A View of the Woods" or "A Circle in the Fire" come quickly to mind as illustrations. The city may confuse and disorient both characters and readers, whereas the woods fascinate and frighten because of what they appear to promise and, conversely, to threaten. Although Gabriel wants to go into the woods on the hunt for the wildcat, left behind alone, he is haunted by a cat that stalks through the forest of his memory and his imagination reminding the reader of other animals. Thus the woods represent a specific landscape and possess mythic dimensions as well.

The people who occupy O'Connor's spaces rarely stay contentedly in one space. Both Gabriel and Ruller enter the woods in order to hunt or chase. Sometimes different visions or wills compete in the woods, as they do between grandfather and granddaughter in "A View of the Woods" and between Mrs. Cope and the three visitors in "A Circle in the Fire." At still other times characters journey into, around, or out of the wilderness. In "A Good Man Is Hard to Find," for example, an auto accident interrupts the family journey, which itself ends in individual journeys into the woods and to death. In this particular story, the journey implies both a physical sojourn and a psychic or spiritual pilgrimage.

As a space set apart from social interaction, the wilderness as well as the journey separate the journeyer from those who remain behind. Wilderness and journey experiences, which move us outside social boundaries or orthodox religious practice, occupy the center of O'Connor's creative attention. In "A Temple of the Holy Ghost" neither woods nor wilderness but rather the carnival isolates the outsider hermaphrodite from the socially conventional and biologically normal—the insiders—who enter the "wilderness" of the tent.

Within the woods or wilderness and the carnival environments O'Connor embodies symbolically the mythic dimensions of her region—and of human beings in general—in a concrete location. There she stages the endless contest between order and disorder, between perfection and limitation, between life and death. The wilderness connotes the natural and the primitive elements of human history and experience—wildcats, hermaphrodites, cripples, and refugees—which threaten to destroy as well as promise to renew communities and the conventions on which communities depend. We may perceive better the promise for renewal in the carnival space, for in the deliberateness of its construction, the carnival circumscribes the wilderness; it is a place of play inviting openness to the mysterious or uncontrollable in life. As the hermaphrodite running from one side of a curtain to another illustrates at the carnival, common behavior, conventions, rules, and expectations can be lifted to permit the entry of the unruly or of another "order."

When the physical reality or spiritual symbolism of the wilderness diminishes in a culture, the carnival becomes the place where traditional orders can be turned on their heads and the authority and respectability of insiders challenged and potentially renewed by those who live beyond the acceptable bounds. Flannery O'Connor understood the perpetual need for ritual inversions that might humble the self-righteous, revive flagging faith, or even lead to conversion; she had learned from her own Catholic tradition that, in addition to everything else it is, the holy ritual of the Catholic mass is "at the same time a form of human play and game."[25]

In the backwoods wilderness and the carnival O'Connor harmonized two apparently dissonant interests: she securely placed herself on Georgian soil, and she filled her southern landscapes with mythic overtones and representatives through which she transcended the arbitrary boundaries of both place and time.[26] Talking with Harvey Breit about the importance of the South in her fiction,[27] O'Connor said that an author's greatest contribution to her writing is self-knowledge and knowledge of her region. She did not consider herself a southern writer but believed that the South was the *accent* that led to the *essence.* To know yourself is to know your region and then to be an exile from it for life. From the Georgian woods and farms and small towns, O'Connor's fiction reveals the paradox of commitment. O'Connor's interest in the paradox of time, place, and the eternal appears in an early burlesque of Proust, written during college and entitled "Recollections on My Future Childhood." In it she contrasts Proust's preoccupation with past time to her own preference for "any old time."[28] Thus with deceptive flippancy, O'Connor foreshadows her intention to lead her readers—with skill, humor, and tough-mindedness—into spaces and time that are both ours and all others.

Characters

In considering the role of O'Connor's characters in the structure of her stories we observe that, usually, the principal characters live on the edges of their families or communities. Existing on the fringes, relying heavily on sight—a less intimate sense than touch or taste, for example—each is to some extent a passive spectator distant from the world and not responsible for it. Because of their onlooker stance, these characters often become obsessed with matters of conscience. By interpreting their seeing through consciences shaped by their perceptions of others' wishes and expectations, these spectators live themselves with a partial, indirect experience of reality.

In the three stories mentioned, O'Connor conveys the problem of partial vision through spectators' eyes that are not fully reliable. Repeatedly asking "Who that?" as he depends on sound and smell as his vehicles of witness, Gabriel is ironically a spectator forced to the edges of his community by blindness. From the moment Ruller spies the turkey at the outset of the story, he chases it with his eyes and actions, trying to capture it, seeing it then losing it, and leading the reader to conclude that Ruller's eyes are not equal to the wily ways of the animal. Ruller's objective in catching the turkey was to gain recognition from those inside his family system whose judgment of him mattered—his brother Hane and his parents. As he lunges around the wild woods he imagines the longed-for recognition in his family's praise: "Ruller gets our turkeys for us. Ruller got it in the woods, chased it dead. Yes, he's a very unusual child."[29] From this anticipated acclaim he egotistically concludes that the turkey is God's sign that God wanted him to be a preacher. O'Connor weaves several levels of spectating together in "A Temple of the Holy Ghost," each spectator moving the story from the outermost alienated ring of observation, carried out by the girl child, to the bizarre sight of the hermaphrodite in the carnival tent witnessed by Joanne and Susan, and finally to the mystical vision stimulated by the girl child's psychological obsession with the freak.

Because many of O'Connor's characters are chronologically young people or adults psychologically and spiritually arrested by consciences formed by distorted vision, they seem bizarre and easily dismissed. Yet their very penchant to impute meaning beyond sense impression, to trick others and themselves, to invert and distort events, turns these spectators into spectacles, making them interesting to us. Many of the objects with which these spectators are obsessed resonate or are associated in the spectators' minds with a mysterious power or presence: God "speaks" through the turkey; the wildcat is a hunter after "folks' blood"; the report of the hermaphrodite so consumes her imagination that the girl child "prays" a vision of the hermaphrodite accepting her-himself as a temple of God, which leads to the concluding spectacle of the red sun as an elevated Host in the sky.

By exhibiting some outrageous behavior, changing form, or attributing almighty power to particular objects or other characters by which he or she is obsessed (e.g., the wildcat, the turkey, or the hermaphrodite), the character himself or herself may turn into a spectacle.[30] For example, Ruller begins as an imaginary, self-appointed posse to protect wild game from poachers, turns into a turkey-chasing outlaw himself in order to gain recognition, is often outwitted by the veering fowl, and is finally stripped of his prize by the deceit of the country boys.

Mockery and deceit occur more complexly in "A Temple of the Holy Ghost." Laughing at biblical injunctions to regard their bodies as temples and at their convent training to keep their minds off boys, Joanne and Susan label themselves Temple One and Temple Two. Behind this guise they ridicule the religious conventions of Wendell and Cory, giggle at the appearance and social position of Alonzo Myers, and condescendingly try to shock the girl child who hangs around them. Through this ability to change form from teen-age girls to figurative holy temples who ridicule everyone not like themselves—this play of spectacle charged with sexual energy[31] between insiders and outsiders—O'Connor moves the characters as well as the reader beyond the geopolitical or architectural space to another mythic or mysterious dimension, one beyond the fringes yet strangely accessible to the constraints of material reality. Such antics dimly reflect the more appalling trick the two temples and the readers will encounter in the hermaphrodite who proclaims himself-herself an offspring of God.

Linguistic Devices

As we examine more of O'Connor's works we will observe how the linguistic devices contribute to the activity that occurs in the spaces in which spectators and spectacles interact. We will keep our ears attuned to the multiple layers of narration in the stories: narrators to readers, characters to other characters, to themselves, or to the Unseen. In short, we will consider briefly here and in greater detail in subsequent chapters how the following language devices sustain the narrative structures: (1) the function of incantations, obsessive ruminations, and outrageous behavior; (2) the narrator's position and language in relation to the story; (3) the importance of the *as if* territory toward which O'Connor pulls us through language; and (4) the function of irony.

Usually outrageous behavior, repetitive gestures, or changes in form accompanied by obsessive ruminations, rationalizations, or incantations uttered by the spectator trying to orient himself in uncertain circumstances expose the tension within a character, between characters, or between social groups and differing views of reality. For example, Gabriel's certainty that the wildcat "comin' out the woods . . . [to] git itssef some folkes blood" torments his memory as he mumbles and groans thinking, "gonna git him," "gonna hit it," "gonna git him tonight."[32] Ruller's obsessive thought that "he was going to get it if he had to chase it out of the county . . . he was going to have it. He was going to have it if he had to run it out of the state," fuels his outrageous turkey chasing. Near exhaustion after colliding with the tree, Ruller cants defiantly, "God dammit . . . God dammit to hell, good Lord from Jerusalem . . . Good Father, good God, sweep the chickens out the yard."[33] Within the girl child's consciousness, fragments of the cook's admonition that "God could strike you deaf dumb and blind" coalesce with images of a hermaphrodite intoning "God made me thisaway and I don't dispute hit" as a carnival congregation shouts "Amen, Amen."[34] In addition to signaling the complication of language levels that put the text under pressure, such incantations also open dialogue between the manifest and resonant levels of the text's structure.

The narrator's position in this so-called dialogue between the levels of a story is critical, for the verbalized incantations as well as the obsessive thoughts common to O'Connor's characters are usually available through the narrator whose stance in relation to the characters and actions shift subtly from story to story or even within stories. Initially in most stories, the third person narrator begins the tale at the descriptive remove of an observer-reporter, mirroring the spectator position of many of the characters. But, frequently without the reader's awareness, the narrator circumvents or leaps the distance, moving to limited omniscience, and encircles the reader like a traditional storyteller. When he submits to the actions and messages he is conveying, the narrator becomes, as it were, a channeler or medium through whom messages from another dimension may pass.

In "Wildcat," "The Turkey," and "A Temple of the Holy Ghost," O'Connor's narrators illustrate such narrational shifts in three slightly different forms. The narrator of "Wildcat" introduces the reader to Gabriel with a one-sentence descripton of his sound shuffling across the room and then immediately reports the hunters' conversations blended with minor-toned laughter, groans, and the frogs' hum. Throughout part 1 of the narrative, the narrator views and interprets the unfolding plans of the hunters. The initial distance of the narrator makes us as readers watchful of Gabriel. Only in Gabriel's response to the mocking question about how many wildcats he has killed does the narrator hint at the shift to occur in the narrative stance in part 2. Between part 1 and part 2 the narrator leaves the external, present-time world of the hunters and enters Gabriel's past through his memory. This realm of memory mirrors the present world, thereby disorienting the readers initially as the narrator moves back and forth between reporting Gabriel's recollections of what others did and said in past time and space, and Gabriel's fearful ruminations on those events.

The reader's immersion in Gabriel's memory and heightened imagination prepares her for the collision of the past and present in part 3—the point at which Gabriel becomes a spectacle. Following this confrontation the narrator resumes the distance of part 1 but brings a disillusioned and agitated Gabriel back to present time. With skillful construction, the narrator takes the present reality of Gabriel's disappointment not to be going on the hunt, evokes a past memory of fear and challenge, and turns Gabriel and reader toward a new territory—the metaphoric *as if* territory—where Gabriel responds to his real disillusionment on the basis of conditions no longer actually present. Gabriel ends up with a broken shelf incapable of being transformed because he lacks adequate awareness of the relationship between his inner tormented longing and fear, his outer condition of being left behind, and the importance of the intersection of the two. In the end we wonder whether or not we judge Gabriel through the conscience of the narrator who, at the end, returns to spectator.

In contrast to "Wildcat" where the narrative change between reporting and limited omniscience parallels the events in the three parts of the story, leading only in the third section to the ambiguous, unresolved tension of the actual and the imagined, the narrator of "The Turkey" immediately drops the reader into the internal reflections in Ruller's mind as he physically bumps around the brush in pursuit of the turkey. The difficulties Ruller faces are signaled by the narrator's report that Ruller wishes his real conditions vis-à-vis the turkey were otherwise. "If he only had a gun, if he only had a gun," the narrator reports from Ruller's angle of vision and with the privilege of Ruller's inner thoughts. Then surveying the ground for a stone, Ruller notices that it looked "as if it might just have been swept."[35] With these reports, the narrator informs the reader that Ruller is not on "ordinary" ground; he is undertaking a chase that moves between the physical opportunity to capture a turkey and the compulsion to invest that feat with meaning beyond itself, through words containing resonances of other holy ground experiences; it could help him acquire inner stature and security through such a victory.

In the central section of the story the narrator depicts the tension, embodied in Ruller, between looking for and seeing the turkey, on the one hand, and dealing with its tricky elusiveness, on the other. Immediately after hitting the tree face-first, Ruller wonders "why he had seen it [the turkey] in the first place if he wasn't going to be able to get it." Unable to handle the ambiguity of this tension, Ruller concludes that "it was like somebody had played a dirty trick on him."[36] At that moment, he collapses the metaphoric *as if* territory of ambiguity—is this merely a real turkey he wants?—into an identity: the turkey is a trick played on him by some force beyond his ken. When he interprets the turkey to be a representative of God, he first attacks God for deceit and trickery and then bargains with him. As the narrator brings Ruller out of the woods into the town with the turkey slung over his

shoulder, Ruller must face a trial of confirmation. Will his interpretation of the events that have taken place in the *as if* region of the woods
and his mind be confirmed by community perceptions and judgments? Will he receive the acclaim "due" him? Having collapsed the
conditional into the comparative—the turkey *as* (not *as if*) God's generous blessing—Ruller sets himself apart from the community, making himself vulnerable to being stripped of the illusion he has created
through his misapprehension.

"A Temple of the Holy Ghost" is animated by shifts in narrative
voice similar to those just described, and here we can see yet more
clearly how the author's choice of narrative stance impacts the narrative structure. Although the narration is primarily objective, the
narrator's adoption of the girl child's angle of vision reduces the space
between the narrator and the central events, between the insider (the
girl child's perception of events) and the outsiders (those who merely
visit carrying news of outside events). The narrator relies heavily on
words of seeing and watching in the opening scenes of the story;
together, in fact, the narrator and the girl child survey from a safe
distance the activities unfolding as the two temples settle in for the
visit.

Gradually the narrator moves us closer to the girl child's inward
experience first by reporting through the metaphoric *as if* the child's
interpretation of Wendell and Cory's frowning stares when they are
uncertain about whether they are being ridiculed. The narrator further reduces the space between narration and direct experience of the
girl child's internal perceptions not simply by reporting what the child
sees but by anticipating for us the child's anagogical vision: "past the
wall of woods [she saw] . . . the speckled sky where a longer finger of
light was revolving up and around and away, searching the air as if it
were hunting for the lost sun."[37] Immediately from this vision the girl
child distills her "calling" to be a martyr.

The narrator repeats this back-and-forth pattern of moving from
the distance of observer-reporter to the inward reflection of the central character throughout the story, each time bringing us closer to the
final "vision" of the riddle. For example, first the narrator reports
Joanne and Susan's dialogue about the freak ending with the description of the way Joanne uttered her words: "as if she had bit into
something she didn't know if she liked or not." Then, in presenting
the words of the hermaphrodite, the narrator slides into the girl
child's consciousness confessing, "The child felt every muscle strain as

if she were hearing the answer to a riddle."[38] From that point until the end of the story, the narrator leaves us in the girl child's inner region of imagination and introspection. Through the figure and experience of the hermaphrodite, we have crossed the nebulous time and space boundaries between an ordinary summer town, an entertaining circus tent, and the mysterious hermaphroditic incarnation of God.

The narrator's shift from observer to omniscient seer parallels the movement in the girl child's stance as spectator at the outset of the story to her condition of obsession as she incorporates the vision of the hermaphrodite into her own imagination and prayers. These linguistic devices reinforce the author's creation of the architectural spaces in which each more intense stage of encounter and confrontation occurs leading ultimately to a transcendent space of mystical vision where the girl child, herself now more a spectacle than a spectator, sees the sun as a spectacle, "like an elevated Host."

Through the shifting narrative voice and the metaphoric *as if* territory, which functions as a structural hinge between levels of perception and consciousness, O'Connor links two levels of her narratives—the physical world of time and space and the mystical and metaphoric realm. For O'Connor's characters the *as if* perception might be called a structural metaphoric territory and is fraught with ambiguity because it always threatens to confuse or at least complicate appearance and reality.[39] Most of O'Connor's characters are vulnerable in this region because they rely so singly on sight, the sense most remote and prone to distortion but also the one on which modern human beings rely most heavily. Sometimes a character's perceptions and interpretations of his or her experiences are radically altered through the associations suggested by *as if.* Often in the *as if* territory O'Connor brings the conditional and the comparative into struggle and reveals connections through resonances from other times, spaces, and stories and with aberrant, though not purely negative, aspects of her characters. As subsequent analysis of O'Connor's stories will illustrate, her manipulation of these narrative devices makes possible a dialogue with unknown or lost parts of ourselves, our human relatives, and our shared past. In addition, the play among these devices—particularly the ability and inability to perceive metaphorically—produces irony, "the one language befitting [the] image of the imagination in dialogue with all being."[40] Kierkegaard explained irony as contradiction or ambiguity; "its structure [is] dialectical, its medium the language of reflection, its style antithetical, and its aim self-discovery." Irony does not establish anything but rather calls forth something that lies behind irony.[41] In its attempt "to mystify the surrounding world not so much in order to conceal itself as to induce others to reveal themselves," irony is a means of revelation.[42]

Through irony in O'Connor's narratives and her reliance on *as if* constructions, narration and incarnation intersect along two axes, the horizontal (or comparative and analogical) and the vertical (the conditional and anagogical).[43] Taking place along a horizontal axis, narration relies on comparisons and possibilities to convey the known. In O'Connor's fiction a vertical axis, expressing the urge toward incarnation of the unreal or unknown through impossibilities and conditionality, intersects the horizontal axis. Through the *as if* construction, O'Connor puts characters, narrators, and readers under pressure of the mysterious. Narrators reporting omnisciently appear superior or broader in understanding to those who know only one perspective on reality or to characters trapped in their subjective viewpoints. But both narrators and characters are capable of optical distortions along the geographical or psychological horizontal axis created through distancing. Gabriel's blindness, Ruller's eyes that try to follow a "disappearing" turkey, or the girl child's vision of an elevated Host drenched in blood remind us of other O'Connor characters who feign blindness, look with only one eye, or use telescopes to see far things near. In short, the horizons on which O'Connor's stories unfold depend on the position and perspective of the spectator, be that person the narrator or character, and on how open that spectator is to interventions along another axis. These axes are additionally complicated because, running through memory, they also run across time and texts. They link the historical with the mythologic, the temporal with the spiritual. Just as the incarnation of God in the human form of Jesus Christ was a mystifying and ironic act in which not only did the divine break through to the human, but also human beings were revealed to themselves, O'Connor's hermaphrodite, her references to saints and martyrs, her images of pursuit, struggle, and war provide modern, inverted, even grotesque "repetitions" of the original event of God's invasion into history.[44] As J. Louis Martyn points out, for St. Paul Christ was the invasion that produced a cosmic conflict. "What has been made visible is not some *thing* previously enclosed behind curtains, now revealed by pulling the curtains aside. Rather, the *One* who has been on the other side rips the curtain apart, steps through to our side, altering irrevocably our time and space."[45]

Signs of the Trickster

By examining the structures of O'Connor's narratives we will discover a presence (sometimes embodied in a figure, sometimes hinted only through language and actions), which presides over the *as if* territory, buttressing the spatial and psychological boundary conditions that dominate O'Connor's stories. The *as if* territory to which the narrator brings the reader resembles a *limen*,[46] the border area or threshold where collision or intersection between two worlds or orders of existence occurs. Here in this area, where characters turn from spectators to spectacles and the vertical and horizontal axes intersect through irony, resides a presence who often appears in the form of the mythological trickster. Through his actions "the anomalous and ordered, the sacred and the profane, the absurd and the meaningful are joined to create, not merely an ironic symbol, but an image of irony and of the working of the ironic imagination."[47] As an agent of reversals, a master of guile and disguise, the trickster reflects the "experience of the human mind in its imaginative operation as itself radically ambiguous, essentially anomalous, inescapably multivalent—facing both out and in, linking above and below, animal-like and god-like, social cog and individual solitude, shaped and shaping, part of all that is but only as a subject knowing its own apartness."[48] Living through the imagination in tales from diverse times and places, the trickster is an interpreter, who weaves a textile out of words into tales. He is the maker of language and literature because of his capacity *"to imagine the real"*[49] or "to embody mystery in manners."[50] In his ability to see the *what is not* through the *what is,* he is a servant of anagogical vision.

The imagination's ability "to imagine the real" through irony, which allows human beings to be transformed into symbols and thereby to become participants of all the experiences of the cosmos, is prefigured in the magico-religious experience.[51] The "trickster ironically symbolizes the symbolic reality of man, that 'freak,' as Pascal calls him, who is the 'glory and the refuse' of the universe."[52] Moving in the ironic imagination, the trickster struggles with God against stasis and against false, distorted human images of the sacred. In so doing he potentially makes plain (ironically through double talk, inversions, or riddles) the "counteractive patterns of the culture." These are "elements of a culture's own negation which in an ordinary, quite un-Hegelian fashion are included within it."[53] Such "counteractive patterns" are generally repressed in the individual or collective psyche or classified, only apparently, out of existence. However, in ritual, in drama, and in the narrative, these hidden elements may begin to emerge into the manifest elements of life. Thus in Flannery O'Connor's fiction, readers may confront "counteractive patterns" existing in Judeo-Christian religion—such as the deceitfulness or jealousy of God, the disorderliness of the world, or the evil capacities of God's emissaries—which have been repressed or reified from our contact.

Because the archetypal trickster's activity is cloaked in irony and motivates the ironic imagination, he is a likely guide through O'Connor's landscape and interpreter of her narrative secret. In his varied historical manifestations, the trickster appears as a mediator, an imitator, and a figure of the peripheries—taking animal forms as well as the form of a god such as the Greek Hermes—who makes possible relationship not by forcibly exerting power but by challenging authority and power, even as an infant, through phenomenal cunning and secret action.[54] All of these activities overlap, increasing narrative density and deepening the mystery of every myth, legend, or tale that depends on his presence and action.

The trickster mediates by going between one region and another, one realm of experience and another, or things manifest and things hidden. As a figure of energy who goes between apparent oppositions, he opens a path between inward and outward contradictions experienced in the soul of every human being, between the individual and the community, and between the human (or material) realm and the divine (or spiritual) realm. The fool, the clown, the madman, the seer, and the prophet—as offspring of the trickster—have all mediated oppositions like these.

In O'Connor's fiction we will find a sometimes entertaining, sometimes revolting, sometimes confusing, but always provocative blending and blurring of the prophet of Hebraic tradition with the trickster. Robert Brinkmeyer argues that O'Connor was influenced heavily by extreme Yahwist thinking that regarded Hebrew prophets as serving a skeptical, demythologizing function in their societies; "they probed and called into question the basic structures of thought and belief that guided humanity's life in the everyday world." The Hebraic prophetic vision not only offered critiques of the culture, separating profane and sacred, but also alienated human beings from themselves. Yet to be taken out of the center of self-preoccupation—to be de-centered as Herbert Schneidau describes it in *Sacred Discontent*—is the beginning of insight.[55] However, O'Connor's prophets belong not purely to the

Hebraic tradition; they do not always stand firmly above culture con-
demning it and unequivocally calling people to separate from their
vainglorious ways and to repent. Sometimes they appear in strange
guises of the culture or in bestial behaviors; through their grotesqueries, they inform human beings about the ambiguities and complex-
ities of identity. It is this complication of the prophet-like figure in
O'Connor's narratives that forms a central preoccupation of this book.

Despite specific cultural or historic differences among these various
forms of the trickster, each has the unselfconscious ability to see things
as if from another realm or with a set of eyes not limited to "objective"
vision. Each has the capacity to dissolve rather than to focus events
because he stands apart from the main action or between the opposing
perceptions or regions.[56] While mediating contradictions internal or
external, these figures are always on the side of human beings who
suffer in their uncertain relationship to the world and point toward a
binary quality in the universe or in the human soul perpetually in
need of reconciliation. In the ironic imagination the trickster capacity
for mediation enables the mind to overleap the arbitrary and artificial
boundaries erected against the anomalous and chaotic to preserve
stasis. The trickster's usefulness as an interpreter depends on his capacity to imitate, his location in any contest or opposition, and his
penchant for cunning words and secrets.

Through his capacity to manipulate language and to mediate,
he facilitates dialogue in place of monologue within the individual
self, between the self and others, and between the self and the world
by presenting consciousness as multiple. Whereas a Hebrew prophet
might press an individual away from monologic self-absorption
through self-alienation, the trickster introduces individuals to the
polyphony of voices and impulses within themselves.[57]

The capacity for imitation is visible in the story of Job when Satan as
a *simia dei*—ape of God—desires to trick Job and gets Yahweh to agree
to test Job. The contest over Job, and within him, hangs on the identification of Satan with God, depicted in the story as a pact or an
agreement between the two. And it is through that imitation that Job
and God overstep former barriers into a new relationship. Brer Rabbit, whose antics are collected among Creek Indian tales as well as in
the Uncle Remus stories, masterfully turns imitation to his own advan-
tage by usurping the authority of God or posing as a spokesman for
someone else.[58] Brer Rabbit uses such imitation for his own survival in
threatening circumstances. In O'Connor's "The Turkey" Ruller imag-

ines the turkey to be, if not an imitation of God, at least an agent sent
by God at once to trick him and to send him a message that maybe he
should be a preacher. As Ruller chases the lame turkey around the
woods, it becomes in his imagination the means by which he passes
between the surface realities of his life and the mysterious interventions of the divine.

The trickster effectively mediates because he locates himself along
the edges rather than at the center of any contradiction or tension. In
that respect, he is always an outsider ready to go between the boundaries of any given realm, social order, or mental category. He is like
"an amphibian, equally at home in the world of reality and the world
of the imagination."[59] We find an example of this indefinite, fringe-
like location represented in Ananse, the spider trickster in the *anansem*
of the Ashantis of West Africa.[60] As an animal, who flees to the ceiling
(the fringes of the prevailing social order) in several stories when he is
humiliated or caught in his trickery, Ananse mediates between the
animal and human worlds because he has "a primordial intimacy with
the human world. . . . [He] is a metamorph, an embodiment of liminality, . . . a living connection between the wild and the social, between the potentially and the actually human."[61] As an embodiment
of margins, he both establishes boundaries and opens passages; he
seizes the forces of incoherence and disorder for order; he stands
between what is and what is coming, what is manifest and what is
hidden. The wildcat in O'Connor's "Wildcat" also exists in a woods on
the remote edges of human society. Threatening Gabriel's world with
disorder and Gabriel with death, he stalks in Gabriel's imagination as
an embodiment of the mysterious boundaries between the terrors in
the human heart and those of the wilderness and between the divine
and the human.

Finally, mediation is also conducted through the trickster's facility
with cunning words that disclose secrets. We expect those who are the
makers of language and literature to be fascinated by words. The
madman or seer throughout history has been depicted as "an awe-
inspiring figure whose reason has ceased to function normally because
he has become the mouthpiece of a spirit or power external to himself,
and so has access to hidden knowledge."[62] In the Hebrew tradition
there are hundreds of prophets, some wild ecstatics, who are called
nabi. The root of this word, which identifies "inspired people" or a
state of being "beside oneself," means "to call or to proclaim." Among
the Greek Hermes' several gifts, the one that binds him most closely to

the trickster is his skill at persuasion, especially when that skill depended on the saying of oaths or the chanting of incantations or whispered words. Hermes' role as herald or messenger reinforces his dependency on words, for "heralds are called public workers . . . , a term which is applied also to seers, healers, woodworkers, and bards and which connotes a socially useful and respected craft. The special knowledge they possess is emphasized in a series of stock epithets meaning 'wise,' or 'knowing.'"[63] The etymology of *herald* links it with a Greek word meaning "expert sound maker," underscoring further the connection between the herald and the bard.

In his tendency to chant certain words or phrases and in his preoccupation with magical or ceremonial rites, Hermes brings Flannery O'Connor's Gabriel and the hermaphrodite to mind. In chant-like proclamation Gabriel says or thinks repeatedly "I been smellin' it," thus bringing ever closer the confrontation between this figure of the wilderness and his own heart. Similarly, in "A Temple of the Holy Ghost," the words uttered by the hermaphrodite—first to the men's side of the tent, then to the women's side—move insistently to the center of the child's litany as she lies in bed: "God made me thisaway and I don't dispute hit." "Amen. Amen." This enigmatic incantation mediates between a freakish earthly form and the spiritual mystery of being a temple of the Holy Ghost.

The capacities to imitate, to live on the boundaries, and to disclose secrets through cunning words and riddles are all activities necessary for mediation. In the hands of O'Connor these mediatory images become her means of weaving a rich narrative fabric in which she fills negative spaces—holes left by our denial and loss—with mythological-historical fragments of wide variety, thereby showing us affinities between what we think we are and what we might be. When we keep our eyes on such activities in O'Connor's stories, we will find behind them the trickster's presence mediating apparent contradictions in the texts, pulling near and far spaces—Georgia and mythic wildernesses—together, binding in kinship fundamentalist fanatics, animals, and freaks with the biblical prophets and with God. As we follow these activities embedded in and animating her story structures, we ourselves will move into deeper conversation with these narratives and closer to Flannery O'Connor's secret.

2

Episodic Tales of Sin

Yes'm, . . . Jesus thown everything off balance.
—The Misfit

In December 1954, Flannery O'Connor informed Sally and Robert Fitzgerald that she had dedicated her first collection of stories, *A Good Man Is Hard to Find,* to them: "Nine stories about original sin, with my compliments."[1] Later she added "The Displaced Person" to the collection. Despite this characteristically humorous admission of the collection's unifying, apparently serious theme about human imperfection and O'Connor's careful selection, arranging, and rewriting of one or two of the stories for publication,[2] many literary critics have faulted O'Connor's stories for their inconsistency between comedy and seriousness and for tonal shifts that run out of control.[3] Such charges highlight the technical and imaginative problems O'Connor undertook for herself when she decided to convince the unbelieving modern mind of the reality of sin. This chapter investigates how this challenge shaped O'Connor's stories in *A Good Man Is Hard to Find* and why her techniques have drawn unwarranted criticism.

O'Connor's explicit statement about the subject of the stories in this first collection arouses readers' propensities for symbol-hunting and doctrine-sleuthing. Such questions as what did she mean by original sin? or what theological doctrines of sin and grace are evidenced in these stories? are apt to claim our early attention. However, taking Sarah Gordon's warning against too-early symbol-hunting seriously,[4] we turn aside from these intriguing questions. Instead, the task of this chapter is to tease from the narrative structures O'Connor's representations of original sin. More specifically, we investigate here in which ways the story structures themselves convey the nature and causes of original sin. How do her techniques of indirection take us from "a safely recognizable world to the realm of mystery where we are baffled, challenged, and ultimately heartened"?[5] Only at the end can we ask what these structures reveal about sin.

In *A Good Man Is Hard to Find* there are at least five narrative devices through which O'Connor shapes the structures of these stories. Refined for our examination of this first story collection from those techniques introduced in the preceding chapter, the devices include: (1) O'Connor's juxtaposition of southern backwoods speech with biblical or classical allusions; (2) incantations that anchor the stories, focus the events, link characters, and become recurring metaphors or images that deepen and complicate the symbolic dimensions of speech and action; (3) doubled characters whose language and behaviors personify contradictions and suggest a relation between consciousness and the unconscious; (4) an arc-like movement or circular operation of the story structures that mirrors the dance between spectators and spectacles, those characters who confuse short-sighted preoccupations and mysterious visions; and (5) the frequent presence of an ambiguous figure who moves between the center and the fringes of the stories preparing for ironic reversals that baffle as often as they transform characters. Although it is the *interaction* of these five devices within each story that yields the shimmering and often shocking life of the story, for the purposes of analysis we will examine the illustrative examples of the operation of each device separately.

Backwoods Speech and the Bible

Over and over in *Mystery and Manners* Flannery O'Connor reveals her belief that "a distinctive idiom is a powerful instrument for keeping fiction social." Speech, particularly a shared idiom, provides a structure through which people are connected not only to a place but also to each other. O'Connor explains that "when one Southern character speaks, regardless of his station in life, an echo of Southern life is heard. This helps to keep Southern fiction from being a fiction of purely private experience."[6] In a panel discussion in January 1961 moderated by Louis D. Rubin, Jr., in a May 1962 interview with Granville Hicks, which appeared in the *Saturday Review*, and in a conversation reported by Joel Wells in *The Critic* for August–September 1962, O'Connor acknowledged the power of the Bible on southern language. "The Bible is what we share with all Christians, and the Old Testament we share with all Jews. This is sacred history and our mythic background. If we are going to discard this we had better quit writing at all." But in addition to the biblical influences on southern language, O'Connor asserted that the interest in telling a concrete story set southern fiction apart from other fiction. Illustrating this distinctive characteristic of southern fiction she said, "I have Boston cousins and when they come South they discuss problems, they don't tell stories. We tell stories."[7]

What is most interesting in all O'Connor's stories, not simply these of the first collection, is the way she builds a dialogic structure in the narratives, extending and deepening the community in her fiction, through deflected speech and overlays of backwoods and biblical talk. By juxtaposing southern idiom with biblical-sounding prophecy, excerpts of scripture, or fundamentalist preaching—which are, in fact, a still audible though remote part of the southern idiom—she establishes a fictional community rooted in Judeo-Christian history and myth in the midst of an age that belittles such history and myth as viable modes of knowing.

O'Connor creates this larger community by using language in two different ways. In the first way, she employs words expected to foster dialogue to perpetuate disconnection. Such disjunction leads characters toward isolation, making them vulnerable to spectacular excesses, and turns readers' attention to another level or kind of communication implied by the *absence* of shared meaning between characters. The second method involves reinforcing the manifest level of the story with resonant images, central sacral events, and prophetic messages drawn from the Bible, classical, or national mythic history. In both methods of using language, O'Connor relies heavily on the auditory as well as visual senses of her characters and readers. For example, conversations taking place between two characters often depend on hearsay evidence or gossip of at least one character. Frequently meetings between characters may be observed from a distance and conclusions drawn by assumption or relayed by rumor. When either narrators or characters fill their talk with allusions to remote prophetic biblical messages or classical events, O'Connor requires of her hearers/readers a severer, more discerning listening. This combined appeal—at one moment to our eyes and another to our ears—puts O'Connor's stories under peculiar pressure. As the auditory sense implies a taking into confidence, the visual sense grants distance and immunity, turning characters or readers into spectators. Each story in *A Good Man Is Hard to Find* illustrates through these two techniques O'Connor's defiance of standard language conventions and enlargement of our expectations of communication, but we will examine how they function together in "A Good Man Is Hard to Find," "The River," and "A Late Encounter with the Enemy."

From the opening conversations in "A Good Man Is Hard to Find" taking place among the family members preparing for their Florida trip until the grandmother is shot, the characters bombard each other with words that never carry a message across the space between characters but ricochet off each other, leaving each person alone. The grandmother who rails against a trip to Florida tries to influence the family plans through fear of an escaped convict. Her state of alarm ("Yes and what would you do if this fellow, The Misfit, caught you?") is met by flippant retort from her young grandson ("I'd smack his face") and by an appraisal of her grandmother's character from June Star ("She wouldn't stay home for a million bucks. Afraid she'd miss something. She has to go everywhere we go").[8] Apparently forgetting the intention of her original comment, or else effectively sidetracked by the verbal barrage that hasn't acknowledged her real interests, the grandmother now retaliates, "Just remember that the next time you want me to curl your hair."[9]

This same process of deflection occurs when the grandmother and The Misfit sit on the ground talking. After assuring him that he's a good man, "not a bit common," the grandmother listens to The Misfit tell her his daddy's appraisal of him—"it's some that can live their whole life out without asking about it and it's others has to know why it is, and this boy is one of the latters."[10] In the midst of this self-disclosure The Misfit interrupts himself to demonstrate a bizarre concern for social convention: "I'm sorry I don't have a shirt on before you ladies. . . . We buried our clothes that we had on when we escaped and we're just making do until we can get better. We borrowed these from some folks we met."[11] And though following the literal meaning of the words and being herself concerned with social approbation but ignorant of both the criminal and religious implications of wearing borrowed clothes, the grandmother responds, "That's perfectly all right . . . maybe Bailey has an extra shirt in his suitcase."[12]

Into a maximally alarming situation O'Connor has inserted exchanges of words that disclose family history, defer to social manners,
and remind us that The Misfit, reminiscent of Job who could not make
his crime match his punishment, asks hard questions of life and identifies himself with Jesus: "Jesus thown everything off balance. It was
the same case with him as with me except He hadn't committed any
crime and they could prove I had committed one because they had the
papers on me. . . . I call myself The Misfit . . . because I can't make
what all I done wrong fit what all I gone through in punishment."[13] A
scream from the woods interrupts The Misfit's flow of words, but he
resumes undisturbed, "Does it seem right to you, lady, that one is
punished a heap and another ain't punished at all?"[14] Yet as such
philosophizing occurs, recalling age-old debates about theodicy, the
murders proceed without question.

Through words, filled with references to Jesus, that do not fit the
actions and through cheap faith, these two southerners are locked in
their private perceptions. Witnessing emotionless on the edge of the
woods the horrors transpiring inside it, these characters turn increasingly into spectacles through whom O'Connor shifts the readers'
attention to her real interests: the nature of sin and the movement of
salvation or grace. The sin binding the grandmother and The Misfit is
their egoism, which leads them into grotesque distortions of Christian
virtues like goodness, charity, and reconciliation. These distortions
manifest themselves in multiple murders that violently incarnate the
abstract ideal of sacrifice and redemption embodied in Christ's death
and resurrection. The ironic movement of grace in the story occurs
when the grandmother claims The Misfit as one of her own—thereby
acknowledging a shared guilt in the world's evil—and when The Misfit
testifies that she would have been a good woman if someone would
have shot her every moment of her life.

Baptism and receiving a new name—central events of Christian
tradition—resound through O'Connor's story about a city child's outing in his baby-sitter's country. Through words rich with religious
images and fundamentalist preaching, O'Connor creates linguistic
dissonance and disconnection, which lead to young Harry's shocking death by drowning in "The River." According to Mark Sexton,
"O'Connor's narrative consciousness carefully delineates the dangers
inherent in the vernacular milieu, even while presenting this world as
a refuge for the affection-starved Harry." Sexton asserts that "readers
of 'The River' perceive vernacular religion as both sincere and obsessive, according to the way O'Connor manipulates the narrative dis-

tance between her readers and the believers."[15] How O'Connor achieves such distance will become part of the focus subsequently in "Shadows and Contradictions."

Enraptured as a spectator at the water's edge, the child watches and listens to the preacher tell the gathered body that "There ain't but one river and that's the River of Life, made out of Jesus' Blood. That's the river you have to lay your pain in, in the River of Faith, in the River of Life, in the River of Love, in the rich red river of Jesus' Blood, you people! . . . If it's this River of Life you want to lay your pain in then come up, and lay your sorrow here. But don't be thinking this is the last of it because this old red river is good to Baptize in, good to lay your faith in, good to lay your pain in, but it ain't this muddy water here that saves you."[16]

Taking the child from Mrs. Connin's arms, the preacher asks him, "'Have you ever been Baptized?' . . . 'What's that?' the child asks. 'If I Baptize you, you'll be able to go to the Kingdom of Christ. You'll be washed in the river of suffering, son, and you'll go by the deep river of life. Do you want that?'" "'Yes,' the child said, and thought, I won't go back to the apartment then, I'll go under the river. 'You won't be the same again,' the preacher said. 'You'll count.'"[17]

In the invitation by the preacher to the river congregation and in his conversation with the child, O'Connor mixes metaphoric and denotative language. By so doing, she heightens the confusion between image and reality embodied throughout the narrative as a tension between faith in a vision beyond oneself and self-centered "hedonism and sophistication" or skepticism,[18] central to the story. A backwoods revivalist, himself a spectacle to those who do not understand his experience of reality, acknowledges this confusion by warning the company of witnesses that the red river is symbolic.

But among the witnesses stands the child who does not make subtle distinctions between image and reality, between rivers of blood and muddy ones; he knows only that he wants to count. When Harry returns to his city home—the ashfield where the sun comes into the apartment "palely, stained gray by the glass";[19] where there are no sharp contrasts as there are in the country, no one to help him discern even the outlines, let alone the meaning of his life; where there is no human activity in his home except at night; and where everything, even Jesus, is a joke—and discovers nothing has changed after his baptism, he decides "not to fool with preachers any more but to Baptize himself."[20] Recalling the preacher's words, but now without an intermediary, Harry wants "to keep on going this time until he found the Kingdom of Christ."[21] This decision turns the child from a spectator into a spectacle whose actions are guided by his subjective interpretations of a sacrament intended to lead one into a community of faith. However, moments before the river current finally takes him under, Harry recognizes that the river might not take him and concludes that this promise of baptism too was another joke.

Through backwoods fundamentalist preaching and his own misperceptions of promises and jokes, Harry makes two discoveries that, in turn, point readers, whose conventional sensibilities have been offended by the drowning, to another logic. Harry finds out first that one learns more by releasing or distancing from those places and things with which he identifies than by grasping them to maintain security. The second thing readers discover through the image-reality distortions of Harry is that life is shot through with deceptions that help one preserve exactly the opposite posture—of trying to achieve security by hanging onto one's surroundings and pulling everything close to oneself. Harry makes both discoveries through the summons from Mrs. Connin and Bevel Summers to count, to *be*. This call runs directly counter to his experiences at home where his life matters little. Through the confusion of figurative and denotative language, "The River" implies that one can respond to such a call only by distancing, by separating from that with which he identifies too closely—his family, his possessions, his self-image, his deceptions and misinformation—and by expanding consciousness even unto death.

O'Connor increases the ironic power of her story, as she outrages adult rationality, by having a little child, who has no substantial attachments and whose ability to distinguish between image and reality is unreliable, lead to this discovery. Addressing disturbed readers about the ending of "The River," O'Connor explained that "Bevel hasn't reached the age of reason; therefore he can't commit suicide. He comes to a good end. He's saved from those nutty parents, a fate worse than death. He's been baptized and so he goes to his Maker; this is a good end."[22] Bevel's is the inevitable sacrifice necessary to overcome the "sins of the fathers," the absence of a community of meaning. Those who live by the rational skepticism and hedonism depicted in Harry's parents find such sacrifice incomprehensible. Infusing the ancient Christian sacrament of baptism with images suggestive of primitive rites of passage and setting the story just outside a modern urban center, O'Connor shifts our attention to a disturbing, new environment to suggest the enigmatic, unitive nature of reality.

Although the words spoken and heard in "A Good Man Is Hard to Find" and in "The River" distorted and deflected meaning, leading to confusion, they still held the *potential* for communication. However, in "A Late Encounter with the Enemy," O'Connor builds a tomb-like narrative construction with words that bring an old conquering hero to his death because they no longer connect him to any reality besides himself. Sally Poker Sash wants her grandfather, the General, to attend her graduation because he represents to her the traditions of family and place: "Dignity! Honor! Courage!" Through these variations of the cardinal virtues (justice, prudence, fortitude, temperance) and theological ones (faith, hope, and charity), O'Connor constricts her character. This man who embodies the old virtues for Sally, O'Connor describes as "pure game cock" and, later in the story, as a "frail dried spider."[23]

Between these two images exists the shell of one who "didn't have any use for history because he never expected to meet it again. To his mind, history was connected with processions and life with parades and he liked parades. . . . There was only one event in the past that had any significance for him and that he cared to talk about: that was twelve years ago when he had received the general's uniform and had been in the premiere." The old General would recount the event to anyone giving him the least attention because "it wasn't a thing local about it. It was nothing local about it. Listen here it was a nashnul event and they had me in it—up onto the stage."[24]

The landscape that O'Connor creates in the General's isolated recollection of beautiful girls, ten-dollar gatherings, tuxedos and uniforms, and his desire for national attention is, ironically, a very private, egoistic one in which Sally tries to root her own present life. Processions and parades generally signify passage from one stage to another, or they mark achievements of change. In this environment, however, they permit no such growth; in fact, the sweltering heat at Sally's black graduation procession prohibits even a breeze, thus contributing to the stifling, constricted atmosphere shaped principally by the arrested ego of the spectacular Old General.

Words in this story, as in "A Stroke of Good Fortune," possess a palpable reality, for, in the form of history, they become the final enemy the General battles. As a collection of words, history symbolically links isolated individuals to each other and separated centuries or groups to some common experience. Because the General acknowledges no such connections, the word battle rages tortuously and uncontrollably in the hole in his head. Words enter the hole against his will and chase cyclically around his head where he must finally confront, in near exhaustion, the faces of his wife, his sons, his mother, and past places whose reality and meaning he has forgotten or denied. What we may understand from this labyrinthian chase in the deep regions of the General's mind is that passage into the future or expansion away from egocentrism must lead through the recesses and crevices of a buried past. For the General, words have been his self-protection against that past; instead they have sustained his illusions. But they are also, O'Connor implies ironically at the end of the story, capable of taking on life that shatters deception and makes transference from life to death possible.

The final irony occurs when Sally Poker Sash does not recognize what has been taking place in the General's head during her commencement. Following her grandfather's example, she has been isolated in a world of illusions—"she wanted to show what she stood for, or, as she said, 'what all was behind her,' and was not behind them"[25]—which she has built on old virtues and ideals cut off from historical, institutional, and mythic roots. Not only does Sally not recognize that it is the *corpse* of her grandfather who looks on as she receives her diploma, but also she fails to understand that ideals without physical form or words without some informing reality or presence "is the Great American Joke that allows for the triumph of the banal . . . that paved the way for numberless religious eccentrics . . . and for an equal number of abstracted or sentimental idealists."[26]

Each of the stories in *A Good Man Is Hard to Find* depends on O'Connor's similar manipulation of language to express truth indirectly. By showing us the almost limitless potential in language for distortion and disconnection, for illusion and isolation—often through words spoken by preachers or prophets or generals, by a carpenter con man, a Bible salesman, and a convict conversant with the sacrifice of Christ—O'Connor intrudes her artistic and religious interest in an original Word that came in unexpected form to stand "in-between," partaking of both the human and the divine, the accent and the essence.

Incantation as Recurring Metaphor

Understanding that the fiction writer "can't create compassion with compassion, or emotion with emotion, or thought with thought . . .

[but] has to provide all these things with a body," Flannery O'Connor confesses that writing fiction requires "the habit of art" in which "the whole personality—the conscious as well as the unconscious mind"—participates.[27] Reading her fiction summons a similar participation from the reader. One way O'Connor moves our attention in her stories to some informing presence or mystery that stands behind, between, or within all our words, even failures to communicate and distortions, is to shape the words that obsess or plague her characters—their incantations or confessions—into metaphors, thus giving the *verbal* expression of obsession, of piety, or of rebellion a "body" or pattern to be wrestled with. Victor Shklovsky has described this technique as "defamiliarizing the object—that is by adding more 'weight' to it—and thus emphasizing its properties."[28] By emphasizing the grotesqueries of words, O'Connor turns them into metaphoric objects. Again, readers will find examples of this technique in every story of this collection, but "A Stroke of Good Fortune," "A Circle in the Fire," and "Good Country People," illustrate its operation and effect.

In "A Stroke of Good Fortune," a story she did not count among her favorites, O'Connor illustrates how "words . . . take physical shape and function as separate dramatic entities . . . [and become] forces to be struggled with at least in the mind of the protagonist."[29] In fact, O'Connor intensifies the sense of exertion in "A Stroke of Good Fortune" by linking Ruby's psychic struggle with words that unwittingly describe her true condition to her personal effort to climb the stairs. The irony of the story depends on words—*cancer, good fortune,* and *motherhood*—which simultaneously allow Ruby to deny her actual condition while forcing the reader to recognize her pregnancy.

The word *cancer* illustrates this double capacity of language to hide and to reveal, for Ruby concludes that the pain in her stomach is a growth of cells forewarning not life but death. The word haunts her every time she feels the pain. "She had felt [the pain] before, a few days ago. It was the one that frightened her most. She had thought the word *cancer* once and dropped it instantly because no horror like that was coming to her because it couldn't."[30] Ruby temporarily dispels this palpable fear of cancer through her faith in the incantations of Madam Zoleeda who promised Ruby the pain would end in good fortune. So, with two words turned to metaphor for an unacknowledged pregnancy, *good fortune,* Ruby destroys the word *cancer,* which is ironically eating away in her imagination as it develops new life in her womb: "she slashed it [cancer] twice through and then again until there were only pieces of it that couldn't be recognized."[31] The physical reality of *good fortune* is increased by O'Connor's personification of it in Hartley Gilfeet, a child known to Ruby as Little Mister Good Fortune, through whom O'Connor informs us about the true nature of Ruby's cancer.

The good fortune Ruby denies is motherhood, a state she associates with death. "She remembered her mother at thirty-four—she had looked like a puckered-up old yellow apple, sour, she had always looked sour, she had always looked like she wasn't satisfied with anything . . . all those children were what did her mother in—eight of them: two born dead, one died the first year, one crushed under a mowing machine. Her mother had got deader with every one of them."[32] Ruby's mother reminds Ruby of her own whole nature, a wholeness she rejects in ignorant preference for a vegetable-like dependence on Bill Hill's birth control measures and a house in the suburbs. The shadow of motherhood, which resides in Ruby's memory as well as in her own blooming body, takes on tangible reality as Laverne Watts, chanting and dancing ritualistically sings, "Put them all together they spell MOTHER."[33] By shaping words like *cancer* and *good fortune* into metaphors and juxtaposing them with pregnancy, O'Connor embodies, through Ruby's struggle, human resistance to and distortion of the inbreaking of new life.

In "A Circle in the Fire," O'Connor again rivets our attention on a concrete, circumscribed world and simultaneously distracts that attention toward her real interests: the sins of piety and possessiveness. She achieves this double focus through the language of conversation marked by long monologues, which are interrupted by non sequiturs and repeated phrases sounding similar to incantation. Speculating, for example, about how a woman could conceive and give birth to a baby in an iron lung, Mrs. Pritchard asks, "'You know that woman that had that baby in that iron lung?'"

> "I read about her," [Mrs. Cope] said.
> "She was a Pritchard that married a Brookins and so's kin to me—about my seventh or eighth cousin by marriage."
> "Well, well," Mrs. Cope muttered and threw a large clump of nut grass behind her. She worked at the weeds and nut grass as if they were an evil sent directly by the devil to destroy the place.
> "Beinst she was kin to us, we gone to see the body," Mrs. Pritchard said. "Seen the little baby too. . . . She had her arm around it in the coffin."[34]

Mrs. Pritchard's monologue is interrupted briefly when a Negro, driving a tractor and wagon around rather than through the gate, diverts Mrs. Cope's attention from weeding. Exasperatedly Mrs. Cope reflects that "her Negroes were as destructive and impersonal as the nut grass."[35] Hardly delayed in her rumination, however, Mrs. Pritchard continues:

> "I don't see myself how she had it *in* it. . . ."
>
> Mrs. Cope was bent over, digging fiercely at the nut grass again. "We have a lot to be thankful for," she said. "Every day you should say a prayer of thanksgiving. Do you do that?"
>
> "Yes'm, . . . See she was in it four months before she even got thataway. Look like to me if I was in one of them, I would leave off . . . how you reckon they . . . ?"
>
> "Everyday I say a prayer of thanksgiving," Mrs. Cope said. "Think of all we have. Lord . . . we have everything. . . ."
>
> Mrs. Pritchard studied the woods. "All I got is four abscess teeth. . . ."
>
> "Well, be thankful you don't have five," Mrs. Cope snapped and threw back a clump of grass.[36]

In conversations spoken over nut grass between one woman intoning thanks as a charm against fear and the other captivated by "calamitous stories," O'Connor incarnates two psychological orientations as she turns nut grass into a metaphor for anything that threatens Mrs. Cope's control of herself and her property. By turning nut grass into a metaphor, O'Connor prepares us for the intervention of three nutgrass-like "prophets"—inverted from three biblical prophets—who come from beyond the borders of her farm to harass Mrs. Cope and her land. Their presence forces her to expose the weedy underside of her optimistic piety for what it truly is: idolatry of herself and her land. Whereas Mrs. Cope worships her own power and control, Mrs. Pritchard is the one who repeatedly reminds Mrs. Cope, after Powell and his friends begin to torment her, that "there ain't a thing you can do about it,"[37] thereby ironically anticipating what becomes "the new misery"[38] for Mrs. Cope whose incantations of thanksgiving cannot save "her" woods.

O'Connor originally intended "Good Country People" to be the concluding story of her first collection because, as she wrote with typical irony to Robert Giroux, "It is really a story that would set the whole collection on its feet."[39] That O'Connor believed this story, in which an atheist loses her artificial leg to a thieving Bible salesman, would set the collection firmly on its feet is not only a measure of O'Connor's imaginative subtlety but also a hint that her artistic intentions may be rendered to her satisfaction here. This humorous story about seduction exposes the sterility of language and life either stripped of metaphors, which disclose mystery, or dependent on clichés, which preserve illusions in place of mystery.

As in "A Circle in the Fire," O'Connor frames "Good Country People" with cliché-ridden conversation between Mrs. Hopewell and Mrs. Freeman, displaying Mrs. Hopewell's limited vision and perception. Though she recognizes "nothing is perfect,"[40] Mrs. Hopewell hopes superficially in the goodness of everything and everyone. Her sentimental hope makes her gullible to a Bible salesman who confesses, "Well, lady, I'll tell you the truth—not many people want to buy [a Bible] nowadays and besides, I know I'm real simple. I don't know how to say a thing but to say it. I'm just a country boy. . . . People like you don't like to fool with country people like me!"[41] Taken in by a "good country person" as she believes herself to be, Mrs. Hopewell exclaims that "good country people are the salt of the earth."[42] Through these two repeated phrases—"good country people" and "salt of the earth"—O'Connor turns Manley Pointer and Mrs. Hopewell into a composite metaphor for all those who make their way in the world through illusions held in place by fixed categories and glib labels, structures built in the air.

Mrs. Hopewell's daughter, however, is intent on avoiding such illusions; thus, when her mother interrupts her conversation with the Bible salesman to check on her dinner cooking in the kitchen, Hulga tells her to "get rid of the salt of the earth" so they can eat.[43] Frequently feeling impatience for her mother's vacuity, Hulga expresses it finally with her mouth half full: "Woman, do you ever look inside? Do you ever look inside and see what you are not? God!"[44] From Hulga's efforts to strip language of its illusory capacity and religion of its sentimentalism, O'Connor fashions a metaphoric nihilist.

O'Connor lays bare the sterility of sentimentalism and nihilism alike in the seduction episode in the barn. Rose Bowen finds in the violation-initiation ritual that transpires in the barn resonances of the baptismal liturgy in which candidates are given a taste of salt, symbolizing wisdom, to preserve them from sin. Bowen takes Manley Pointer's status as "the salt of the earth" seriously, considers his curiosity about where Hulga's wooden leg attaches to her body as desire to "enter into her uniqueness," and credits him with leading her to

grace. Although these associations with baptism enrich our appreciation for the direction in which O'Connor presses us, they overlook
what happens to Manley as well in the process of preparing Hulga for
"baptism."[45] Through words and images carrying both religious and
sexual meaning, she intensifies the encounter in which, ironically, the
sentimentalist con man and educated nihilist exchange positions. In
the barn we learn that the atheist, who would strip away all illusions,
associates her wooden leg with her soul. When she took it off "it was like
losing her own life and finding it again, miraculously, in his."[46] Quickly
Hulga realizes that without her leg her brain seems to stop thinking;
the soul is dependent solely on her rational faculties. For Manley, the
leg has sexual significance. When Hulga asks him to put it back on,
he resists, explaining, "Not yet. Leave it off for a while. You got me
instead."[47] Without replacing her leg, Manley instead presents gifts—a
flask of whiskey, a pack of playing cards bearing obscene pictures, and a
box of condoms—to this half-souled goddess. Through these gifts,
ironically reminiscent of the wise men's gifts, the Bible salesman—now
himself having given up his religious pose—mocks the nihilist's confession that salvation comes by taking off one's blindfold and seeing
nothing. He climbs down from the loft with his vision apparently
burned clean to nothingness, and Hulga remains legless in the loft—
her life still miraculously lost in his—with her words, "Woman, do you
ever look inside?" echoing in the readers' ears, if not in her own.

Using strain and violation in the loft at the uppermost boundaries
of the farm, O'Connor creates a new language environment from the
physical and psychic soil of her characters. Through her own ironic
vision capable of imagining through to everything, she twists passages
of Christian scripture into platitudes, turns a Bible salesman into a
con man, grafts Christian festivals with pagan or secular rites, and
obscures the conventional conceptions of good and evil to show that
simple faith in good country people and faith in nothing are equally
deceptive. By setting this bizarre confrontation on the edge of the
farm beyond the view of the good country people, O'Connor makes
the episode a large metaphor for the human tendency to prefer deception to truth when the material and the spiritual are not mutually
informed.

Through recurring metaphors reflecting psychological states that
abstractly threaten, plague, or secure her characters, O'Connor constructs the geographical and architectural landscapes of these stories.
When words take on concrete shapes, we see them as outward mani-

festations—projections—of inner, invisible states. Thus the apparently
clear distinctions among various characters' perceptions or professions—used to justify, to protect, and ultimately to isolate them—
become grotesque and more ambiguous when they are embodied.
Through this language technique O'Connor moves repressed contents
of our collective history and psyche to the conscious level, thereby
challenging our inherently one-dimensional interpretations of reality.
Indeed, the foggy familiarity of O'Connor's landscapes invites us to
expose ourselves.

Shadows and Contradictions

O'Connor's ability to turn repeated phrases into metaphors sustains
her ability to present doubled characters who personify the contradictions that so preoccupied her or disclose the shadow cast by obfuscating the light of truth. As we examine this technique in "The River,"
"The Life You Save May Be Your Own," and "Good Country People,"
it will be obvious that character doubling occurs in most of O'Connor's
fiction, as Frederick Asals has demonstrated, and is reinforced by all
the other language devices O'Connor employs.

In "The River" O'Connor presents two pairs of doubled characters,
one which discloses the confusion resulting from opposing innocence
(a literal interpretation of reality) and experience (an ability to interpret reality symbolically), and one which mirrors the contradictions
between the city and the country and conducts young Harry's passage
between the two and to his final rest. The more ironic and obvious
doubling occurs when Harry chooses *Bevel*, the preacher's name, as
his name when he goes to the country with Mrs. Connin. Through the
name *Bevel*, O'Connor implies the contrary notions that meet in these
characters, making them a symbol of an oblique divine-human intervention. Much as a bevel gear conveys motion by means of bevel
wheels from one shaft to another at an angle, Bevel Summers, whose
surname suggests fecundity, leads young "Bevel" from his ashfield to
the restorative water, from his no-count spectator life in the city to the
spectacular experience of death. But through his innocence, young
Bevel—unable to distinguish symbolic from literal language—drowns
himself in these restorative waters, thus suggesting the innocence ever
present especially in intellectual sophistication and religious fervor.
This preacher of experience unwittingly invites the child Bevel to

move from innocence to experience achieved in fleeting moments before he is swept under the river.

Harry tempers his innocence with experience in the country, a place where he notices rich variety—a red and gold grove of sassafras, a pasture dotted with black and white cows, a pine woods, crackling red leaves, and "the reflection of the sun . . . set like a diamond," which creates an orange stream.[48] And among the country human beings there are also sharp contrasts in a pair of characters who guide and threaten him: nurturant Mrs. Connin, a pious preacher, and shoat-like Mr. Paradise. Mrs. Connin is Harry's central caretaker; throughout the story she conducts him safely from the city to the country—introducing him there to her large family, to her animals, to Jesus, and to the possibility of "counting" through baptism—and back to the city. When the preacher questions Harry at the river on the day of his baptism, Mr. Paradise scoffingly watches from the outermost edge of the congregation. His faithlessness stands as contradiction to Mrs. Connin's faith in such rites. However, when Harry returns alone to the river the next day, Mr. Paradise, who has been fishing in the river with an unbaited line, leaps from the fringes to the center—shifting from spectator to spectacle—in order to become Harry's guide or would-be savior. Just before Harry drowns in his act of self-baptism he sees "something like a giant pig bounding after him shaking a red and white club and shouting."[49] O'Connor intensifies the irony of this pair by naming a cynic, who assists in Harry's baptism into eternal life, Paradise, and by connecting skeletal images with Mrs. Connin—who initiated Harry's journey by taking him away for a day—that imply the paradoxical passage that she guides from death-in-life to life-in-death.

In "The Life You Save May Be Your Own," O'Connor also offers us two pairs of doubled characters. Although sharing the same name, the mother and daughter Lucynell Craters present opposite character traits. "The mother is a hard-bitten, leathery, and toothless country widow whose toughness has enabled her to survive but has taken its toll. . . . The daughter is a moron whose vapid beauty . . . serve[s] as a strange and distorted symbol of spiritual innocence."[50] Together these women not only caricature the mother-daughter relationship, asserts Louise Westling, but also reveal O'Connor's sardonic attitude toward sexuality. O'Connor further complicates the character doubling by encouraging, through inverted shadow and suggestion, the reader's association of one character with Jesus Christ. Again in this story O'Connor focuses on the sin of delusion and builds the language environment, like flimsy scaffolding, on the ironic juxtaposition of moral platitudes and blunt honesty expressed by her doubled characters, Tom and Lucynell. After ambiguously announcing himself through his shadow that forms a crooked cross against the setting sun, Tom T. Shiftlet tells Lucynell Crater in words who he really is: "Lady, . . . nowadays, people'll do anything anyways. I can tell you my name is Tom T. Shiftlet and I come from Tarwater, Tennessee, but you never have seen me before: how you know I ain't lying? How you know my name ain't Aaron Sparks, lady, and I come from Singleberry, Georgia, or how you know it's not George Speeds and I come from Lucy, Alabama, or how you know I ain't Thompson Bright from Toolafalls, Mississippi?"[51] Immediately after offering this riddle that presents Tom as Everyman, he tells Lucynell that he is a carpenter.

O'Connor confounds the too-easy association of this carpenter with the Nazarene one and deepens the deception of the story by doubling an itinerant con artist with a rooted one. Both want to use the other for their own ends. Lucynell "was ravenous for a son-in-law";[52] Tom "had always wanted an automobile but he had never been able to afford one before."[53] The secret desires of these two bring them into collusion, linking Lucynell's deaf-mute daughter with a mechanical object. Through these two characters, O'Connor contrasts the operations and consequences of partial vision, one practical and down-to-earth, the other pervertedly spiritual and grandiose. Lucynell schemes and openly negotiates a marriage for her innocent, ignorant daughter basing her negotiations on material security: "Listen here, Mr. Shiftlet . . . you'd be getting a permanent house and a deep well and the most innocent girl in the world. You don't need money."[54] Tom, however, philosophizes and moralizes his ambitions, pretending to a spiritual stature that leaves him still half a man. "Lady, a man is divided into two parts, body and spirit. . . . The body, lady, is like a house: it don't go anywhere; but the spirit, lady, is like a automobile; always on the move, always. . . . I'm only saying a man's spirit means more to him than anything else."[55] Through their egoistic interests, they embody contradiction not simply between them. The interests themselves additionally expose the contradiction inherent in their individual desires. For example, Lucynell wants her daughter's marriage not for human intimacy but for material security, and Tom cunningly suggests that the car will transport him to some spiritual horizon or at least as far as Mobile.

We return to "Good Country People" for a final example of the way

O'Connor could complicate character doubles within single narratives as well as across stories. The daily, repetitive gossip between Mrs. Hopewell and Mrs. Freeman—the repetitious nature of which is heightened because Mrs. Freeman reflects the opinions of those around her and "could never be brought to admit herself wrong on any point"[56]—encircles the story to present an illusion of conventional farm life and a backdrop for the shockingly unconventional encounter between the Bible peddler and the atheist. Although both Mrs. Freeman and Mrs. Hopewell have daughters, Mrs. Freeman's Glynese and Carramae are sexually attractive and active compared to Hulga, who seemed to Mrs. Hopewell every year to grow "less like other people and more like herself—bloated, rude, and squint-eyed."[57] Mrs. Freeman's fascination with "secret infections, hidden deformities, assaults upon children,"[58] not only anticipates Manley Pointer's obsession with Hulga, which was "like a child watching a new fantastic animal at the zoo."[59] Accepting Mrs. Hopewell's cliché-filled speech as a mouthful, the Bible salesman also mirrors these two farm women. Through Hulga's intense impatience with her mother's shallowness and Hulga's belief in nothing, O'Connor not only incarnates the contradiction between their philosophies but also prepares for the contest between Manley, a shadow of the good country people, and Hulga, the in-the-flesh contradiction of such goodness and decency. For Mrs. Hopewell, Manley Pointer represents the goodness she espouses and looks to her like an optimistic aspect of her daughter's cynical rejection of everything. By linking Hulga and the Bible salesman through their weak hearts, Mrs. Hopewell unconsciously suggests the pregnability of pure categories and the troubling coexistence of faith and doubt.

Similar character doubling across stories not only increases the company of those afflicted by various manifestations of original sins—such as delusion and inflation—but also contributes to an episodic quality in these first collection stories. In her obsession with "secret infections and hidden deformities," Mrs. Freeman recalls Mrs. Pritchard's voyeuristic attraction to "calamitous stories" and Mrs. Shortley's penchant for visions and prophecy. Although Mrs. Hopewell and Mrs. Cope both protect themselves with platitudes, Mrs. Cope and Mrs. McIntyre struggle willfully to maintain control over their land and themselves. O'Connor's shadowy reference to biblical figures—like Shadrach, Meshach, and Abednego—or association of a character like Tom Shiftlet with Jesus Christ extends and deepens the cross-story doubling. The children in all these stories are spectator-victims who—like the girl child in "A Temple of the Holy Ghost," Mr. Head's grandson, Mrs. Cope's daughter, Young Harry, and even thirty-two-year-old Hulga—initiate us through contradiction into the real contest for the human heart going on at the center of the world. When such similar pairs of characters appear in several stories, we have the sense that we as spectators—just as O'Connor's characters who talk in circles that rarely interconnect—are hearing echoes or watching spectacular reruns. These sensations should not surprise us, for they are characteristic responses to episodic tales, but they do arouse our interest in how O'Connor's story structures themselves reinforce the contest taking place within or among characters.

In her examination of the fiction produced by Eudora Welty, Carson McCullers, and Flannery O'Connor "in a society which officially worshipped womanhood but in its imaginative life betrayed contradictory undercurrents," Westling provocatively adds a further dimension to our understanding of O'Connor's doubling. Through sexual imagery drawn from pagan fertility rites, classical mythology, and Christian tradition, O'Connor identifies her women with the land and implies "that male incursions amount to a kind of rape," thereby etching more deeply the "often excruciating picture of . . . female self-loathing, powerlessness, and justified fear of masculine attack." According to Westling, O'Connor "presents fictional doubles of herself . . . who express the rage and frustration which is too dangerous for women to admit in ordinary life." But the ultimate irony of O'Connor's treatment of her women—the trickster tricked—is that "she punishes them with a finality which restores a balance with the dominant values of the world in which we all must live."[60]

Arcs and Circles

All the stories in *A Good Man Is Hard to Find* turn on circular structures that arise from a central tension either revealed within the life of one character or, more commonly, expressed as an apparent contradiction between a pair of characters. This tension is set in motion by the forces of resistance and attraction the characters manifest toward their own or others' inner states, which when projected, influence their outer circumstances as well. Through these interpersonal and spatial centripetal-centrifugal pulls, O'Connor does not simply reflect the earth's movement and balance between expansion and contraction; rather, using these natural forces as metaphor, she incarnates what she believed was an ongoing struggle for the world between God and the devil and between human faith and doubt.

She reveals her sensitivity for such motion in human beings in her ideas on conversion: "I don't think of conversion as being once and for all and that's that. I think once the process is begun and continues that you are continually turning inward toward God and away from your own egocentricity and that you have to see this selfish side of yourself in order to turn away from it."[61] We might conclude from an observation like this and from the perpetual tension in her characters, carried into the story structures, that O'Connor intends to make our selfish side visible to us. But artistic intentions, like the intention to believe, are never simple. And so we find that often the centripetal-centrifugal strain in the stories arises as much from characters' not knowing the difference between egocentric afflictions "that you can get rid of . . . and must bend every effort *to* get rid of, and 'passive diminishments,' . . . those afflictions that you can't get rid of and have to bear,"[62] as from stubbornness to turn and be changed. O'Connor embodies the confusion between self-inflation and balance—which is realized by living from a divine center—in her stories' structures. Built on exaggerations and inversions, the structures mirror the distortions that paradoxically preserve human beings from discerning the truth about themselves and their real condition.

In "A Good Man Is Hard to Find" the doubled characters (The Misfit with cynical doubt and the grandmother with sentimental faith) are pulled irresistibly together by the centripetal force of events leading to the accident—the newspaper article about The Misfit and the grandmother's desire to avoid a meeting with his kind; the grandmother's attention to being well dressed so that, in case of an accident, people would know she had been a lady; the graveyard which the grandmother informs her family is a family burial plot as they pass it; the cat, hidden deceptively by the grandmother, that lurches out of its basket causing the accident when the grandmother recognizes she has deceived herself about the location of the plantation. Built like a tight house-that-Jack-built, the story pulls to the central confrontation—an inversion of the inward turning toward God—between these two characters, reflections of each other, whose respective journeys from and to Florida have converged in Georgia. As they squat on the ground discussing goodness and suffering, the horrors explode around them pulling them to another plane of experience, toward fuller self-consciousness, which is touched for a mere instant by the possibility of conversion in an instant before The Misfit shoots the grandmother.

"The Displaced Person" also depends heavily on a centripetal-centrifugal tension made progressively apparent through the landscape and characters of Mrs. Shortley, Mrs. McIntyre, and Mr. Guizac. O'Connor gives Mrs. Shortley a mountain-like power to preside over the centrifugal changes threatened by the Guizacs' arrival from over the ocean. In the opening paragraph, Mrs. Shortley, followed by the peacock whose tail was "full of fierce planets with eyes that were each ringed in green and set against a sun that was gold in one second's light and salmon-colored in the next [and looked like] a map of the universe,"[63] climbs to her lookout. As "the giant wife of the countryside,"[64] she immediately possesses mythic proportions. O'Connor sets the whole first part of the story on the strength of this "priest"-protector who turns prophet and displays stubborn intolerance of everyone. Coming down from her hilltop perch after the Guizacs arrive, Mrs. Shortley's "look first grazed the tops of the displaced people's heads and then revolved downwards slowly, the way a buzzard glides and drops in the air until it alights on the carcass."[65]

O'Connor consistently places Mrs. Shortley on the edge of activity. She drives to the edge of the cane field with Mrs. McIntyre to see how Mr. Guizac operates the silage cutter. She approaches the barn from oblique angles so she can see before being seen. Even her husband, whose illegal whiskey-making Mrs. Shortley defends, carries on his business on "the farthest reaches of the place."[66] Yet, because she regards herself as the resident guardian of morality, she seems always omnipresent implying the doom to come through visions of warring words and "fiery wheels with fierce dark eyes in them, spinning rapidly all around [the gigantic figure she saw in the sky.]"[67] We find in this story, as in ones previously cited, how O'Connor juxtaposes a biblical prophet with Mrs. Shortley, using images central to the story of Ezekiel as an organizing principle of her own narrative. Mrs. Shortley's Sunday vision connects her with Ezekiel, also renowned for his strength, whose ministry was to Babylonian exiles. Mrs. Shortley thinks of the exiled ones in her midst as the Whore of Babylon. Through her character, her judgments, and visions, Mrs. Shortley embodies the human problem of displacement served on humanity as punishment for arrogance and intolerance (sin).

The second and third parts of the story revolve on the wheel images established in the first section. With the Shortley's departure at the end of part one, Mrs. McIntyre takes up the circular refrain, "We've seen them come and seen them go."[68] In its impersonal, even fatalistic tone, the refrain inverts Job's personal lament: "Yahweh gave, Yahweh has taken back. Blessed be the name of Yahweh."[69] Although this refrain forewarns Mrs. McIntyre's final loss in part three, it first prepares the way for Mr. Guizac's gradual exposure of death that lies at the farm's center. O'Connor presents that exposure in the physical activity of corn cutting. Looking like a fallen angel dressed in her black hat and smock, Mrs. McIntyre interrupts Guizac's cutting to inform him that he cannot bring his cousin to her country to marry a black and thereby make her job of fighting the world's overflow harder. Guizac, who began cutting in circles at the edge of the field, ends at the center. When he finishes, the graveyard stands in the center, "risen like an island . . . where the Judge lay grinning under his desecrated monument."[70]

In section three, Mrs. McIntyre's faith in Mr. Guizac as her mechanically adept miracle-worker has turned to doubt as she contemplates his dismissal. To Father Flynn she rationalizes, "'He's extra and he's upset the balance around here,' she said, 'and I'm a logical practical woman and there are no ovens here and no camps and no Christ Our Lord and when he leaves, he'll make more money. He'll work at the mill and buy a car and don't talk to me—all they want is a car.'"[71] Mr. Shortley's return to the farm implies the centripetal pull now underway in Mrs. McIntyre who confesses "she should have been content with the help she had in the first place and not have been reaching into other parts of the world for it."[72] Convinced that the Pole killed Mrs. Shortley, Mr. Shortley is pulled back to the farm as he unwittingly prepares to participate in the final displacement of Mr. Guizac. The tractor wheel, which had formerly made Guizac Mrs. McIntyre's savior, breaks Guizac's backbone as Mr. Shortley's, Mrs. McIntyre's, and the Negro's eyes come "together in one look that froze them in collusion forever."[73] The prophetic wheels have locked in death leaving Mrs. McIntyre alone on her desolate land with steadily worsening eyesight, no voice, and a weekly visit from Father Flynn who would "sit by the side of her bed and explain the doctrines of the Church."[74]

Using the downward circling of buzzards, the visual impression of orbs on a peacock's tail, Ezekiel's visions of wildly spinning wheels, the mechanical wheels necessary for farm efficiency and profit, O'Connor tells a gyrating tale of human displacement. She thus molds the psychological-religious tension between ever-expanding consciousness that has no center and the consciousness that seeks security in facile conventions—money, war, racial and national superiority.

We find in "A Circle in the Fire" a similar confluence of circular images, allusions to Judeo-Christian history, and narrative movement, through which O'Connor exposes a centripetal-centrifugal tension. On the concrete level, this is a story about resistance to centrifugal forces like Mrs. Pritchard's obsessive preoccupation with calamities and about the barriers constructed against purification brought through light and heat. At the outset of the story O'Connor describes the blank sky as if it were "pushing against the fortress wall, trying to break through."[75] The only way that light can possibly break into the dark, constricted center of Mrs. Cope's world is through fire, through the consumption of everything she protects and desires to preserve through her words of thanksgiving.

O'Connor prepares for the fire that burns the woods encircling the farm largely through eye and sun imagery. The narrator implies the approaching threat to Mrs. Cope when in her anger with the laziness of her Negro help, "her eyes, as she opened them, looked as if they would keep on enlarging until they turned her wrong-side out."[76] Mrs. Cope's entire world is turned upside down, or inside out, when the three vagabonds arrive. Although "all three boys had white penetrating stares,"[77] Powell's eyes become the dominant vehicle through which O'Connor moves the narrative. Mrs. Cope observes Powell's one roving eye and his other stationary eye cautiously: "One of his eyes had a slight cast to it so that his gaze seemed to be coming from two directions at once as if it had surrounded them. . . . One of Powell's eyes seemed to be making a circle of the place, examining the house and the white water tower behind it and the chicken houses and the pastures that rolled away on either side until they met the first line of woods."[78] Within the head of one person—in Powell's eyes—O'Connor places the contending centripetal-centrifugal forces that give this story its dynamic quality.

The boys test the patience of Mrs. Cope, threaten her world, and move closer to the earth-shaking question of ownership. The movement occurs not alone through Powell's eyes, which "looked as if he were trying to enclose the whole place in one encircling stare."[79] Westling reminds us that for Powell, Mrs. Cope's farm is "a paradise lost when his tenant farmer father moved the family to Florida."[80]

Returning now with two friends, O'Connor associates the boys with snakes whose function is ambiguous in this story, for they exhibit a misogynist spirit bent on invading and reclaiming the place. Also, the boy's gestures intensify Mrs. Cope's uneasiness and anger, moving the story toward its climax and Mrs. Cope toward judgment. Fearful that people will get hurt on her place and terrified of fire in the woods, Mrs. Cope erupts angrily when she sees one of the boys spit a cigarette butt in an arc. This defiant gesture arches over the rest of the story, gradually riveting the reader's attention on fire.

Changes in the sun forecast the approaching destruction-purification. Its color is no longer glaring white but flame-colored as it settles prophetically on top of the tree line. Almost as if anticipating the ritual burning of the woods, "the sun burned so fast," observes the narrator for Mrs. Cope, "that it seemed to be trying to set everything in sight on fire."[81] However, as the child crashes through the woods determined to confront and beat the boys, "the sun had risen a little and was only a white hole like an opening for the wind to escape through in a sky a little darker than itself, and the tops of the trees were black against the glare."[82] This image anticipates the earth as a fiery furnace from which smoke escapes through the hole made by the sun. In this strange light from the edge of the woods, Sally Virginia watches the boys undergo a preparatory symbolic baptism in a cow trough, which O'Connor likens to a coffin. Joining their watery romp with incantations about possession, the big boy exclaims, "Listen, it don't belong to nobody." And the little boy responds, "It's ours." Powell then jumps from the trough and begins racing around the field.

O'Connor completes the narrative circle, begun with the three boys' entrance into the farm, through their ritual-like circling of the field. The arc made earlier by a spewed cigarette butt bursts forth now into a fire. By alluding to the boys as "prophets [who] were dancing in the fiery furnace, in the circle the angel had cleared for them,"[83] O'Connor, albeit through inversion, joins this circular narrative to the larger religious story of three prophets who turn King Nebuchadnezzar from idol worship. With his one roving and one steady eye, Powell has encircled and judged the whole place, ironically offering the land for purification. The big boy's suggestion that he would make a parking lot on the land if it were his pulls these inverted prophets and Mrs. Cope into the same circle. On Mrs. Cope's land O'Connor has incarnated the struggle between a techno-industrial expansionist spirit symbolized by the automobile and the preservationist defense of agrarian property rights and tradition. Though the boys expose the distortion of vision Mrs. Cope's self-righteousness causes, the use to which they would put the land—a place for cars—reveals their own constriction of vision. By exhibiting Mrs. Cope's idolatry through the narrow self-interests of her visiting prophets, O'Connor makes clear the power of sin, subverts the possibilities for conversion, and leaves the reader wondering how much expansion of consciousness a human being can tolerate.

In "The Artificial Nigger," the story Flannery O'Connor considered her best, we can observe further how three devices—placing the classical and biblical in the backwoods psyches of Mr. Head and Nelson, doubling characters, and containing the story's movement in an arc that turns full circle—contribute to a total environment that, in effect, challenges the convention of self-preservation so central to human beings. The Dantean images of the underworld, the biblical allusions to Raphael's awakening by God's trumpet to go to Tobias, Peter's denial of Christ, the labyrinthine quest in the city, and the classical unity of its structure have been noted by most critics.[84] Together these features, plus the persistent omniscience of the narrator coupled with a narrative tone inconsistent with the characters' mentality, give the story its mythic dimensions and "situate Mr. Head's sin in the history of the race."[85]

But what we are specifically interested in here is how all these features simultaneously generate and reflect the movement of the story. The actions of the story occur within one day, beginning in the still-dark morning hours and ending at night. The story opens with the narrator's description: "Mr. Head awakened to discover that the room was full of moonlight. He sat up and stared at the floor boards—the color of silver—and then at the ticking on his pillow, which might have been brocade, and after a second, he saw half of the moon five feet away in his shaving mirror, paused as if it were waiting for his permission to enter. It rolled forward and cast a dignifying light on everything."[86] After their dreadful sojourn in the city, the train bears Mr. Head and Nelson home accompanied by the narrator's description: "ten minutes before [the train] was due to arrive at the junction, they went to the door and stood ready to jump off if it did not stop; but it did, just as the moon, restored to its full splendor, sprang from a cloud and flooded the clearing with light."[87] Using the moon's movement, O'Connor frames the circular journey from country into city and back again in the space of one day. This natural rotation of the earth anchors the centrifugal movement to the city.

O'Connor also uses the doubled characters—Mr. Head and Nelson—as mirrored images, even shadows, of each other to reinforce the movement with the human life cycle. Early in "The Artificial Nigger" she describes them: "They were grandfather and grandson but they looked enough alike to be brothers and brothers not too far apart in age, for Mr. Head had a youthful expression by daylight, while the boy's look was ancient, as if he knew everything already and would be pleased to forget it."[88] And she reproduces that portrait after they have been reconciled through the statue. "The two of them stood there with their necks forward at almost the same angle and their shoulders curved in almost exactly the same way and their hands trembling identically in their pockets. Mr. Head look like an ancient child and Nelson like a miniature old man."[89]

While the moon arches over the story, the train is the moving center that binds the inner tensions of the story together. First, it is the mechanical means by which grandfather and grandson shuttle between country securities and the baffling city. Second, the train station is the center on which Mr. Head focuses his attention when they venture into the city streets.

> At the second corner, Mr. Head turned and looked behind him at the station they had left, a putty-colored terminal with a concrete dome on top. He thought that if he could keep the dome always in sight, he would be able to get back in the afternoon to catch the train again. . . . At the end of two more blocks he turned to the left, feeling that he was circling the dome; and he was correct for in a half-hour they passed in front of the railroad station again. At first Nelson did not notice that he was seeing the same stores twice but when they passed the one where you put your feet on the rests while the Negro polished your shoes, he perceived that they were walking in a circle.[90]

When they are lost from the dome, they circle aimlessly in a suburb. "For blocks they didn't pass even a dog. The big white houses were like partially submerged icebergs in the distance. There were no sidewalks, only drives, and these wound around and around in endless ridiculous circles."[91]

Their loss of physical moorings is foreshadowed in the grandfather and grandson's consideration of the city sewers. Directly in the middle of the story about two country men exploring the city's labyrinths, O'Connor inserts a passage filled with Dantean images of Hell.

> "Lemme show you one thing you ain't seen yet," he said and took him to the corner where there was a sewer entrance. "Squat down," he said,

"and stick your head in there," and he held the back of the boy's coat while he got down and put his head in the sewer. He drew it back quickly, hearing a gurgling in the depths under the sidewalk. Then Mr. Head explained the sewer system, how the entire city was underlined with it, how it contained all the drainage and was full of rats and how a man could slide into it and be sucked along down endless pitchblack tunnels. . . . He connected the sewer passages with the entrance to hell and understood for the first time how the world was put together in its lower parts. He drew away from the curb. Then he said, "Yes, but you can stay away from the holes," and his face took on that stubborn look that was so exasperating to his grandfather. "This is where I come from!" he said.[92]

In his projected pride, Mr. Head, whose purpose in taking Nelson to the city was to give "a lesson that the boy would never forget, . . . that he had no cause for pride merely because he had been born in the city,"[93] recalls Lucifer. The above passage gives the Heads' journey mythic proportions, reminding us that such trips occur endlessly in human history.

Flannery O'Connor does more, however, than join a contemporary trip, organized by a headstrong old man, with an ancient mythic journey. She intensifies the story's circular movement by associating the images of an underground sewer system with visions and images driving up from Nelson's unconscious as he sleeps restlessly against a building: "The boy was dozing fitfully, half conscious of vague noises and black forms moving up from some dark part of him into the light."[94] O'Connor compresses the ageless tension between father and son into a troubled sleep, thus preparing for Nelson's frantic eruption into waking that leads to his grandfather's denial and their subsequent alienation. These two human spheres, revolving always in each other's shadow, now split apart and ironically come back together through the mediation of an artificial nigger.

Figures on the Fringes

In this first collection of stories, peripheries inhabited by figures who move from the fringes to the center of action are central to O'Connor's artistic intention to convince an audience who thinks God is dead about the ultimate and present reality of the spiritual realm.[95] Sometimes these figures mediate an opposition or reconcile characters or world views at the center of the story; sometimes they simply heighten the central distortion or conflict by reflecting it in their own form and behavior. Usually these peripheral figures initially are or become spectacles because they live on the margins of the story landscape outside the domain of most conventional social discourse. Although these figures more often than not are deluded by the limits of their subjectivity, their actions and presence provide a counterpoint to the prevailing assessments and assumptions about reality. Sarah Gordon describes such figures as "newsbearers" who enter the world of the "managers," those characters who are "apparently at home in [the modern] world and 'calling the shots.'"[96]

Examples of the first kind of peripheral figure—the mediational one—are Harry in "The River," Tom Shiftlet in "The Life You Save May Be Your Own," the boys in "A Circle in the Fire," the previously discussed hermaphrodite in "A Temple of the Holy Ghost," the statue in "The Artificial Nigger," Manley Pointer in "Good Country People," and Guizac in "The Displaced Person." On the other hand, the Misfit in "A Good Man Is Hard to Find," Ruby's good fortune in "A Stroke of Good Fortune," and the General in "A Late Encounter with the Enemy," existing on the edges of the stories to mirror the fears and illusions that plague the central characters or distort their vision, illustrate the second type of peripheral figure.

Moving back and forth between the city and the country, Harry Ashfield lives on the fringes of both worlds, aware that his life does not count in the city and longing to make it count in the country. This innocent child not only goes between the hedonistic skepticism of his parents and the fundamentalist faith of Mrs. Connin and Bevel Summers, but also mediates between a pale, literalistic interpretation of reality and a variegated, symbolic representation. With a child's consciousness, Harry associates misinformation—including the promise that he would be different after his baptism—with trickery but, ironically, he shockingly tricks himself and readers onto another level of consciousness by baptizing himself without an intermediary. Harry's experience of being caught in between two worlds and two perceptions of reality portrays the common human experience from which there is no apparent release or movement when the material and spiritual do not inform or break-in upon each other.

Tom Shiftlet comes onto Lucynell's land from the outside offering himself as a servant to fix up the place; in this offer he appears on the surface to be a mediator between Lucynell and the demands of her

rural life. By marrying the young Lucynell he mediates between am-
bitious mother and ignorant daughter, but his moralizing delusions
permit him to steal a car, money, even a human life from others and
justify those actions through his partial vision. Tom's pious words,
borrowed or stolen from others, make him an imposter from beginning to end and therefore an impotent mediator.[97] At the end of the
story when the hitchhiker, another outsider, confronts Tom with the
ugly truth about his moralizing life—"You go to the devil! My old
woman is a flea bag and yours is a stinking pole cat!"[98] Tom becomes a
victim of his own deceit, praying for the slime of the earth in which he
does not include himself. Although Tom is powerless to usher Lucynell into fuller vision because of his own partial vision, he can stand
between the story and the readers as a mirror for all those who distort
reality for their own ends.

In "A Circle in the Fire," a clear mediation seems to be performed
by the boys, who come from the unknown peripheries to land that is
like heaven to Powell, between Mrs. Cope and land that is not hers but
God's. Through the devilish harassment of Mrs. Cope and wanton
destruction of her woods, these boys expose the human impossibility
of ultimately subduing the stubborn, disruptive aspects of our environments and ourselves. For three upright prophets—willing to suffer the fire of torture for proclaiming faith in one God—who went
between God and King Nebuchadnezzar, O'Connor substitutes the
arsonists to bring low the mighty Mrs. Cope, thereby revealing the
spectacular deceit in every attempt to claim possession of anything
and the peripheral nature of everything.

In only one of these first collection stories does O'Connor use an
object as an apparent mediator or reconciler of differences. Ironically,
here Mr. Head and Nelson, the central characters, seem to come from
the rural periphery to the heart of the city. They are outsiders whose
pride, fear, and ignorance lead to a protracted walk in the city and
subsequently to Mr. Head's denial and their alienation. Only after Mr.
Head's desperate admission that he is lost does some kind of reunion
become possible between grandfather and grandson. The object in
the heart of the city which facilitates the reconciliation of two living
human beings is a plaster statue of a black man. It derives its pure,
albeit ironic, mediational power from its inability to distort and its
capacity to mirror the consequences—lifeless forms—of all conventions like pretense, judgment, prejudice that separate people from
their true nature and origins, in this story embodied in the blood
connections between one generation and another.

Like Tom Shiftlet, Manley Pointer in "Good Country People" comes from the outside onto the Hopewell farm. Bearing similarities to Mrs. Hopewell by fulfilling her view of good country people and to Mrs. Freeman through their mutual attraction to deformities or artificial limbs, Manley peddles a book filled with stories of insiders and outsiders. In the early part of the story, Manley appears to be a potential mediator between Mrs. Hopewell's shallow hope in everything and her daughter's belief in nothing. With his backwoods mispronunciation of the word "Christian," Pointer "tells Mrs. Hopewell that he plans to devote his life to 'Chrustian' service." Both Pointer's parlor Bibles and "his hollow Bible, containing condoms, whiskey, and pornographic cards" represent "'crusts' covering a core of emptiness or evil."[99] However, at the center of the story O'Connor casts Hulga and Manley out to the barn loft, the outermost and uppermost edge of the farm, where they trick each other into exposing the contradictions they both hold within themselves. The importance of the periphery in this story is that it is the place of greatest vulnerability and of least resistance, a place where religion and sexuality are associated, and the place most likely for a breakthrough or change of perception to occur. Though Manley and Hulga are left on the periphery when the story ends— Hulga still in the barn and Manley walking away altogether from the farm—and the state of their consciousnesses remains ambiguous, they have together performed a mediational function for readers. They show us our vulnerability to deception present in both intellectual sophistication and sentimental religious optimism and thereby potentially transport us, through irony, toward a larger, if less comfortable, vision of ourselves.

Guizac, as a displaced person, arrives at the center of the McIntyre farm as a figure from far away over the ocean. Appropriately, the priest, as world reconciler and agent of salvation, brings Mr. Guizac and his family to the farm where he becomes Mrs. McIntyre's salvation and Mrs. Shortley's devilish torment. On the farm this figure of foreign distances occasions an apocalyptic confrontation, which O'Connor embodies in resonances of biblical prophecy and images of war drawn from newsreel clips and from Mrs. Shortley's imagination of Polish words and English words doing battle: "She saw the Polish words, dirty and all-knowing and unreformed, flinging mud on the clean English words until everything was equally dirty. She saw them all piled up in a room, all the dead dirty words, theirs and hers too, piled up like the naked bodies in the newsreel."[100] This mysterious, usually silent outsider, Mr. Guizac stands between a woman who resists and one who welcomes his services. Despite their connection through him, both women equally misunderstand his existence. Coming from the outside, speaking an unknown language, living on the edge of the farm, offering his services sacrificially, even extending an altered interpretation of humanity—black and white are the same—Guizac also recalls the trickster.

The ambiguity of Mr. Guizac's proposal to marry his cousin to a black man is central to the insider-outsider tension O'Connor creates in "The Displaced Person." At the center of the McIntyre world lies the grave of the judge bearing the naked granite cherub Mrs. McIntyre refers to as an angel. Associating Mrs. McIntyre with the statue through her "aging cherubic face"[101] and the report that the judge bought it "partly because its face reminded him of his wife,"[102] O'Connor turns Mrs. McIntyre into a living statue, a spectacle hardened into stone who, through her connection with the naked stone cherub, stands guard as an anagogical symbol over *her* territory. For people like Mrs. McIntyre and Mrs. Shortley, Guizac's plan is an offensive trick to infiltrate their already overpopulated world. A world with a center transcending arbitrary national or racial boundaries, making no distinction between insiders and outsiders, offers a radical vision requiring a deepening of consciousness impossible for the Shortleys and Mrs. McIntyre. Although Guizac does not resolve the differences between Mrs. Shortley's and Mrs. McIntyre's views while he lives, he does expose the inevitable conflict created by self-preservation, narrow loyalties, and arbitrary divisions between insiders and outsiders. Even the outsider is affected by this conflict when Mrs. McIntyre discovers Guizac's interest in bringing more of his family to a social and cultural "inside" she wishes to protect.

Paradoxically, the only way to be released from the war between insiders and outsiders is to stand outside conventional boundaries; living from a reality that encompasses all "insides" renders every distinction between the inside and outside meaningless. But in a world of Shortleys, McIntyres, and extermination camps, O'Connor implies that death is the only sure release from partial vision and artificial boundaries.

The Misfit, Ruby's pregnancy characterized as good fortune, and the General possess less capacity to mediate because they are trapped by their defiance, fear, and rebellion that produce constrictive circumstances from which there is no passage or outlet. The Misfit characterizes their permanent peripheral status when he describes his own life:

"Turn to the right, it was a wall. . . . Turn to the left, it was a wall. Look up it was a ceiling, look down it was a floor."[103] For Ruby the good fortune she fears is motherhood, a state she associates with the threat of death through her own mother's experience, not with the promise of life announced to and accepted as a sign of blessedness by the biblical Mary, mother of the world's good fortune. As a "frail dried spider," the General also has no mediational power not simply because he is old but because he recognizes no reality behind words and no experience other than private, self-aggrandizement. Although Sally Poker Sash tries to use her grandfather to mediate between her and "all the upstarts who had turned the world on its head,"[104] he can only mirror her own illusion.

Whether these figures on the peripheries actually go between characters or perceptions in some way to mediate and expand the consciousness of characters or readers or simply isolate themselves on the fringe because of their own distortions, all the figures who come into the stories from the outside or the edges possess the capacity to embody contradictions or at least to reflect them from others. They are the vehicles for Flannery O'Connor's irony. Thus, they are able to show convention-dependent insiders their own potential for outsiderliness, unruliness, displacement, and loss. The figures on the peripheries who break into the stories are incarnations, albeit often inverted ones, of God's breaking into the center of time and space. They are ironic agents of grace. Because they are outsiders themselves exposing the outsiderliness of characters, they invite us—as outsiders—*into* the stories. These figures on the peripheries are created in O'Connor's ironic imagination "to recover in her audience that experience of the tensional In-Between which has been eroded from public consciousness by historicism and scientism since the Renaissance."[105]

Techniques of Indirection

As we finish examining the structures of O'Connor's first collection stories, we must be disturbed by what seems to be an obliqueness or unevenness in these narratives on original sin. Why do only a few stories seem to suggest any resolution of ambiguity, however difficult that resolution, or any conversion and redemption? Why do others end in deception? Are O'Connor's characters who cannot see the am-

biguity in their own gestures failures of artistic creation? Or do the
imaginative structures which O'Connor created, when more fully apprehended, settle some of the disturbance engendered by the stories?
These questions turn us to investigate the way the author works with
the narrators to achieve this state of irresolution, before we condemn
the stories as artistic failures.

Robert Brinkmeyer's analysis of O'Connor's narrative devices reflects his interest in such questions as well and helps to explicate the
methods O'Connor employs to produce her slanted tales of truth.
Although the aims of his study and the present one are similar, the
emphases differ. Drawing heavily on Mikhail Bakhtin, Brinkmeyer
works out his interpretation of O'Connor's narrative form largely as
an "interplay between narrator and author, which in effect gives us
two stories in a piece of fiction."[106] Both Brinkmeyer and Marshall
Bruce Gentry investigate the ways O'Connor puts both her Catholic
and fundamentalist visions under pressure in her narratives to expose
all manner of pretensions whether located in the liberal, secular intellectual or the authoritarian, religious fundamentalist. Confining his
examination first to pressures he finds in the stories between the author's and the narrator's voices or between these voices and a third
which he vaguely identifies as the narrative consciousness,[107] Brinkmeyer then moves on to demonstrate how the artist's internal pressure
shapes the story and puts her secular and religious readers under
pressure of her dialogic vision.

Whereas Brinkmeyer investigates the dialogic nature of the stories
through the artist's imagination that erupts into story, we have here so
far been examining the architecture or landscape of the narrative
structures that render the reader's engagement as significant as the
artist's imagination. What Brinkmeyer identifies as a narrative consciousness different from the narrator's and author's voices, I suggest
may be the trickster's presence mediating among the narrator, author,
characters, and readers, thereby significantly extending and opening
up the "dialogue." There are at least two bases for considering this
possibility. First, although Brinkmeyer acknowledges that O'Connor
never explicitly identifies this narrative consciousness, he asserts that
"its language and commentary clearly indicate that it embodies a level-
headedness and general sanity that the other two perspectives in their
own ways lack."[108] Later, however, he associates this narrative consciousness with the fundamentalist vision, which seems on the surface

at least a contradiction of his previous assessment of this consciousness.

Because of the difficulty of pinning down this narrative consciousness to the author's or the narrator's voices (to the genteel-Catholic or vernacular-fundamentalist perspectives) and because of the way it offers an alternative vision that moves between the Catholic and the fundamentalist visions, which operate dialogically in O'Connor's stories, we might consider it a product of O'Connor's own desire to communicate through the vision and language of irony. This ironic vision, which is not cruel and brutal but potentially sacramental in nature, may lodge in this narrative consciousness that is O'Connor's response to readers she imagined reading her stories incredulously or skeptically.

Because O'Connor was highly conscious of her readers, their limitations and confusions, and because she equated success as a writer with being heard, we seek in her fiction the means she thought most likely to communicate. Her desire to have her readers see from her angle of vision turned O'Connor's art increasingly toward irony or toward a language that would encourage readers to see reality whole. Longing to communicate her sense of Incarnation, O'Connor implies a role for readers *in* the narratives, which is almost as important as the characters' roles. In this first collection of stories her techniques are ones of indirection, of showing by telling the truth slant,[109] so that the stories might meet us where we are as readers.

Effective indirect communication, which enables a subject to see his or her true condition more accurately or comprehensively, depends on two requirements. First, there must be a correspondence between the communicator and the content of the communication. In O'Connor's stories about original sin this means that her communicators (characters and narrators) should themselves be familiar with the propensity to sin. Second, since the intention of the indirect communication "is to bring about an existential communication through the agency of the receiver himself," the communicator and the receiver must remain separate from each other.[110]

The first of these two requirements of indirect communication O'Connor fulfills within her stories through characters whose communication to those around them is deflected, distorted, or incomplete, corresponding to or mirroring their intellectual or spiritual condition; in short, their egoism separates them from their own integ-

rity and bars them from redemptive or conciliatory relationship.
These are conditions of original sin. The second requirement is less
frequently met in the stories in *A Good Man Is Hard to Find* because
those characters receiving messages are equally locked in some form
of egoistic deception that makes existential reflection difficult. Consequently, within many of these stories themselves the goal of indirect
communication is not realized if we expect to find it reflected in the
transformation of the characters. Instead, ambiguity, irresolution, or
despair often dominate the ends of the stories.

However, O'Connor's incarnational purposes in writing and the particular theme of the first collection stories press us, in the face of this
apparent failure, to fulfill the requirements of indirect communication
within the stories, to investigate the stories themselves as the communicator and the readers as receivers of O'Connor's indirect communication. When we consider the stories in this light, we find that both
requirements of indirect communication are more nearly fulfilled by
O'Connor. The content of the stories—the various guises and dis-
courses in which original sin appears in human beings—is presented
by the communicator, in this case the stories themselves. Related by
narrators who are under the authority of the author's imagination, the
stories deliver "possibilities to be considered" to us as readers.[111] We
are delivered not only to the fallen states of O'Connor's characters but
also led, through her indirection, to see these as possibilities of our
own condition.

O'Connor maintains a distinct separation between the communicator (the stories) and the receivers (the readers)—so essential for
our existential engagement—by presenting penetrating variations or
"possibilities to be considered" on the theme of original sin. In con-
structing the relationship between her theme and the narrators,
O'Connor depends on eyes like Powell's in "A Circle in the Fire." Her
one steady eye remains stationary, committed to presenting the reality
of sin in fiction. Her roving eye, which has the subtle capacity to
reproduce deception or perceive the spectacular, she implants in narrators whose shifting angles of vision—by discerning shadows and
disguises, reporting movements between centers and fringes, and de-
tecting the nuances of inflation and constriction—give us the experience of being encircled by evil and human sin.

What we learn about O'Connor's vision of fiction and faith from her
narrative landscapes in *A Good Man Is Hard to Find* depends heavily on
our ability and willingness to leap the conventional boundaries be-

tween reader and story and between sin and immunity from it. Our conclusions about the vision driving these stories also depend on having our senses pulled in somewhat contradictory directions. The strikingly visual character of the stories allows us to observe as spectators from a safe distance. We watch the alternating angles of vision, moving back and forth between centers and peripheries; we attend to the play of light and shadow just as a visionary or seer might. Yet, in her reliance on our ears—the more intimate sense—Flannery O'Connor resembles more the raconteur of folk traditions than a self-conscious twentieth-century artist. Through the recurrence of circular narrative patterns, the recasting of ancient myths in contemporary regional dialects, the doubling of characters, and the omnipresence of a trickster element that almost makes the stories dance, O'Connor invites the reader into a subtle, episodic journey with the characters compelled to struggle with sin.

In the end, O'Connor's narratives reveal that "ironic literature begins with realism and tends toward myth."[112] She achieves such movement from the recognizable to the mythic or mysterious by drawing characters who are familiar country people but who "live outside the boundaries of customary experience."[113] Although unmistakable families inhabit her stories, there are—finally, at least—"no families and neighbors with a common, albeit fictive history and locale . . . no equivalent of Yoknapatawpha County to provide links in time, place, and custom between one narrative and the next."[114] The fact that O'Connor's stories graphically recount personal dramas acted out "in a common milieu, but without knowledge of each other,"[115] hints at a community of outcasts trying to maintain their balance through egoism. Requiring her characters to distance from their precious self-images and cherished illusions in order to draw closer to mystery, O'Connor uses irony also to encourage us to stand apart from conventional religious doctrines of sin and suspend our reliance on literary theories that break reality into discrete, fragmentary categories.

In their episodic character in which discordance threatens to overpower concordance, the stories in *A Good Man Is Hard to Find* resist the configuration associated with emplotment—where "a sense of finality, stability, and integrity"[116] reign—and push the reader to the brink of an ambiguous abyss or to breakthrough.[117] Whether the episodes of sin presented in these O'Connor stories lead to deceit or transformation depends in part on the condition of our predispositions as readers. Those who undertake O'Connor's journey into sin by clinging tenaciously to psychological, religious, even literary, explanations that distort reality in their pretense to render it accessible will be deceived. O'Connor's narratives are grounded in religious myth for an audience whose cynicism paradoxically arises from sterile Christian conventions and the denial of mystery. Readers who allow these narrators to move them off balance and lead them beyond dogma and conventions may be transformed.

3

A Story Cycle of Communitas

By gesture he had lived his lie;
he had never deigned to tell one.
—"The Comforts of Home"

The preceding chapter examined principally the narrative devices that influence the shape of the story lines—or the spatial elements—in Flannery O'Connor's first collection of fiction.[1] Although the same techniques operate in the second collection, the author's imagination more overtly controls both the forms and the narration of these narratives. The narrative landscape, shaped by the techniques of indirection, in the first collection stories reflects O'Connor's search for a form adequate for her "goal of alerting an ignorant and unreceptive audience to the possibilities of the ineffable."[2] Her ambivalence, however, about a writer's responsibility to this audience influences her narrative techniques and exposes her concern with the proper point of view in reading her works. Sometimes she believed that "the writer whose vocation is fiction sees his obligation as being to the truth of what can happen in life, and not the reader—not to the reader's taste, not to the reader's happiness, not even to the reader's morals."[3] At other times she wrote directly for the puzzled reader over her shoulder: "When I sit down to write a monstrous reader looms up who sits down beside me and continually mutters, 'I don't get it, I don't see it, I don't want it.' Some writers can ignore this presence, but I have never learned how. I know that I must never let him affect my vision . . . yet I feel I must make him see what I have to show, even if my means of making him see have to be extreme."[4] The narrative implications of O'Connor's concern with her reader, essential to our understanding of her notion about incarnational art, will be discussed toward the end of this chapter and further in chapter 4.

Because O'Connor did not trust readers' *willingness* to be thrown off balance by indirection, she appears in her second collection fiction to try to tip us toward the right point of view to take in reading and judging her work. This chapter then will analyze more closely the devices of narration, especially those affecting time, point of view, and the narrator's discourse,[5] through which O'Connor tells her stories in *Everything That Rises Must Converge* in hopes of making her readers see. From such investigation we can assess first how O'Connor's narrative techniques are reinforced or altered between her two story collections, second how the trickster aids interpretation, and third how these narrative devices affect the reader's engagement, thereby moving us closer to the secrecy or mystery embodied in these narratives.

O'Connor's preference for what *can* happen in life (the possibilities) rather than what is expected (the probabilities) ties her, of course, more closely to the romancer than to the modern novelist. And her use of conventions which we associate with the probable in service of the possible contributes to an essential discontinuity in us as readers and pushes us toward some space between the material world of customs and conventions and a spiritual one her readers may refuse to acknowledge. In effect, O'Connor's fiction arises from her attempt to embody a "space between" or what Nathaniel Hawthorne described in "The Custom House" as "a neutral territory, somewhere between the real world and fairy-land, where the Actual and the Imaginary may meet, and each imbue itself with the nature of the other."[6] This "neutral territory" is like the *limen* characteristic of rituals of passage. In O'Connor's stories it is the place where the movement of spiritual grace is most likely to occur.

From Indirection to Direction

In *A Good Man Is Hard to Find,* Flannery O'Connor tried to create and reveal this "space between"—this place on the periphery—through techniques of indirection. Her subtle insinuation of religious themes or biblical characters into vulgar circumstances; her mixture of pagan with Christian allusions; the episodic, even repetitive, character of the stories; and the persistent threat of deception in the very conditions that promise insight all contribute to a baffling environment that seems liminal and heightens mystery. When O'Connor collected her second group of stories in *Everything That Rises Must Converge,* she turned thematically from the private sphere (depicting individual manifestations of original sin) to the public realm (exploring "man's relationship to his neighbor, and therefore to himself and God").[7] O'Connor's rhetorical preoccupations become even more apparent in this volume. While she sustains aesthetic subtlety in these stories through many of the techniques employed in the first collection, her desire to communicate turns her from suggestion toward greater direction.

Paul Ricoeur's provocative discussion of the metamorphoses of plot through which literary genres have passed—imitating or expanding the actions in the world—illuminates the tension between indirection and direction we find in Flannery O'Connor's works and sets that tension in a historical context. Tracing the changes in the modern novel, Ricoeur observes that "the wearing out of the paradigm of concordance,"[8] is signaled by the shift from governing principles of unity, completeness, and closure in fiction to principles of inconclusion and irresolution. O'Connor's assessment of her audience's lack of any "paradigm of concordance" in the form of religious conviction is embodied throughout her fiction, which is governed increasingly by narrative techniques that undermine coherence, unity, and closure in favor of fragmentation, disintegration, and irresolution. Paradoxically, however, as inconclusiveness is heightened, as it was particularly in stories like "The Life You Save May Be Your Own," "A Late Encounter with the Enemy," or "The Displaced Person" in the first collection, we find O'Connor exerting greater control over or direction of the narrative process in the second collection. Such interest in direction, Ricoeur points out, is necessary lest either "the reader's expectation that some form of consonance will finally prevail" is undermined or "the reader's work of composition . . . [rendered] completely impossible."[9]

There are three ways in which O'Connor's concern with direction in *Everything That Rises Must Converge* becomes apparent; the first is thematic, the second structural, and the third linguistic and stylistic. The thematic direction of these stories was first noted by Forrest Ingram who suggested that seven of the stories form a story cycle. He excludes

"Parker's Back" and "Judgment Day," arguing that they were added later by an editor and publisher.[10] Ingram links the stories in the second collection on the basis of "geometrical relationships among independent units brought together in a single book."[11] Although such grouping does not account adequately for the density within and among the stories, it does give readers a rudimentary map of the collection's terrain. "Everything That Rises Must Converge," "The Enduring Chill," and "Revelation" form a unit because they "explicitly treat the relationship of blacks and whites."[12] In their treatment of generational conflict, "Greenleaf" and "A View of the Woods" form another unit. And Ingram asserts that "The Comforts of Home" and "The Lame Shall Enter First" form another unit, exposing the follies of intellectualism and maudlin charity.

The notion that these second collection stories form a cycle is supported first by the relationship and development one discovers between the two story collections. The episodic recurrence of "theme, motif, character or character-type, setting, symbol, and myth"[13] apprehended in *A Good Man Is Hard to Find* forms an identifiable pattern of development associated with cycles and particularly reminiscent of one like the Winnebago Trickster Cycle, for example. By transferring and elaborating upon some of the themes, narrative shapes, and actions that occurred in her first collection in the second, O'Connor writes like a cycle-maker.

Second, O'Connor's ideas about convergence, which she took from Pierre Teilhard de Chardin, also support the thematic direction of this volume. Acknowledging her indebtedness to Chardin, O'Connor confessed, "I'm much taken . . . with Père Teilhard. . . . I've even taken a little from him—'Everything That Rises Must Converge' and am going to put it on my next collection of stories."[14] Julian Huxley explains that usually Teilhard "uses *convergence* to denote the tendency of mankind, during its evolution, to superpose centripetal on centrifugal trends, so as to prevent centrifugal differentiation from leading to fragmentation, and eventually to incorporate the results of differentiation in an organized and unified pattern."[15]

O'Connor gives visible life and form to this idea of convergence in these narratives, Ingram asserts, principally through her characters; thus, the presentation of character reinforces theme. Each story is dominated by a proud human spirit whose centrifugal extensions are either interrupted or turned back on themselves at the edges of the stories. Ingram claims that "every story in *Everything That Rises Must*

Converge treats man's relationship to his neighbor, and therefore to himself and God. . . . Every rising in the stories is a rising to some new level of consciousness—a process which O'Connor typically conveys through the metaphor of seeing."[16] Unfortunately, Ingram's focus on the concept of convergence illustrates the limits of thematic interpretation because it gives the impression that taken together these stories decrease centrifugal fragmentation through an increase of consciousness or enlightenment in the characters. In fact, this impression is challenged when we examine O'Connor's metaphors of seeing more closely in these second collection stories.

Continuing the technique used in *A Good Man Is Hard to Find* of giving physical substance to metaphors, here O'Connor turns metaphors for seeing into particular objects that become ironic vehicles of enlightenment. By so doing she both highlights the importance of seeing and demonstrates the difficulties and distortions that are possible with vision. In addition, metaphors that take on physical form reinforce the centrifugal-centripetal tensions of the narrative structures. For example, in "A View of the Woods," old Mr. Fortune and his granddaughter Mary Fortune Pitts are joined by the presence of "his very light blue eyes . . . and his steady prominent scowl" on the young girl's face; and O'Connor embodies the tension between them through a mirror metaphor: "He had frequent little verbal tilts with her but this was a sport like putting a mirror up in front of a rooster and watching him fight his reflection."[17] Through the telescope in "The Lame Shall Enter First," Sheppard tries to redeem Rufus by making it "possible for this boy's vision to pass through a slender channel to the stars."[18] Ironically, Rufus resists such enforced enlargement of vision, while Sheppard's son Norton, trying to launch himself into outer space to be with his dead mother, hangs himself above the telescope in the attic. "Revelation" presents Mrs. Turpin's distorted vision, which is confronted by "the girl's eyes [that] seemed lit all of a sudden with a peculiar light, an unnatural light like road signs give."[19] Through Mary Grace's ugly eyes, which see through the surfaces of Mrs. Turpin's life, O'Connor prepares for the action—the propelled textbook—which strikes Mrs. Turpin just above the eye, radically altering her vision.

All of these characters involved in seeing or trying to make others see are vulnerable to the monologism that vision, which grants one the distance of spectator, threatens. Each falls victim to the myopia of the partial, individual perspective. However, some of the narrators appear to challenge such singular perspective by insinuating that to see fully requires contrary motions or a total inversion of one's viewpoint. For example, the narrator in "The Lame Shall Enter First," speaking from Sheppard's point of view and describing Sheppard's redoubled efforts to help recalcitrant Johnson "see," says, "If he couldn't impress the boy with the immensity [through the telescope], he would try the infinitesimal [through the microscope]."[20] The narrator in "Revelation" depicts a similar realization that seeing (or convergence as Ingram suggests) must be preceded by some inverting disturbance when she summarizes the effects of the book's blow on Ruby: "All at once her vision narrowed and she saw everything as if it were happening in a small room far away, or as if she were looking at it through the wrong end of a telescope."[21]

Finally, all these thematic, character, metaphoric, and structural elements that suggest a cyclic quality in O'Connor's *Everything That Rises Must Converge* are not simply supported but significantly complicated, as O'Connor's use of seeing illustrates, by the techniques of narration, which O'Connor used more persistently here to undermine the monologism of her central characters and to put her works and her readers under pressure. As noted previously, both Gentry and Brinkmeyer investigate the means O'Connor used to produce such pressure. Whereas Gentry "sees the characters in O'Connor's fiction as participants in an ongoing struggle against authoritarian narrators," Brinkmeyer argues that such pressure results from the interaction between the author and the narrator, which produces two stories: the author's story behind the narrator's story.[22]

Although the association of O'Connor's stories with a story cycle certainly is deepened further by the suggestion of such layering or interplay of narratives, neither Brinkmeyer's nor Gentry's interpretations of the narrational devices pay adequate attention to the interactions among time, the narrator's point of view, and the type of discourse used by the narrators, all of which complicate the narration. Despite the compelling features of Brinkmeyer's analysis, particularly the way it accurately locates the fundamentalist-Catholic tensions portrayed in her works in O'Connor's own faith and thought, it paradoxically risks its own monologism by focusing essentially on the themes the narrators present instead of attending more closely to the actual operations of narration that occur in the stories and by performing a procrustean feat of fitting O'Connor into a Bakhtinian construct. Brinkmeyer's conclusion that O'Connor's narrators express a tenacious fundamentalism that is challenged by the stories governed by the Catholic vision of the author must be tested against the actual techniques of narration.

Under such scrutiny, O'Connor's second collection stories reveal that particularly her techniques of narration, not simply her use of characters, repetition of themes, or reliance on metaphors of seeing, embody the cyclic human attraction and resistance to transcendent mystery. Indeed, we find that the narrational techniques themselves pull us as readers in sometimes opposing directions.

The narrative devices on which O'Connor relies to tell these second collection stories not only reflect her struggle to give greater direction to these stories but also contribute to the cyclic shape of the narratives individually and collectively. In the following discussions we will examine the operations of the shifting narrative voice, the more sharply delineated trickster figures, and the discourse of conditionality in the service of the holy unconditional in *Everything That Rises Must Converge*. The shifting narrative voice is itself a subtle and comprehensive metaphor for seeing. O'Connor refines the narrative voice she uses throughout her fiction by juxtaposing qualities of omniscience with qualities of objective reporting in her narrators. The effect of such juxtaposition is that the narrator can see everything from several angles of vision, and readers feel themselves simultaneously inside and outside characters' minds and experiences, though often offended or uncomfortable with the unreliability of the narrative voice.

O'Connor actually complicates the alterations in narrative voice by reshaping several of her techniques of indirection from the first collection. For example, the projections of characters' inner states of consciousness, which in *A Good Man Is Hard to Find* become recurring metaphors, are more often absorbed into and reported through the omniscience of the narrator in *Everything That Rises Must Converge*. Doubled figures still remain in the second collection stories, but shadows—to which the omniscient narrator has access—may more often remain inside characters. O'Connor captures the circular or arc-like motion so important in the earlier stories in the narrator's movement between omniscience and reporting in the second collection and through the layered tale, a device we will discuss more fully in relation to selected stories. In short, the narrator's widening and narrowing focus offers readers an inclusive, if fluctuating, vision of the stories' landscapes and the characters' inner and outer circumstances.

Two other techniques O'Connor seems to transfer from *A Good Man*

Is Hard to Find and to reshape in *Everything That Rises Must Converge* are the figures on the peripheries, who become more clearly mediating tricksters in many of the second collection stories, and her use of the language of conditionality through which she creates a putative reality and brings her proud characters to silence. Functioning together in the narratives, all three of these techniques yield a greater direction that paradoxically holds readers in tension between the centrifugal visions of the proud spirits in the stories and the narrator's voices or tricksteresque mediating actions which centripetally pull them back toward some center of judgment. This double pressure for disintegration and reintegration contributes to the quality of illusionism Caroline Gordon associates with O'Connor's stories. We will understand this quality better as we examine each of the techniques of direction O'Connor employs in shaping the structures of the second collection narratives.

The Shifting Narrative Voice

The role of the narrator or the narrative voice in O'Connor's fiction presents difficulties for critics of realistic fiction because it is unpredictable and uneven; yet this very difficulty contributes to illusionism. Though O'Connor presents her stories from an external point of view through a third person or omniscient narrator, the tone of the narrator, the characters' information, or the quality of insight attributed to the characters is frequently inconsistent with the characters' own environments, background, or education. Because we expect an omniscient narrator, for example, to use the access she or he has to the inner as well as the outer life of a character, we are thrown off balance by the incongruity between the narrator's insight or knowledge and the character's apparent lack of awareness or inner motivation. Commonly in O'Connor's stories an omniscient narrator offers information or judgment about the characters which seems unmotivated or for which the reader is unprepared by the characters' actions or thoughts. Such narrative unevenness unsettles the reader's expectations and leads critics like Carol Shloss to consider it a sign of O'Connor's artistic weakness rather than a central device of her purposes and view of art. Others, like Brinkmeyer, underestimate the multiple perspectives expressed in the narrator's voice and interpret it largely as a singular, fundamentalist voice.

Despite her confession, in the preface for the second edition of *Wise Blood,* that she was "an author congenitally innocent of theory,"[23] Flannery O'Connor knew, even if instinctively, what makes a story "expand in the mind." It expands in the "neutral territory" through techniques that masterfully produce the illusionary quality of the stories. Gordon contends that illusionism depends on readers' abilities to master those techniques that lure them "into that world of imagination which exists only in the author's imagination."[24] Both Henry James and O'Connor "had a vision which demanded a revolutionary technique, a technique which had never been used before."[25] The region to which James and O'Connor—and Hawthorne before them—went in their imaginations was "the subterranean chambers of the human spirit,"[26] where characters struggle "to view life in the light of eternity."[27] James developed the method of the Central Intelligence to get to that region. Influenced by James's method as well as by "the Hebrew genius for making the absolute concrete,"[28] O'Connor's "central intelligence" moves back and forth between an omniscient narrator whose distance "is almost clinical" and an inward "restless obsessiveness [that] can be indicated only indirectly."[29] O'Connor's management of the narrative voice in her stories creates both the awesome power of her tales and, as we shall consider later, the communitas among the characters who have turned into spectacles and between characters and readers.

There are at least six ways in which O'Connor manifests the shifting narrative voice in these second collection stories and through which she turns characters' and readers' attention toward some "space between" or toward an intersection of the finite and the eternal. The first, most obvious manner of depicting narrative voice shifts is by balancing a narrator's objective report with omniscient reflections. Thus, in a short passage from "A View of the Woods," we find external details—the age difference between Mary Fortune and her grandfather or the color of the old man's eyes—provided alongside revelations on the shape of the old man's inner life. "She was now nine, short and broad like himself, with his very light blue eyes, his wide prominent forehead, his steady penetrating scowl and his rich florid complexion; but she was like him on the inside too. . . . Though there was seventy years' difference in their ages, the spiritual distance between them was slight. She was the only member of the family he had any respect for."[30]

In "Greenleaf" and in "Parker's Back," O'Connor similarly and consistently juxtaposes objective description and omniscient commentary. First the narrator reports in "Greenleaf" that "the animal pawed the ground and Mrs. May, standing bent forward behind the blind, closed it quickly lest the light make him charge into the shrubbery." Following immediately after such objective description, the narrator moves inside Mrs. May's consciousness confessing that "she had been conscious in her sleep of a steady rhythmic chewing as if something were eating one wall of the house."[31]

The narrator of "Parker's Back" possesses this same capacity for moving from the outside circumstances to a character's inner state. After he conveys the factual outlines of Sarah Ruth and Parker's environment—that they lived in a rented house which "sat alone save for a single tall pecan tree on a high embankment overlooking a highway" and that "at intervals a car would shoot past below"—he comments on Sarah Ruth's inner suspicions, a characteristic called to mind by his reference to passing cars. "One of the things she did not approve of was automobiles. In addition to her other bad qualities, she was forever sniffing up sin."[32] This kind of shifting occurs in every story and generally continues throughout the entire story.

Furthermore, by giving readers access both to concrete, external details and to subjective states of mind, the shifts between objective and omniscient narration enable O'Connor to span distances of time and space. The reporting or objective narrator creates psychic distance for characters and readers while generally reporting events and actions in the present, near time. When the omniscient narrator tells the story, he can move to far times—the past or the future—while bringing those distances psychologically close. Two examples will illustrate this contrary motion, though the principle works in all the stories. The omniscient narrator in "Everything That Rises Must Converge" takes the reader inside Julian's head where he frequently retreats to see the idiocy of his mother's prejudice and of the world more clearly. From this point of distance "he could see her with absolute clarity."[33] In this mental room "his soul momentarily expanded but then he became aware of his mother across from him and the vision shriveled."[34] The objective narrative voice takes over again in present time on a bus, emotionally distancing Julian and readers: "He studied her coldly. Her feet in little pumps dangled like a child's and did not quite reach the floor. She was training on him an exaggerated look of reproach."[35]

O'Connor contrasts present time experiences in which one feels safely in control with inner visions that threaten to disturb one's psychic peace in "Parker's Back" as well. Again through the shifting narrative voice O'Connor moves back and forth between near things reported with objective remove (Sarah eating the apples O.E. had brought or O.E. objectively surveying her shortcomings) and far things presented by the omniscient narrator as spiritual stalking (vast vistas that stretch indefinitely on the horizon or actions carried out from somewhere inside him without his rational consent). The contrast is captured in the following paragraph: "[Sarah Ruth] chewed the apple slowly but with a kind of relish of concentration, bent slightly but looking out ahead. The view from the porch stretched off across a long incline studded with iron weed and across the highway to a vast vista of hills and one small mountain. Long views depressed Parker. You look out into space like that and you begin to feel as if someone were after you, the navy or the government or religion."[36]

Sometimes O'Connor complicates the movement between objectivity and omniscience in the narrative voice in a second way by interjecting conversation in the shifts between reporting and omniscient review of inner or unobvious conditions. In "Everything That Rises Must Converge," O'Connor demonstrates this method of complication. When Julian and his mother leave for the Y, Julian says, "Some day I'll start making money." But before he promises "and you can have one of those jokes [a hat] whenever you take the fit," his conversation is interrupted by the omniscient narrator's judgment of his thought that he knew he never would start making money. Julian's mother takes up the conversation, "I think you're doing fine. . . . You've only been out of school a year. Rome wasn't built in a day." Then the narrator intervenes with the objective report that Julian's mother "was one of the few members of the Y reducing class who arrived in hat and gloves and who had a son who had been to college."[37] Again, then, Julian's mother resumes her conversation with Julian, complicating it further with reports of her earlier conversation with the clerk who had sold her the hat.

Likewise in "The Enduring Chill," O'Connor uses conversation and reporting to advance the surface action of the story while the narrator's omniscient reflection deepens the implications of the external details. Through conversation between Mrs. Fox and Dr. Block, Asbury learns that he has undulant fever. "Found theter ol' bug, did ol' Block," said the doctor. Asbury's mother replies to the doctor, "I think you're just as smart as you can be!" and then continues to Asbury, "you have undulant fever. It'll keep coming back but it won't kill you!" Block's satisfaction in announcing, "You ain't going to die," is greeted by the omniscient narrator's assessment of Asbury's response: "Nothing about Asbury stirred except his eyes. They did not appear to move on the surface but somewhere in their blurred depths there was an almost imperceptible motion as if something were struggling feebly. Block's gaze seemed to reach down like a steel pin and hold whatever it was until the life was out of it."[38] Conversations added to an already shifting narrative voice perplex readers who may not be sure whose words to trust, while they simultaneously expose the ignorance or folly of some character's partial vision. Dr. Block's parting comment, "He must have drunk some unpasteurized milk up there,"[39] not only illustrates Asbury's myopic foolishness but also highlights his ignorant resoluteness that he had come home to die.

A third way O'Connor uses the shifting narrative voice to turn our attention to the mysterious dimensions of human existence is by reinforcing the alternations between objectivity and omniscience with similes or allusions that encourage associations beyond the limits of the story. Such allusions in the perpetually shifting narrative voice produce an unforgettably surreal atmosphere in stories like "Greenleaf," "A View of the Woods," "The Enduring Chill," "The Comforts of Home," "Revelation," and "Judgment Day."

The narrator opens "Greenleaf" by comparing the bull munching steadily outside Mrs. May's window to "some patient god come down to woo her."[40] The mythical overtones of the simile—to "Jupiter, the bull as disguised God-lover" and to Christ as the suffering lover of humanity—have been widely acknowledged.[41] However, the story acquires its surrealistic atmosphere through the interaction of simile, objective reports about a farm bull, and the omniscient view of Mrs. May's inner state. The narrator does not merely report that a stray bull is eating shrubs below Mrs. May's bedroom window, nor does he compare that bull to a divine presence. Capable of entering Mrs. May's unconsciousness, the omniscient narrator turns the bull into a devouring monster that chews up people, houses, and land, leaving only the detestable Greenleafs on a tiny island that formerly belonged to Mrs. May. In just one and a half pages, the narrator's shifting voice has linked physical realities to spiritual ones, revealed the psychological anxiety of the main character, and foreshadowed the inevitable destruction of the fearfully proud Mrs. May.

The narrator in "A View of the Woods," like the narrator in

"Greenleaf," implies the story's mythical aspects by reporting that old man Fortune "was always very careful to see that [Mary Fortune Pitts] avoided dangers. He would not allow her to sit in snakey places or put her hands on bushes that might hide hornets."[42] Yet he himself thrived on business transactions, which threatened to change his Edenic woods into a filling station, with Tilman who "sat habitually with his arms folded on the counter and his insignificant head weaving snake-fashion above them. He had a triangular-shaped face with the point at the bottom and the top of his skull was covered with a cap of freckles. His eyes were green and very narrow and his tongue was always exposed in his partly opened mouth."[43] The snake-like mark-ings of Mr. Tilman remind readers of another snake whose tempting proffer changed the face of the earth. Through additional slanderous associations—Mr. Fortune refers to his stubborn granddaughter as a Jezebel and she retorts by labeling him the Whore of Babylon—the narrative expands the Fortune-Pitts struggle by suggesting ancient religious dimensions in it.

Sitting in a doctor's waiting room in "Revelation," Mrs. Turpin dis-dainfully observes impolite behaviors, the commonness of other patients, and above all the crude ugliness of Mary Grace. Self-righteously appraising her own station in life, Mrs. Turpin comments on all facets of her life, including the hogs (which are "cleaner than some children I've seen")[44] she and Claud keep. All her observations and reflections prepare for Mary Grace's comparison of Mrs. Turpin in her message, "Go back to hell where you came from, you old wart hog."[45] The omniscient narrator subsequently moves the comparison to Mrs. Turpin's interior as she first lies on her bed staring at the ceiling and denying, "I am not a wart hog. From hell."[46] And as she repeatedly asks herself at the pig parlor, "How am I a hog and me both? How am I saved from hell too?"[47] her vision is turned back with humbling centripetal force.

In "The Comforts of Home," the connection of Thomas with Star Drake is subtly suggested, not through simile but through direct, al-beit fearful, association of the two individuals in Thomas's mother's mind. Striving to be a paragon of virtue, Thomas's mother wants to help the helpless, a desire about which Thomas is cynically critical. "Can't I make you see . . . that if she can't help herself you can't help her?" His mother murmurs, "Nimpermaniac." Thomas corrects her pronunciation and her behavior fiercely. "Nymphomaniac. . . . She doesn't need to supply you with any fancy names. She's a moral mo-

ron. That's all you need to know. Born without the moral faculty—like
somebody else would be born without a kidney or a leg." And then his
mother expresses her true anxiety: "I keep thinking it might be
you. . . . If it were you, how do you think I'd feel if nobody took you
in? What if you were a nimpermaniac and not a brilliant smart person
and you did what you couldn't help and. . . ."[48] Such a bizarre association reinforces the surrealism of the story achieved through the shifting narrative voice reinforced by allusions. In addition, it prepares for
Thomas's own obsessive resistance to Star Drake that finally and ironically makes them seem more alike than different.

Sometimes the associations O'Connor's narrators suggest are neither
mythical, religious, nor even human, but natural phenomena or material objects through which she depicts the spiritual-mental states of her
characters. Immediately before Mrs. Turpin marches off to the pig
parlor for her encounter with the wart hog in herself, the narrator
reports objectively that "the dark protuberance over her eye looked like
a miniature tornado cloud which might any moment sweep across the
horizon of her brow."[49] Such a comparison anticipates the devastating
change about to level the proud Mrs. Turpin. In "The Enduring Chill"
the omniscient narrator changes water spots on the bedroom wall into a
fierce bird with icicles in its beak threatening to Asbury both in his
childhood past and in the present. This "Holy Ghost, emblazoned in ice
instead of fire," offers no solace only "purifying terror" as Asbury
watches it continue, "implacable to descend."[50] By comparing Mr.
Fortune's heart to a car racing forward—an inanimate object associated
with the technological progress Fortune himself admires—the omniscient narrator reflects the inner rage that drives the old man and will
eventually consume both grandfather and granddaughter. Perhaps the
most entertainingly surrealistic and most theologically significant allusion a narrator makes in these stories occurs in "Judgment Day."
Tanner's concern about his burial site leads the narrator to compare his
eyes to those of an angry corpse. Later, inside Tanner's imagination, the
omniscient narrator relays an imagined scene among Hooten, Coleman, and a wood box containing Tanner's corpse. At the end of the
scene, corpse-Tanner jumps up, like a resurrected jack-in-the-box to
proclaim "Judgment Day! Judgment Day!"

Through all these allusions that accompany the shifting narrative
voice, O'Connor moves between present time and all time. This potential to be in the present and backward or forward from it allows her to
juxtapose two specific historic periods, differing philosophical out-
looks, or contrasting realms of experience—each manifesting some

centrifugal-centripetal tension. Through the shifting narrative voice and supporting allusions in "Greenleaf," O'Connor discloses the limits of rational control through Mrs. May's fear of Mrs. Greenleaf's fundamentalist fervor. At one moment the narrator objectively reports the difficult circumstances under which Mrs. May tries to run her farm and family. At the very next moment, through the narrator's omniscient capacity to enter inside and beyond Mrs. May's head, O'Connor can reveal the woman's fear of religious fervor and sacrifice that signal a loss of control. By incorporating religious and mythic allusions, the story contrasts faith and rational control.

A similar contrast, here between a mythic and a modern-technological world view, lies at the center of "A View of the Woods." Once again, O'Connor's shifting narrative voice manifests this contrast. By moving the narrative back and forth among the present familial tension about how to use the Fortune land, the mechanical clearing of the land that preoccupies both grandfather and granddaughter, and the land sale to Mr. Tilman, O'Connor brings the reader to the center of the deadly contest she depicts as a centrifugal-centripetal one. That contest is the struggle for dominance that the omniscient narrator presents through mythic allusions.

O'Connor strengthens the centrifugal-centripetal tension present in the shifting narrative voice through yet a fourth way that deliberately frustrates both characters' and readers' ability to discern which perceptions are trustworthy from those that are unreliable because they are deceitful. Usually O'Connor applies the narrator's omniscience principally to the central proud spirit of the stories. By reporting the inner states of these characters or their private, apparently hidden, response to their circumstances, O'Connor not only produces a more complete picture of pride and self-delusion but also complicates the story. Thus, for example, our external view of Mrs. Turpin as concerned, friendly, even gregarious—if a bit condescending—is enlarged by inner reveries reported through the narrator's omniscience. Ruby's saccharine observations of and conversations with people in the doctor's waiting room are a thin veil hiding her inner fascination with the ranking of human beings: "On the bottom of the heap were most colored people, not the kind she would have been if she had been one, but most of them; then next to them—not above, just away from—were the white-trash; then above them were the home-owners, and above them the home-and-land owners, to which she and Claud belonged."[51]

The narrator's omniscience exposes Mrs. May in similar fashion, through her own comments and behavior juxtaposed with interior reflection. After driving her car to the center of the pasture—the perfect place to corral the terrorizing centrifugal movement of O.T. and E.T.'s bull—Mrs. May unwittingly exposes her own weariness from fear and anticipates a permanent, centripetal rest in death. "For some time she lay back against the hood, wondering drowsily why she was so tired. With her eyes closed, she didn't think of time as divided into days and nights but into past and future. She decided she was tired because she had been working continuously for fifteen years. She decided she had every right to be tired, and to rest for a few minutes before she began working again. Before any kind of judgment seat, she would be able to say: I've worked, I have not wallowed."[52]

In several stories in *Everything That Rises Must Converge*, however, the omniscience of O'Connor's narrator is not confined to the proud spirits but may spill over into the minds of other characters as well. When O'Connor employs this fifth variation of the shifting narrative voice, we are appropriately confused by the addition of other conflicting perceptions and illusions and may justifiably conclude that no few people have a corner on arrogance or self-delusion. In the opening scene of "Everything That Rises Must Converge," the narrator seems to have his omniscience turned toward Julian's mother as she prepares to go to her reducing class; however, quickly Julian's become the eyes through which we will see his mother: "Julian thought he could have stood his lot better if she had been selfish, if she had been a hag who drank and screamed at him."[53] The narrator's omniscience shifts decisively to Julian, reporting what went on in his mind when he withdrew behind the newspaper or "retired into the high-ceilinged room [in his mind] sparsely settled with large pieces of antique furniture." Here as we have already noted, "his soul expanded momentarily but then he became aware of his mother across from him and the vision shriveled."[54] By showing us Julian's mother's inner nature through Julian's disdainful eyes and simultaneously laying bare Julian's interior, the narrator locks them both in the sin of pride, thus confounding the preferences of those who see ignorance and enlightenment as distinct states of mind.

Flannery O'Connor uses this technique in every story where two major figures embody a conflict or tension between perceptions. By revealing Mary Fortune Pitts's spirit through the mind of old Mr. Fortune to which the omniscient narrator has access—"She didn't move an inch. She had a habit of his of not hearing what she didn't want to hear and since this was a little trick he had taught her himself, he had to admire the way she practiced it"[55]—O'Connor again connects proud spirits and uncovers the seeds of disaster that lie hidden in the human tendency to ignore the mutual necessity of centrifugal-centripetal forces at work in the human mind, in nature, and in human societies.

In "The Enduring Chill" and in "Judgment Day" the omniscient narrator has increased access to the inner states of the two main characters. As the narrator omnisciently expresses both Asbury's and his mother's reflections, the tension between them is heightened. Believing he has come home to die, Asbury thinks he should have contacted the priest whose card he carries with him, for "as a man of the world, [he is] someone who would have understood the unique tragedy of his death, a death whose meaning had been far beyond the twittering group around them."[56] When Asbury tries to shock his mother into facing his true condition by saying that what was wrong with him was way beyond the local doctor, we learn from the narrator: "His mother knew at once what he meant: he meant he was going to have a nervous breakdown."[57] From continued counterbalancing of distorted perceptions, readers conclude that there is no perception impregnable to inflation and distortion.

One of the best stories in which to see how the extension of the narrator's omniscience confuses the standards for judgment or the authority by which judgments are made is "The Lame Shall Enter First." From the beginning O'Connor prepares us for a contest between idealism and realism through Sheppard's relation to his son Norton. Trying to acquaint his selfish going-on-eleven-year-old child with the hard realities of life, Sheppard tells Norton about seeing Rufus rummage for food in a garbage can. Blindly idealizing the conditions of his own son's life, Sheppard says, "when I saw him yesterday, he was skin and bones. He hasn't been eating cake with peanut butter on it for breakfast." Without illusions, Norton innocently and realistically retorts, "It's stale. That's why I have to put stuff on it."[58]

Sheppard's self-deceptive pride in his realism and pragmatism are apparent in all his social scientific explanations for Rufus's past and present behavior and his misinterpretations of Norton's attitudes reported through the narrator's omniscience. But only through Rufus's religious literalism ("I ain't going to the moon and get there alive, and when I die I'm going to hell . . . and if you die and go there you burn forever"),[59] his defiance, and his mockery is the full extent of Sheppard's illusion exposed. We are again baffled (thrown off balance as I suspect O'Connor intended) by a narrative voice that, by showing us the inside of fanatic faith and malicious acts, strips another man of his pretense and condescending charity. Confusing her reader's expectations, distorting moral categories, or clouding our ability to judge truth simply, O'Connor's shifting narrative voice, in effect, forces us to wander in some "space between" the limited perceptions of the proud characters, or of those through whom their perceptions are reflected, and a larger dimension or a spiritual realm that might acquaint such characters with a fuller experience of their true nature.

O'Connor signals the importance of this neutral territory, or "space between," where the material and the spiritual intersect or where limited perceptions are illumined by a moment of truth, through all the varieties of movement in the narrative voice already discussed and in a final device—the tale-within-the-tale. These tales-within-tales are not simple flashbacks nor incidents that could be removed from the stories because they merely supplement our information about a character. Rather, O'Connor's tales-within-tales undergird and motivate the central action of the stories, for they are inward manifestations of experiences either forgotten or ignored. One might think of these tales as clues to or evidences of an orienting framework through which an O'Connor character attempts to give meaning to his or her life. Charles Taylor describes the framework as inescapable for a moral ontology and some sense of self-identity.[60] Even when O'Connor presents these tales as partial, anxiety-ridden, or perverse in their defiance of or deviance from an overarching framework, they function in the narratives as a window into a character's moral order. They prepare for or precipitate the ironic inversion in the story.[61] As another sign of her greater direction in the second collection of stories, O'Connor develops the episodic features of *A Good Man Is Hard to Find*—the hermaphrodite in the carnival tent or the seduction scene in "Good Country People"—into tales-within-tales. Like geological layers of human landscape, these tales show us how human perceptions and actions become embedded in cultural institutions reflecting our technological projects and our psychological, religious, or sociological rationalizations that claim our fundamental allegiance over time and beyond time.

The tale-within-the-tale, which simply extends O'Connor's custom of narrating her stories principally in the past tense, also rivets attention on particular events as it heightens contrasts in perceptions be-

tween characters and narrators. In addition, this device complicates
the sense of time in these narratives, illustrating how time past and
time future exist in and affect the present narrative moment. In varying degrees, all the stories in *Everything That Rises Must Converge* use
some form of flashback to motivate action or to provide information to
the readers. For example, in four stories O'Connor shapes a flashback,
anxiety, a dream, and memory of a fair into significant portions of
the total tale to which readers need access in order to be illumined
by the irony. The omniscient narrator, sounding like a prophetic
Greek chorus, in "The Enduring Chill" reports about Asbury's "communion" in the milk parlor with Randall and Morgan a year earlier
when he was home trying to write a play about the Negro. Defying his
mother's orders not to smoke in the barn or to drink the warm fresh
milk, Asbury invites Randall and Morgan to join his rebellion. Refusing his invitation to commune, the two hired men watch Asbury drink
alone. The inserted tale ends with the narrator reporting a private
conversation between Randall and Morgan about Asbury's inexplicable ugliness.

In a story about a failed playwright who imagines himself to be dying,
this tale of defiance draws the reader more fully to the inside of Asbury
and provides information that prepares for the ironic reversal: Asbury
is not dying but suffers from undulant fever contracted by drinking
unpasteurized milk, not up North as Dr. Block would believe, but in his
own milking parlor. Asbury's commitment to his dying, his mother's
specific ignorance of Asbury's earlier actions and general illusions
about her son, and Randall and Morgan's thoughtless compliance to
what is expected render them all incapable of the distancing necessary
to produce insight. Until the very end only the readers are enlightened
by this tale in which the rebellious Asbury of the past and the now
shattered Asbury meet in an ironic moment of grace.

Most of "The Comforts of Home" presents the tale of events that lead
to Thomas's final action, an action resulting from his dependence on
words that render him morally impotent. Remembered by Thomas,
these events are transmitted through the narrator. The tale reveals the
mother's illusions both about charity and about her son as it displays the
obsession of this historian-intellectual, whose rationalizing words possess no power to produce action, with his dead father's powerful gestures. In the tale readers see Thomas clearly caught between the ghost
of a father who "had never deigned to tell [lies]" but acted them and a
mother who tries to care for a nymphomaniac because "I keep thinking

it might be you."[62] Though his mother's emotional associations of Thomas with Star Drake upset him, they do not disturb his illusions about his own moral superiority. On Thomas they have the effect of pushing him closer to his father's ghost. On readers, however, Thomas's mother's words "suppose it were you?" prepare us for the ironic reversal, for as the omniscient narrator reports, "Thomas felt a deep unbearable loathing for himself as if he were turning slowly into the girl."[63] This gradual blurring of moral distinctions, of categories of people, and even of the conventional boundaries between readers and story is characteristic of peripheral experiences. And what the tale-within-the-tale implies, as it also prepares us for the final irony, is that Thomas's entire life was arrested in a "space between."

"Judgment Day" was O'Connor's revision and expansion of "The Geranium."[64] Revision, expansion, or separate story, it operates like a closing for her composite short stories, which together resemble a cycle. In this story the tale-within-the-tale returns Tanner and readers to Tanner's past home in Corinth, Georgia; the tale moves progressively deeper into Tanner's past not simply linking the doubled Tanner and Coleman but also reflecting the institutionalized disruptions in black-white relations, providing insight into a man's connections to a place and implying the dislocations that accompany technological urbanization. This tale of Tanner's true country is framed on one side by Tanner's determination to get to Corinth, Georgia, dead or alive, and on the other side, by his death on the New York apartment stairs. The narrator interrupts the tale with Tanner's encountering a new, New York City black whose anger, focused on Tanner, propels Tanner closer to his departure and death. The tale is Tanner's imaginative effort to make a temporary stay against dislocation. By revealing Tanner's dependence on his black double Coleman, and his "borrowed" land, the tale prepares the reader for the ironic reversal: that in the new order—in the new city and to the new man—the old dependencies mean nothing. Tanner's daughter's change of heart after she has buried him in the city is prepared for by the dialogue—a mini tale—she carries on within herself throughout the present-time parts of the story. While the tale in this story disorients us because of its dreamlike quality, it also serves as a momentary stay against displacement, utter centrifugal fragmentation, for an old man removed from his true country. Even the interior dialogue of Tanner's daughter acts as a corrective to her own willfulness.

In "Parker's Back," Parker's memory of seeing a tattooed man in a fair when he was fourteen serves as flashback, to explain his fascination with tattoos, and as anticipation of a more profound "branding" to come in a later tale-within-the-tale. Through the omniscient narrator's report of his adolescent experience, we learn that wonder was born in Parker only after he saw the man at the fair. Although this birth of wonder at first produced barely perceptible changes, it gradually consumed him with a desire for more and more pictures on his body, pictures that would attract to him "the kind of girls he liked but who had never liked him before."[65] As the narrator traces the progression of Parker's obsession for tattoos—"from lifeless ones like anchors and crossed rifles . . . [to] a tiger and a panther on each shoulder"[66]—we learn that a dissatisfaction that raged within him and inexplicably controlled his life has overcome his former lack of concern about the subject matter of his tattoos.

Though Parker had hoped a change to the country would calm his disquiet, it led instead to his marriage to Sarah Ruth—a woman who bears the names of the mother of Judaism and of a woman converted to Judaism through her extraordinary loyalty—and a gloomier turn of spirit in him. He recognized that there was no containing this dissatisfaction outside of a tattoo. After he hits—or is grasped by—the tree in the field while he is baling, Parker is propelled toward the city, for he "knew that there had been a great change in his life, a leap forward into a worse unknown."[67] His return to his old tattoo artist in the city, his experience of selecting and getting the Byzantine Christ tattooed on his back, his overnight stay in the Haven of Light Christian Mission, and his fight in the pool room—from which he emerges knowing "the eyes that were now forever on his back were eyes to be obeyed"[68]—form an apocalyptic tale-within-the-tale. For Parker, his experience at the fair and all the subsequent tattoos are like rituals that have preserved him and have prepared him for the awe-full encounter with the living God, made possible through the penetrating eyes of the Byzantine Christ imprinted on his back.

All these tales-within-tales occur on the edges of the stories and on the edges of a character's consciousness or in the unconscious. Because they inform the present with remnants or recollections from the past or the unconscious, because they move between concrete reality and a more mysterious reality, these tales must be related by an omniscient narrator whose consciousness can stand in this "space between" realms or realities. These tales-within-the-tale become, in individual stories, the places or moments of intersection between the material and the spiritual, between illusion and truth. When considered collectively, O'Connor's tales-within-tales offer a metaphoric reminder, to her characters and readers alike, that we see only a part of our collective story at one time. Because she embodies the Hebrew belief that to make pictures or graven images of God was idolatry, Sarah Ruth refuses to accept the *image* of Christ on Parker's back. In addition, she is slow to understand that Parker bears the real name of Obadiah Elihu, which means servant of God. The most minor prophet in the Old Testament, Obadiah was charged to condemn Edom and announce a vision of the universal rule of God. Through such peripheral tales, O'Connor implies that our heresy—like Sarah Ruth's of denying the corporeal substance of Christ, the union of spirit and flesh, the influence of the past on the present, the continuing revelation of the divine in the human—is believing in a partial reality that separates a vaporous and ineffectual spirituality from the living, breathing, material world. All of O'Connor's tales in the second collection expose heresies—from egoism, Puritan fanaticism, racism, political or religious authoritarianism to psychological determinism—which rise from the central one. Through the tales-within-tales, she informs us, more directly than in her first volume of stories, that our little tales, however grotesquely distorted, are part of a larger, more mysterious tale or framework.

All the means through which O'Connor creates the shifting narrative voice reflect the tension Asals, Brinkmeyer, Gentry, and others have identified in her stories between a fundamentalist and Catholic vision. Explicating these means, we realize, however, that O'Connor does not merely incarnate a dialogue between a fundamentalist vision assigned to her narrators and her own authorial Catholic vision. Instead, through these she exposes her characters' varied strains of egoism and directs her readers' disorientation. Although narrating the stories principally in the past tense, O'Connor's narrators occasionally move between the recent and more distant past or even insert a snippet of the present into the past. And, as we have seen above, the narrator can lead us through time to the atemporal or to mystery.

As we assess the aspect and mood of the narratives—that is, how the story is perceived by the narrator and the type of discourse the narrator uses to present the story—we recognize further complication. Generally O'Connor's narrators mirror the proud spirits of the egoists who are sometimes religious fundamentalists and sometimes staunch secularists determined to disabuse fundamentalists of their narrowness, and thereby vulnerable to another "fundamentalism." Through the third person, the narrators often appear to judge these characters; however, when the narrators' capacity for omniscience undermines the objective distance required of either reporting or judging, we receive a more sympathetic presentation, which turns ironic.

The types of discourse used by the narrators reflect their perceptions of the story. Usually the narrator begins to tell the story in the language and attitude of the dominant character; if this character is a pedantic materialist like Grandfather Fortune or self-righteous prude like Mrs. May, the narrator speaks in that language and tone. However, either the omniscience of the narrator will intrude to alter the discourse by giving access to interior states of being, or, as we have seen, other characters' modes of perception and speaking will undermine or challenge the dominant discourse. Through the operation of such subversion, the primary mode of discourse ultimately becomes irony. In "Judgment Day" in the narrator's description of Tanner's daughter, O'Connor hints at the way her acts of narration operate in all her stories: "She questioned herself in one voice and answered herself in another."[69]

This dialogical questioning—in the narrator's presentation, within a single character, between characters, or between the author and the narrator—highlights the human susceptibility to blindness or myopia about egocentric sin and O'Connor's concern with a proper point of view in reading these tales. Because neither contesting visions nor authority is clearly demarcated with a shifting narrative voice, O'Connor moves the reader herself to the liminal "space between" where the story, in true parabolic character, begins to question the reader.

The Mediating Tricksters

From the foregoing analysis of her narrational techniques, one is tempted to conclude that Flannery O'Connor was interested only in directing disorientation. Nevertheless, since we know by O'Connor's own admission that she desired to interject actions of divine grace into the lives of unexpecting proud spirits and that she became more deliberate about such intentions as her writing progressed, we proceed further to investigate the functioning of figures who extend grace in bizarre and shocking ways and to assess how the shifting narrative voice assists the mediations of the trickster.

In order to penetrate the defenses of the proud, to embody the mysterious actions of grace, indeed, to disclose a radically different kind of hope—hope in the miraculous rather than in human progress, or in impersonal providence—she uses an increasingly insistent presence or agent in these second collection stories who, through his or her grotesqueness or inversion of conventional assumptions, potentially subverts the protagonist's pride and distorted vision so that he or she might see whole. Whether the prideful characters or readers in fact see differently depends heavily on some minimal perception of a go-between who mediates a conflict between two characters or two perceptions in one being's mind or who interprets a partial view of reality by reference to a larger, if stranger, one. Embodied frequently in O'Connor's fictional world as visionary prophets, these go-betweens, as we have already seen, are relatives of clowns, fools, and tricksters. In the first collection stories, these go-between characters usually reside outside or on the edge of a given community and have access to an unseen and customarily rejected dimension. In the second collection, these mediators often exist right in the center of the plot line, but their perceptions or actions pull the characters and readers off center to a periphery or "space between" the center and the abyss of utter fragmentation where enlargement of vision may occur.

We identify the tricksters in the stories of *Everything That Rises Must Converge* by their actions as much as by their words, keeping in mind that in their "going between" they are not immune from deception themselves. In all except three stories the tricksters are human beings or ghosts of human beings who mediate conflicting pulls within a character or conflicting visions between doubled characters. For example, in "Everything That Rises Must Converge" two sons, living on the edges of their mothers' visions, challenge those visions. Julian, feeling "an evil urge to break her spirit," contemplates ways—short of causing a stroke, he cautions himself—to make her see the foolishness of her outmoded views. On the bus as the black woman crowds into the seat next to him and her son successfully attracts the attention of Julian's mother, Julian fantasizes that the two women have swapped sons, a movement that delights Julian but he suspects would horrify his mother. The son of his mother's black double—linked as the two women are through identical hats but vastly different visions—tests his real mother's sense of dignity by playing peek with Julian's mother. Although the blow that knocks Julian's mother to the ground comes not from Julian but from his mother's black double, it has been anticipated in Julian's imagination. It undermines her pridefulness and reduces her finally to the silence of death, though not without O'Connor's deepening the ambiguity of the shock effects.

Julian's mother's response before she dies from a stroke is to ask for her old black nurse Caroline. On the outermost level, her vision seems unchanged by the blow she has received. Is this final call not a plea for the old order? Or is it ironically an admission of need and a request for human kindness that, despite its inadequacies, the old relationship between blacks and whites provided? John R. May argues that both Julian and his mother are transformed by the blow from the black woman. Supporting his conclusion with Teilhard de Chardin's ideas about convergence, May reasons that Julian's mother's diminishment—her fall to the pavement and her admission of need for Caroline—are necessary for her growth and make possible "a higher level convergence" between conflicting forces or visions.[70] Though May believes Julian, too, is transformed because he suffers "a painful awakening to the complexity of racial tension,"[71] the evidence seems ambiguous. His panic and "the tide of darkness seemed to sweep him back to her, postponing from moment to moment his entry into the world of guilt and sorrow."[72] As a trickster who fantasized, in a "high-ceilinged room . . . where his soul expanded momentarily,"[73] the expansion of his mother's limited vision, he himself becomes a victim of his own fantasy. Ironically, the trickster—a maker of language—is himself also reduced to a silence that, however ambiguously, points to a convergence with a silence deeper than any verbal or racial conventions and realized only through suffering and death.[74]

Perhaps of all the agents in the second story collection who facilitate transformation, the trickster action in "A View of the Woods" is the most complex and difficult to discern clearly. This complexity is caused by the mirror-like identification of the apparently doubled characters, Mr. Fortune and Mary Fortune Pitts. In effect, they are merely human representatives of a conflict over the mythic question of what it means to have dominion over the earth that is also portrayed as a familial, generational conflict between the Fortunes and the Pittses. Throughout most of the story the grandfather moves and acts as a trickster: he watches the bulldozing of the land from the side; as a helpless outsider, he witnesses what he believes are Mary Fortune's beatings; he teaches Mary his own tricks, like not hearing; he clandestinely arranges the sale of the woods with serpentine Mr. Tilman; and he tries to bribe Mary Fortune to support his woods sale. During all this movement Mary quietly absorbs her mentor's habits and yet simultaneously reaches a different conclusion about the Fortune-Pitts land controversy.

In the end, taken into the woods at the edge of his property to be whipped by the old man, Mary Fortune reverses his deception by beating him. At this instant she becomes more fully a mediator in the Pitts-Fortune controversy that has raged in the old man's head and over the land. Though she whips him, he rolls over, gaining enough strength to bring her to deathly silence. At this point it appears that the aged trickster has once again "tricked" his younger contender. But O'Connor deepens the ambiguity when Fortune dies immediately afterwards from the convulsive expansion of his heart. Linked so closely to their separate visions and to each other, both these tricksters are deceived into death. If the face of Fortune's conquered image bore no look of remorse in death it was because her action against the old man was her attempt to save the woods and to restore herself in a Pitts community. In the old man's dying there is no solace; only the ugly pines, a lake that he could not swim, and dark, gaunt trees that "had thickened into mysterious dark files . . . march[ed] across the water and away into the distance."[75] Bereft of any community, all that remains to help him in his passage from life to death is a yellow monster, "gorging itself on clay."[76] In a world where community is sacrificed for domination, the trickster has limited redemptive power.

Whereas we associate the trickster action in "A View of the Woods" with the myth of temptation and the Fall, in "The Comforts of Home" we find it present in psychological form, thus moving the trickster closer to human shadow and farther from a mythological or sociological manifestation.[77] As in many O'Connor stories, several circles of action taking place simultaneously and characters seemingly cross-paired at different times in a story deepen the narrative density. One circle of action occurs among Thomas, his mother, and Sarah Ham; the unfortunate dark Star brings the conflict between apparent doubles—Thomas, who is an intellectual historian skeptical of mindless charity, and his mother, who insists on being morally virtuous to a fault—to a head.

Almost imperceptibly at first readers discern another circle of action that, by the end of the story, becomes a deeper source of the conflict expressed in Thomas's and his mother's lives. This is a struggle Thomas mediates in himself between his father's ghost and his mother's "foolhardy engagements with the devil whom, of course, she never recognized."[78] The narrator reports that Thomas is caught between his father's ghost and his mother, for "at these times . . . [when his mother performed her unreasonable acts of charity] he mourned the death of his father though he had not been able to endure him in life."[79] His father, "untouched by useless passion,"[80] was a man of action, however deceptive, a quality Thomas does not possess. As Thomas threatens action—to leave home—against his mother's charity toward Star, his father's ghost asserts itself in his mind, urging him toward gestures similar to those by which his father controlled his environment. Consequently, Thomas longs to reject his mother's vision and the behavior that his father had resisted in life. His father's voice, growing increasingly louder, leads him forward in that defiance. As his mother slowly dwarfs him by turning him into a "nimpermaniac" through her overidentification of him with Star, his father's ghost ridicules him for letting his mother run over him. Star's presence creates the occasion for action because she disturbs his soul deeply.

Troubled by both his parents' responses to life, which are opposite sides of faith in human effort, Thomas hopes for a miracle. He himself bears increasing resemblance to the trickster when he plots the deception of Star and decides to see the sheriff. He is not self-reflective, repetitively blurts out his business to the sheriff, and leaves feeling that he has delivered his mother over to the sheriff, one of his father's kind. When he returns home he parks the car at a distance from the house, characteristic of the trickster who functions on the edges of his society, and walks in a circle toward the back door. From the moment Thomas discovers that his gun is back in his drawer, his father's voice, now virtually his own, encircles him with direction for further gestures of deception that lead finally to the ironic miracle— Thomas's action that frees him of his mother by reducing her to silence but also tricks him by directly implicating him through irrational violence with Sarah.

In this narrative Thomas's troubled psyche becomes the battlefield—the neutral territory—on which he wrestles with an absent father "squatting in his mind," instead of God, and his own capacity for evil. If there is any transformation afforded by the trickster's struggle between mother and father it must occur to readers who, standing farther on the outside than Thomas, may see the shock of Thomas's action as a grotesque intervention of grace into the daily gestures by which human beings, with dwarfed visions, live their lies.

O'Connor embodies the conflict between goodness and truth as a

contest between freedom and psychological determinism in "The
Lame Shall Enter First." On the manifest level, social worker Sheppard invites a delinquent into his home to teach Norton, his son,
generosity. The help Rufus provides is to expose the bankruptcy of
human goodness when it is separated from divine truth—what is
right. As a crippled social outcast with an intense religious vision of
Satan, evil, heaven and hell, Rufus challenges Sheppard's "clinical
positivism that denies the mysteries of good and evil in the world."[81]
When Rufus Johnson takes up residence with Sheppard and Norton,
he defies Sheppard by offering Norton a belief that his mother's death
may transcend the limits of death. Reminiscent of the traditional trickster, Rufus sojourns between Sheppard's constricted world, through
which Sheppard ironically hopes he will give Rufus "something to
reach for," and the world of petty crime, through which Rufus wants
"to show up that big tin Jesus!"[82] The trickster's movements between
these two realms ironically become Rufus's means of testing Sheppard's capacity for judging goodness and truth. For Sheppard blames
Rufus's lameness for his errantness. Suggestive of Satan who tested
Jesus three times in the wilderness periphery of his society, Rufus also
tests Sheppard three times, each time deceiving him more deeply,
until he exposes Sheppard's faith in psychology as an illusion, really
no more than a superstition. Naively, Sheppard believes human
behavior is the only explanation for good or evil. Sheppard's blind
declaration of Rufus's innocence, after the third test, links in lies the
would-be savior to his recalcitrant subject and reveals that goodness
without reference to truth inevitably yields deception.

Through his disturbing encounter with his psychologist savior,
Rufus moves more deeply toward his religious vision until, having
eaten a page of the Bible, he prophesies the apocalypse to come at the
end of the story and of Sheppard's atheistic world: "The lame shall
enter first. . . . The lame'll carry off the prey!"[83] This lame prophet,
acquainted with the mystery and power of evil in himself, goes between Norton and Sheppard. With all his acts of goodness rejected,
Sheppard reels on the edge of a dark abyss. Without a vision of truth
and with only his generous deeds for questionable self-defense, Sheppard has nothing with which to reproach himself.

Through the mechanical device of a telescope, however, Rufus does
make distant reaches—like heaven—real to Norton. When Norton's
childlike identification of his mother with the moon leads to his attempt to launch himself from the attic rafters to be with her, Rufus's

brutally transforming work has been finished. His vision of truth has been incarnated in Norton's mind. The lame one has carried off the prey, leaving Sheppard to confront Norton hanging from the rafters with his face transformed, "the image of salvation; all light."[84] Through the violent action of grace, the transforming of Norton, a socially delinquent believer in truth that transcends *and* erupts in human affairs deceives Sheppard into recognizing the limits of his own vision. And by those limits he is judged but not transformed because he lacks the imaginative power to accept the displacement of his own pretense to Godhead through human goodness with the mysterious truth that both good and evil lie in the Center.

The trickster action in O'Connor's "Revelation" is more perceptible than in many of the preceding stories because the narrative structure begins and ends with two vastly different visions in Mrs. Turpin's head. The agent who precipitates the transformation of her vision exists psychologically farther on the edge of this story than previous tricksters. Although the reader knows little about Mary Grace that doesn't pass through Mrs. Turpin's consciousness, it appears that O'Connor has exchanged religious obsession for skeptical humanism in this mediating agent. Mary Grace, reading a book entitled *Human Development*, peers through Mrs. Turpin with eyes that "knew her in some intense and personal way, beyond time and place and condition."[85] From this strange sight comes the action—the hurled book which lands above Mrs. Turpin's eye—that promotes Mrs. Turpin's visionary encounter with the incredible mystery that she bears some resemblance to a wart hog. What is changed by this bizarre eruption of grace is Mrs. Turpin's estimate of her position in the universe.

At the beginning she is a physically large presence whose self-pride engulfs everyone else in the doctor's waiting room. In this state she has no genuine community with others there or, apparently, anywhere else. Like Job, she is an upright woman grateful for her "good disposition" and material blessings who mistakes minor gifts for the ultimate gift of human-divine community. At the end, Ruby has been ushered into a true place within the cosmos. Bent over the hog pen, she rails at Mary Grace, or is it God through Mary Grace? "'Go on, call me a hog! Call me a hog again. From Hell. Call me a wart hog from hell. Put that bottom rail on top. There'll still be a top and bottom!' . . . A final surge of fury shook her and she roared, 'Who do you think you are?'"[86] Only after this angry ejaculation is Mrs. Turpin transformed; through the reduction of her size or the containment of her centrifugal drive toward Godhood, "like a monumental statue coming to life, she bent her head slowly and gazed, as if through the very heart of mystery, down into the pig parlor at the hogs. . . . They appeared to pant with a secret life."[87] Through the actions of an ugly skeptic, Mrs. Turpin finds a secret in the hog pen akin to what Job discovered from the voice of God speaking to him out of the whirlwind: that God resides with the mountain goats in their bringing forth, looses the bonds of the wild ass, gives the horse its strength, commands the morning, the rains, and the snow, and, only through encouter, pre- serves both God and human beings from lost community.

"Judgment Day" is manifestly "a parable about an exile's return to his homeland."[88] O'Connor's handling of the narrative shifts both in voice and time make this a multilayered story of deception. The origi- nal and central deception occurs between Coleman and Tanner years earlier when, out of fear, Tanner distorts a revelation of equality be- tween black and white into superiority; by falsely believing he had made Coleman "jump on his back," by showing him "his brains didn't have a chance against yours,"[89] Tanner destroys human community. Both Tanner and Coleman, thus, are locked in this clownish collusion. Because of his belief in the illusion of human inequality and his fear that when "the bottom rail gets put on the top" he'd be working for a Negro, Tanner accepts the banishment ordered by Dr. Foley.

Through Tanner's dream, O'Connor prepares the reader for the transforming deception extended appropriately through a black actor who, when Tanner tries to treat him as he handled Coleman, forcefully challenges his illusion of what it means to be black or white by shoving him back into his daughter's apartment, precipitating Tanner's stroke. In his dream, Tanner's corpse, arriving in a pine box in Corinth, Georgia, jumps out at Coleman and Hooten shouting, "Judgment Day! Judgment Day!" Considered by Coleman and Hooten just another of Tanner's tricks, the dream-corpse anticipates the final trick and real-life judgment proffered through the black actor. When Tanner, suffering the effects of his stroke and longing for burial in Georgia, leaves his daughter's apartment with an identification and destination note pinned to his clothes, he falls upside down on the hall stairs. Confusing the topsy-turvy motion with the tilting of his dream pine coffin, Tanner exclaims the arrival of Judgment Day into the black actor's face, whom he momentarily confuses for Coleman. The black actor mocks Tanner's pronouncement: "Ain't no judgment day, old man. Cept this. Maybe this here judgment day for you."[90] The ambiguity of those words befits the trickster. The judgment Tanner faces is the judgment that races intermix, as the light-skinned woman standing with the black actor and Dr. Foley illustrate, and reveal a common humanity. And the home to which Tanner is going is the radically different home where old conventions—like racial distinctions—do not matter.

"Greenleaf," "The Enduring Chill," and "Parker's Back" have nonhuman agents who function as mediators or agents of grace. Perhaps because these agents are not human we can see more clearly both the world O'Connor tried to penetrate through her fiction and the two realms she sought to reconnect through her vision. In "Greenleaf," the second story of the collection, the revelatory agent is a bull, primitive beast and classical symbol of a love god. Mrs. May's anger and frustration about the bull and the whole Greenleaf family to whom the bull belongs show her vision to be narrowly self-interested; she is an underdeveloped shell who, though deeply committed to social conventions like class, education, professions, and manners, knows herself only by report, by the image she wants to see reflected back to her from others. She worries that the Greenleafs will become society, thus defying all conventions.

In her provocative interpretation of "Greenleaf," Louise Westling notes the troubling paradoxical imagery of this story. While these paradoxical images confuse, they also support the tricksteresque operations we have come to recognize in O'Connor's stories. Westling points out, for example, that O'Connor depicts the earth in contrasting ways in "Greenleaf."

> In the scene where Mrs. Greenleaf performs her prayer-healing in the woods, the earth is presented as a potent masculine entity whose active force charges out of the ground when Jesus is invoked. The bull is the obvious incarnation of this force. But in passages describing Mrs. May's farm, the land is female. The farm is Mrs. May's garden, a cultivated area of gently rolling pastures which had been run-down before the widow came to restore it to productive order. . . . Here, as in so many of the farm stories, the widow's domain is fenced in from the threatening sky by a wall of trees. In the final scene, the precarious integrity of this female place is violated in symbolic rape as the bull, who has paradoxically become the epiphany of sun and sky, breaks through the protective, encircling woods into the "green arena" which symbolizes Mrs. May's own being as well as her hard-won garden.[91]

Westling astutely describes the complications that arise from O'Connor's presentation of the earth as both male and female, from her inversions of traditional Catholic views of the earth and of mythological patterns, from Frederick Asals's unsatisfying comparison of Mrs. Greenleaf to Dionysus and Mrs. May to Pentheus in Euripides' *The Bacchae,* and from O'Connor's failure to give Mrs. May an interior development adequate to warrant her culminating experience.[92] Seeking coherence in O'Connor's use of these various mythological and religious traditions, readers may be as unsettled as Westling is by the symbolism in this story.

However, these apparently tangled threads illustrate the trickster activity in the narrative. Through the inverted allusions and paradoxical images adapted from Greek and Christian religions, the narrator not only mirrors a contest for the world visible in her characters' visions and blindness but also wreaks havoc on both the religious fanatic Mrs. Greenleaf and on the morally upright and conventional Mrs. May. The Greenleaf reverence, which is feared and maligned by Mrs. May, is undermined by Mrs. Greenleaf's worship of a male earth and Mr. Greenleaf's impotence to help Mrs. May control his sons' bull. Mrs. May dies because she is locked in a female garden, fighting to make her land productive. In protecting herself against the Greenleafs, she also shuts herself off from the animating, generative spirit of Jesus on whom Mrs. Greenleaf calls during her healing rituals. The narrative suggests that disorder reigns on the earth and in the human heart where there is no mutuality, no unifying myth, and no community.

Paradoxically, the Greenleaf bull, symbol of fecundity and metamorphosis (and associated with the snake and the sky as well), is a nuisance and threat to Mrs. May's world. Almost simultaneous with his sacrifice, however, he is also the means to enlightenment. Through their ironically mutual pursuit and avoidance, this beast god and woman imply the interdependence of the divine and the human. Typical of O'Connor's general pattern of movement and the traditional trickster, the trickster-bull finally races for Mrs. May from a circle of trees edging a small pasture, reminiscent of the "ancient circular meadow of rape in Greek religion,"[93] at the center of which she has parked her car to await what she innocently, though deceptively, believes will be the death of the Greenleaf bull. Instead, burying its head in her lap, "like a wild tormented lover,"[94] the bull conquers and she succumbs to silence as this elemental force turns her toward a larger center, toward mystery.

Standing near the middle of *Everything That Rises Must Converge,* "The Enduring Chill" may reflect whatever light it sheds on mystery both backward and forward over the collection. Because of its position in the collection and the nature of its trickster agent, it embodies both the narrative's capacity for going-between the story and the reader and the human need for a mediator. Ill and believing he is dying, Asbury returns home to acquaint his mother, through his dying, with a "true" view of herself and the constricted imagination she has bestowed on him. Returned to his childhood room, among the first things Asbury notices are the water stains on the gray walls. "Descending from the top molding, long icicle shapes had been etched by leaks and, directly over his bed on the ceiling, another leak had made a fierce bird with spread wings. It had an icicle crosswise in its beak and there were smaller icicles depending from its wings and tail."[95] He often fantasized that these stain-forms were in motion ready to "set the icicle on his head."[96] To blot out the fear he had always closed his eyes; now he knew he would soon be able to close his eyes on them forever. As a failed artist with no imagination, no talent, no creative capacity— only the desire for these things—Asbury asks his mother to call a Jesuit priest to go between, that is, to interpret him and his dying.

Unable to speak to him about Joyce or the myth of the dying god, the priest insists on talking about Jesus, praying, and the Holy Spirit. Asbury finally convinces himself that he will have no significant experience before he dies just as his mother announces to him that Dr. Block has discovered that Asbury has undulant fever. Though Block brings him this shocking news, inverting all Asbury's assumptions and preparations, it is the movement of a strange chill through his body that shatters the illusion from his eyes. "The fierce bird which through the years of his childhood and the days of his illness had been poised over his head, waiting mysteriously, appeared all at once to be in motion."[97] This frozen figure Asbury now ironically understands as the Holy Spirit. For an egocentric man like Asbury—frozen in spirit, attracted to death—who had himself displaced the dying god, the Spirit comes, in typical trickster fashion, from the ceiling of his room and simultaneously as a purifying chill through his body.

The comforter-interpreter Asbury receives at the end recalls the Holy Spirit promised in the Christian scripture by the God-in-man facing his sacrificial death. Coming out of ice where it has been relegated by visions and worlds like Asbury's, the Holy Spirit unexpectedly interjects itself, breathing on him an animating chill. In this center story O'Connor invertedly discloses the specifically religious content of her fiction and implies yet more fully her narrative secret: that the incarnation of God-in-human flesh repeats itself in endless forms through the actions of the Holy Spirit, the often shocking agent of grace. In orthodox trinitarian terms, the Holy Spirit mediates between the unknowable God and the Christ, God made flesh. Between the mysterious, passionate bull god in "Greenleaf" and the tattoo of a Byzantine Christ on Parker's back, O'Connor has incarnated a fierce Holy Spirit ready to descend and to transform a world full of dying self-gods like Asbury.

Once again in "Parker's Back" O'Connor has given an inanimate object a transcendent living power to turn a vain man into an obedient prophet and to expose Sarah Ruth's vapid religious faith. Perhaps unintentionally using devices of many traditional trickster tales, O'Connor leads Parker and willing readers through a journey-like maze. With Parker, we travel to fairs for tattoos, survive a fiery accident, receive the tattoo of Christ, confront his friends' ridicule in the pool hall, and go home to be turned away. All these experiences parallel Parker's spiritual transition from pride to obedience and rejection. The words that Parker hears "as plainly as if silence were a language itself" as he looks for the right picture in the tattoo artist's book are GO BACK.[98] They echo from the Hebrew prophets who historically called their people to return to God and righteousness, and they characterize the trickster's movement to turn the lost spirit back from isolation or the fringes of society to the center of shared practice and belief.

The tattooed Christ completes the work begun on Parker in his accident; it tricks him, turning him into Obadiah Elihue, making him now "of God" himself. O'Connor turns a phantasmal Christ of distant history into a strange but living presence. However, the narrative, like the two-thousand-year-old incarnation it retells, is not complete with Parker's conversion. Acknowledging the power of blindness, of evil, and of denial, the tale ends in paradox, for Sarah Ruth, the staunch religious fundamentalist, rejects the miraculous intervention of grace, a rejection often repeated in human history nurtured by a faith in a benevolent providence that does not account for evil.

In both story collections proud, often upright characters—Mrs. Hopewell, Mrs. Cope, Mrs. Shortley, Mr. Fortune, Mrs. May, Mrs. McIntyre, Mrs. Turpin—repeat some form of the Pharisee's prayer: "God, I thank thee that I am not like other men, extortioners, unjust, adulterers, or even like this tax collector. I fast twice a week, I give tithes of all that I get."[99] This is a prayer of self-justification spoken as a sign of election or insider status by the self-righteous. O'Connor's tricksters, despite their varied, ambiguous, and often unseemly natures, operate in the stories to subvert the haughty spirited. By turning out such characters' insides or turning up to the light an underside, the trickster intrudes into the proud character's self-imposed isolation that results from having no access to the holy Other, to an enlarged and more unified consciousness, or to human community that includes extortioners, adulterers, the lame, and the blind.

Aided by the narrators' shifting narrative voice, the tricksters in Flannery O'Connor's second volume stories expose contesting perceptions, as between truth and illusion, in the central character; they may also mediate conflicting visions, such as greedy materialism and merciful charity, of two characters. The tricksters' means of intervention usually involve shock or surprise proportional to the proud character's pretense and delusion. In stories like "Greenleaf," "A View of the Woods," "The Lame Shall Enter First," "Revelation," and "Parker's Back" the self-righteousness of the egoist elicits a fiercer interruption from the trickster that, in turn, may produce strong resistance or even defiance in the proud character. Such a stand-off, however, is understandable if we recall that the trickster is a supreme imitator, as well as deceiver, and vulnerable to deception himself. In "Everything That Rises Must Converge," "The Enduring Chill," "The Comforts of Home," and "Judgment Day" the pattern of mediation seems less severe, though not necessarily less grotesque, because in these stories an inexorable undermining of the central character's partial vision is prepared for within the character or through the character's family from the outset of the story.

As a being of the peripheries, or the limen, the classic trickster claims no fixed position or territory. O'Connor's tricksters generally illustrate this characteristic, though with some interesting variations. The Greenleafs' bull most graphically demonstrates the typical trickster behavior. By its inability to be confined in a fixed pasture by either the Greenleafs or Mrs. May and in its relentless, almost sexual, pursuit of Mrs. May, the bull gores her to the portal of danger, death, and possible enlightenment. Asbury's association of a water stain on the wallpaper with the Holy Ghost ironically conveys the human potential for freezing into permanence the Holy Spirit that ranges freely between all regions and people. The ghost of Thomas's father exhibits the similar capacity of going between the material and immaterial realms, though in "The Comforts of Home" he takes up residence in Thomas's imagination guiding him to confrontation and murder. In

"Parker's Back," the Byzantine Christ tattooed onto Parker's flesh represents the culminating claim on Parker who has wandered hungrily but aimlessly most of his life.

Other characters manifest trickster characteristics like Julian and his mother's black double. Mr. Fortune and Mary Fortune Pitts, intercepted by the slithery entrepreneur Tilman; Rufus; and Tanner and Coleman each in specific ways lives on the fringes of prevailing values or disintegrating institutions. They paradoxically struggle against yet are bound by static social categories, by impermeable boundaries between spiritual and material development, by psychological constriction or inflation, and between life and death. Even if the trickster fails to convert O'Connor's protagonist to a narrowly defined religious orthodoxy or to reconcile opposing motives, he does reveal more dimensions of a character's life to other characters, to readers, and occasionally to the character himself or herself.

The emphasis O'Connor places on the physical forms and features of many of her characters, especially those given to trickery or vulnerable to deceit, not only reflects the classic trickster but also serves O'Connor's intention to incarnate mystery. First, in these stories, we usually find the trickster physically standing between a center where truth and harmony potentially exist and the periphery of total disintegration. For example, Rufus stands between or mediates the truth about Norton's and Sheppard's empty lives and the illusions that motivate Sheppard's desperate charity. Similarly, Mary Grace sits stolidly on the edge of the waiting room witnessing Mrs. Turpin's spiraling self-righteousness until she physically intercepts the arrogance and turns the loquacious woman back toward a still center.

Second, the trickster sometimes may bear physical marks that reflect or distort interior divisions that plague the central character(s). We observe this technique in the narrator's description of Grandfather and Mary Fortune: "she was short and broad like himself, with his very light blue eyes, his wide prominent forehead, his steady penetrating scowl and his rich florid complexion; but she was like him on the inside too. She had, to a singular degree, his intelligence, his strong will, and his push and drive."[100] In "Greenleaf," the bull's fecundity and recalcitrance parody the sterile order of Mrs. May's life and garden. Rufus's malformed foot focuses Sheppard's saccharine compassion just as Mary Grace's face blue with acne or Star Drake's nymphomania mirror the inner distortions of Ruby Turpin and Thomas respectively.

Because of his own pronounced physical features, the trickster understands gestures and, through his own movement, can expose the lie O'Connor perceived twentieth-century human beings to be living. Covered with words, justifications, and all manner of social and religious conventions, the lie is arrogance. The trickster uncovers disguises, penetrates gestures, and reduces the arrogant to silence by spinning the tales that acquaint us with the human capacity for duplicity and evil. To become silent is to be able to see and to hear.

In sum, the trickster's activity has the effect of emptying and quieting O'Connor's egoists. The trickster disabuses characters and readers alike of their illusions and stills their rationalizing, justificatory idle chatter. Or, as Anne Doueihi writes in describing the space between discourse and story in trickster narratives, "the trickster shows us a way to see the world by opening our minds to the spontaneous transformations of a reality that is always open and creative. It is only to the closed, ordinary mind that trickster stories seem absurd or profane. It is in the language out of which they are constructed that trickster stories make accessible this deeper wisdom about the nature of reality." [101] Although the trickster cannot save or redeem the stubbornly willful, his interventions prepare the character's spirit for surrender. He opens the inner territory, as it were.

By reading Flannery O'Connor's narratives with an understanding of the trickster, we change the persistent question of critics and readers about whether O'Connor's arrogant spirits *receive* grace and are transformed once and for all. That question reveals our own propensities for judgmental spectatorship, as it also deflects us from recognizing that while the tricksters serve as mirrors for the egoists, they and their tales offer windows to us as readers. Standing further on the fringes of the tale than the tricksters, we readers look into the narrative from the outside. Thus, the trickster also mediates our relation to the story. Through distortion and disorientation, these tales reveal that deception and truth reside side-by-side or, as John Hawkes noted, the demonic and the divine are often threateningly associated. [102] Furthermore, human inclination toward illusion needs perpetual interventions by the trickster, which make us ready for grace that always surprises and throws all our presuppositions and categories off balance. The Misfit recognized our human condition when he observed that the grandmother "would of been a good woman . . . if it had been somebody there to shoot her every minute of her life." [103] Without sensitivity to the operations of the trickster elements in O'Connor's stories, we risk forms of judgmentalism and self-righteousness, akin to O'Connor's egoists, in our interpretation. We fail to understand the importance of becoming silent in order to see, to hear, and perhaps to be changed.

From Language to Silence: The As If Territory

In their dependence on shifting voice and tone, in their use of apocalyptic imagery, in their rendering of characters who are not fully developed,[104] and in defiance of literary conventions associated with realistic fiction, these stories acquire a density reminiscent of Hebrew narratives or Christian parables. Despite Shloss's judgment to the contrary, the similarity of these narratives to biblical ones lies precisely in O'Connor's incarnation—externalization—of mystery. By defying the conventions of both realistic fiction and lifeless Christian orthodoxy, O'Connor acknowledges the hiddenness that exists in all God's revelations and thus moves us closer to living mystery in all its varied manifestations. O'Connor discloses this mystery through pious, humanly initiated religious talk that finally reduces her characters to silence, teaching them the wisdom of Ecclesiastes 5:1: "To draw near to listen is better than to offer the sacrifice of fools." The agent who sometimes interrupts the sacrifice of fools and startles the self-righteous into the secrets of silence is the Holy Spirit embodied variously as trickster in O'Connor's stories.

All the movements in the stories, from the shifting narrative voice to the interventions of the tricksters roving from the story edge to the center of tension, contribute finally to the perpetual turning of the proud spirits who dominate *Everything That Rises Must Converge*—the spectators—into spectacles. Remaining aloof from their families or strangers, these spectators judge others with egoistic protection. However, O'Connor relentlessly pursues these spectators, through the linguistic construction of *as if,* along a path of reversibility into a liminal "space between" or a putative reality where we can infer—if not see or hear—distant things, remote possibilities, the mysterious as if they were at hand. Lifting from the second collection stories several sentences marked by the *as if* construction, we can witness not only the power of this linguistic device but also the necessity of reversibility to O'Connor's ends: "She kept her eyes on the woman *as if* the woman were a monkey that had stolen her hat. . . . The sound was so piercing that she felt *as if* some violent unleashed force had broken out of the ground and was charging toward her. . . . It was *as if* it were *he* that Pitts was driving down the road to beat and it was *as if he* were the one submitting to it. . . . [H]e saw his mother's form *as if* it were a shadow in the door. . . . He felt *as if* he had seen a tornado pass a hundred yards away and had an intimation that it would turn again and head directly for him. . . . The boy looked at him *as if* he were the guilty one, *as if* he were a moral leper. . . . All at once her vision narrowed and she saw everything *as if* it were happening in a small room far away, or *as if* she were looking at it through the wrong end of the telescope. . . . It was *as if* he were himself but a stranger to himself, driving into a new country. . . . And then he looked directly at Tanner and grinned, or grimaced, Tanner could not tell which, but he had an instant's sensation of seeing before him a negative image of himself, *as if* clownishness and captivity had been their common lot."

All *as if* statements defy common cause-and-effect expectations. They wrench characters and readers away from unexamined notions of themselves and from limited perceptions of reality while they and we remain still captive to both. Among endless possibilities that lodge in these phrases, such statements unveil guilt, bring shadows to the light, make far things seem near, turn people into strangers to themselves and freaks into close relatives, expose duplicity, produce laughter and dread, humble the certain through ambiguity, and silence the ceaseless sacrifice of fools. In Edward Kessler's formulation,

> The complex meanings evoked by O'Connor's *as if* center on power, an inexplicable energy acting on the mind and on or through external nature. This power cannot be named; language can only render its effects. If we see metaphor as "saying one thing while meaning another," we can understand why customary metaphor proved inadequate to O'Connor's special needs. Seeking to incorporate power, she required not a condensed simile, confining her to the phenomenal world, but a comparison lying somewhere between a true resemblance and an actual equivalence. What follows the *as if* does not explain what precedes it.[105]

Indeed, the inexplicability of the *as if* throws everyone off balance precisely because it embodies possibilities that lie outside that which we admit into our normal ways of thinking—the possibility of grotesque distortion, mistaken perception, dreadful consequences, or truth and freedom. Collectively the *as if* reflections persistently yet almost imperceptibly create the neutral territory or the "space between" where the Actual and the Imaginary, the material and the spiritual meet. This "space between" is the terrible limen of threat and promise where we are forced to see that evil is not irreversible, as materialists, political ideologues, religious fanatics—yea, most human beings—would like to believe. Through characters who live out their little tales within a greater, somehow mysterious tale, O'Connor invites us to our true country—the *as if* territory—where "evil is not only reversible but it is the proper motive of that mercy by which it is overcome and changed into good."[106] Together these narratives may lead us as the book of tattoos did Parker, waiting for a sign. "He continued to flip through until he had almost reached the front of the book. On one of the pages a pair of eyes glanced at him swiftly. Parker sped on, then stopped. His heart too appeared cut off; there was absolute silence. It said as plainly as if silence were a language itself, GO BACK."[107] In the *as if* territory we are at least silenced if not turned back.

Episode to Ironic Community

Between *A Good Man Is Hard to Find* and *Everything That Rises Must Converge,* Flannery O'Connor's artistic technique becomes more direct without sacrificing the subtlety present in her episodic tales of original sin. In the episodes of the first collection, O'Connor shows us individual characters whose predicaments resemble human dilemmas told and retold in folklore, myth, and history and reenacted in ritual ceremonies of diverse places and distant times. Through the language of irony, which makes it possible to hold apparently contradictory perceptions simultaneously, O'Connor imaginatively invites readers into these earlier tales. By the second collection, however, O'Connor's intentions are more focused and her methods more insistent. If "Revelation" completes a cycle begun in "Everything That Rises Must Converge," as Ingram asserts, and if "Judgment Day" enlarges and fulfills "The Geranium," then "Parker's Back," as O'Connor's closing expression, may be the culmination of her fictional purposes. Caroline Gordon told O'Connor that in "Parker's Back" she had succeeded in writing a heresy.

The heresy of all O'Connor's fiction lies in the persistence with which she sought to incarnate the phantasm, Christ.[108] Through the cyclic character of her narrative structures, O'Connor not only reminds human beings of their continuing need for salvation or return to the still point, which she knew as Christ, but also challenges our assumptions about time and history, a point John Desmond discusses perceptively in his chapter on the biblical view of history and the metaphysical foundations of O'Connor's fiction.[109] What we assume as a linear, progressive movement in Judeo-Christian history culminating in God's one-time intervention in time and space with the incarnation of Christ, O'Connor shapes artistically into an ever-revolving spiral of broken line segments. At every break in the line of her stories, a holy intervention occurs giving her characters a choice to return to the center or still point. When considered with only partial or finite vision, these lines look single and discrete. But writing with eyes tuned to the spirit and to mystery, O'Connor incarnates these segments into a dynamic, cycling spiral into which she gathers her readers as well, linking us with all those in history or fiction who repeatedly face the choice about who and whose we are.

In *Everything That Rises Must Converge,* O'Connor is no longer content to lure readers into her fictional world where she tries to inform the concrete with the spiritual. Instead, her techniques of direction build the world around the readers, leaving *us* to stand in the "space between," in the *as if* territory that is the domain literature and religion share because they both speak—even in paradox and silence—of possibility. Pulled into this territory through the texts, we become part of O'Connor's ironic community. The experience of communitas in the "space between," as characterized by Victor Turner,[110] is liminal and anti-structural. In this space where worship and ritual passage occur, people become acquainted with their own marginality, whether experienced as poverty, loss, illness, disability, or any other form of dislocation. Along with her characters we feel threatened in this "space between" and repeatedly retreat to partial visions and unyielding categories for security. What we learn from and with O'Connor's characters—as they approach and retreat from this "space between"—is that we are paradoxically only free when captive to our true image, that the sublimity of our true condition can be looked at only indirectly through the reflected ridiculousness of our gestures by which we deny that condition, and that the mystery revealed in the "space between" may best be greeted with laughter. This is the laughter not of mockery but of incredulity on the way to faith. It is the laughter that finally invites sympathy, nurtures the imagination, and builds community on a vision of reality whole.

4

The Novels
From Annunciation to Apocalypse

The darkness drops again; but now I know
That twenty centuries of stony sleep
Were vexed to nightmare by a rocking cradle,
And what rough beast, its hour come round at last,
Slouches toward Bethlehem to be born?
—William Butler Yeats

The foregoing analysis of the short stories, those episodic tales that collectively resemble traditional trickster
cycles, has illustrated how Flannery O'Connor's narrative environments challenge all manner of conventions—
social, religious, even literary—thus undermining the
human attachment to categories. Because we, her readers, treat ourselves as categories and O'Connor's works
defy easy categorization, we do not know what to make
of her: "we want our stimuli straight. We want Catholi-
cism or Protestantism; Old Testament or New; Augus-
tine or Aquinas. We want evil condemned or groveled in,
not temporized with. We want gloom and gladness in
separate doses; reality and fantasy dissociated; pleasure
and pain banished to the poles."[1] By analyzing the linguistic and structural devices O'Connor used in her
shorter narratives, we have come face to face with ambiguity, deception, and irony so unsettling to category-
dependents. Furthermore, we have been led to confront
the reversibility of the world through twentieth-century
southern characters and situations that are prefigured in
ancient myths.

Identifying the elements that bind O'Connor's particulars to the universal, the finite to the infinite, the periphery and the center is the heart of religious concern. In her short stories, O'Connor links her particular characters together through their shared displacement; by juxtaposing the moral with the fantastic,[2] she shows these particulars in a world that mysteriously transcends their vision or eludes their grasp. In this chapter we are concerned with O'Connor's fuller and more intricate pattern woven from the episodic tales about original sin into two extended, highly imaginative, surreal works that foreshadow the command to Go Back that Parker experiences in the story O'Connor was refining at the time of her death. *Wise Blood* and *The Violent Bear It Away* together take us backward and inward, through sacred history and myth, to the heart of darkness.

The central purpose of this chapter is to examine the means through which O'Connor's narrative structures intersect with and disclose her metaphysical visions in her two novels. There are two reasons for considering the novels together, despite their differences. First, many useful critical interpretations of each individual novel already exist and do not need to be repeated. Some of these more recent ones are largely thematic or symbolic, like Jill Baumgaertner's *Flannery O'Connor: A Proper Scaring,* John Desmond's *Risen Sons: Flannery O'Connor's Vision of History,* or Richard Giannone's *Flannery O'Connor and the Mystery of Love.* Other critics, such as Asals, Shloss, Kessler, Gentry, and Brinkmeyer, illustrate formal and stylistic interests as well. Second, and more important, the preceding chapters have suggested that a unity of themes and a pattern, if not coherence, of structural devices shape O'Connor's narratives. By juxtaposing the two novels, then, we can extend our investigation, through the principle of analogy, asking how the very structures of her novels are animated by her metaphysical views of the Incarnation. In other words, do the novels give us an analogical model of the activity of Incarnation that while governing the world of the text is directed beyond the text to the world of the reader as well? Examination of the techniques O'Connor employs in these works first helps us understand how she embodies past events—annunciation and apocalypse—in fiction. Secondarily, then, we can consider the implications of that creative act on our religious notions and conventions and on our understanding of language.

The ends toward which the readings of these novels are directed here differ from those readings concerned primarily with the religious or philosophical ideas or the view of history one can infer from the fiction. This explication also pays less attention to any particular critical method through which readers can investigate the author's biography or the mind that created the narratives than to the operations in the works that animate the fictional landscape and open readers' imaginations. It is O'Connor's persistent use of biblical themes, images, and characters, all heavily reliant on folklore patterns found in biblical and classical texts, which has turned my attention away from theological or metaphysical abstractions about the narratives. Instead, these novels filled with "underdogs and tricksters" and with repeated motifs from the Hebrew Bible, which is "rich in underdog tales,"[3] pull this investigation toward the "fresh and flexible improvisation within traditional forms [that lies] at the heart of all folklore."[4] The impulse of this discussion, then, is to resist doctrinal interpretations in favor of a way of reading that releases the imaginative power of the texts for readers willing to accept confrontations with the numinous.

We gain access to these more complex and puzzling novels by recalling that O'Connor's artistic method of amendment repeatedly makes apparent the mystery that old sounds and patterns, remembered tales or songs of earlier traditions, must always haunt later, more complex ones, lest these be empty or shallow.[5] This method of amendment makes possible a process of intertextual relations that in O'Connor's works depends heavily on the principles of repetition and reversibility.[6] We have already identified the trickster's role in imitation, mediation, and reversibility within characters' psyches and in the narration of the stories. Henry Louis Gates, Jr., demonstrates how the concept of signifying,[7] by which "a second statement or figure repeats, or tropes, or reverses the first," contributes to the process of intertextual relations, or what I am describing as O'Connor's amendment method. Gates explicates the characteristics of signifying in black culture and literature in the United States, linking this practice with several African trickster figures. As we have already noticed, O'Connor's narration and dialogues reveal that her own ears were tuned to the turns of mind and phrases associated with signifying in her region. Here we examine the operations of signifying, associated with the trickster, across two novels and between these modern fictions and ancient texts.

In O'Connor's novels there are four devices that support the process of intertextual relations she undertakes. First, the narrative shape of the novels, which recalls both traditional comedy and the Bible; second, the novels' themes, which O'Connor embodies in metaphor; third, the linguistic techniques, which weave myth with realism; and fourth, the interrelating of prophets and tricksters, which together disclose the secrets of these annunciatory-apocalyptic tales. Before beginning a closer examination of the operations of these techniques in the novels, however, some preliminary observations about the resonances of biblical and classical narratives in the novels, which prompt such an investigation, will prepare for the closer scrutiny of the methods through which O'Connor conveyed the actions and consequences of the Incarnation in *Wise Blood* and *The Violent Bear It Away*.

Taking her directions from the Hebrew and Christian narratives of preparation for and disclosure of the Word made flesh, O'Connor "repeats" the human epic in these two novels. Whereas the short stories were episodic, treating dramatic moments or individual incidents of original sin, *Wise Blood* and *The Violent Bear It Away* become both more dense and sweeping. Here O'Connor probes human bondage to anxiety both within her characters' individual psyches and across generations. In the novels better than anywhere else in O'Connor's works, the reader begins to understand her anagogical sense of Scripture, that vision important to the Middle Ages, which reveals itself in her artistic power to portray present realities in light of the eternal or of sacred myth. Unfortunately, "because of her subtlety, many will not know they are reading chapters from an apocalypse,"[8] *apocalypse* referring both to specific allusions to the visions on Patmos contained in Revelation and to any cataclysmic disturbance that precipitates a reorientation of perception.

That O'Connor intended an artistic reincarnation of the radical reorientation that occurred when God entered time and space in the life of Christ, or recurs whenever arbitrary boundaries between divine and human are overleaped, is suggested by the scripture (Matthew 11:12) she affixed to *The Violent Bear It Away*. In Matthew and in Luke 16:16 the writers refer to the violence with which one enters the kingdom of God. This violence is not that commonly associated with mad fanatics—religious or secular—but is rather the violence manifested ironically when the self-sacrificial power of love collides with the old law, temporal powers, and social conventions. Interpreting O'Connor's use of violence in this biblical passage, John R. May associates the violence with the extreme situation "because it is this situation that best reveals to us what we are essentially; it is also clearly *in* the violent situation that our response is purest, drained of all self-interest and especially of that facile optimism which for her is the true enemy of faith."[9] We undertake the interpretation of this apocalyptic fiction remembering that the object of interpretation itself is to retrieve, "if necessary by benign violence, what is called the original event of disclosure."[10]

Apocalypse, yielding revelation and radical transformation, arises from some collision or confrontation between two apparently separate domains. Whenever "two independent matrices of perception or reasoning interact with each other the result is either a *collision* ending in laughter, or their *fusion* in a new intellectual synthesis, or their *confrontation* in an aesthetic experience."[11] O'Connor's novels reflect just such collisions; in fact, she builds the apocalyptic landscape of her second novel from confrontations and collisions she embodies in *Wise Blood* and from what Northrop Frye calls the panoramic aspect of apocalyptic vision. The panoramic aspect is characterized by "the vision of staggering marvels placed in a near future and just before the end of time. As a panorama, we look at it passively, which means it is objective to us."[12] The panoramic vision of the world was acquired at the Fall and perceives the world as subject to a final "judgment" after which it "disappears into two unending constituents, a heaven and a hell."[13]

The shape of O'Connor's narratives is influenced on one level by this familiar panoramic perception of the world. Hence, she repeatedly brings apparently independent domains into collision—the physical and the spiritual, near realities and distances, things of God and those associated with the devil. One sees such collision in Hazel Motes, for example. Throughout *Wise Blood* he denies the existence and power of Christ, preaching "there was no Fall because there was nothing to fall from and no Redemption because there was no Fall and no Judgment because there wasn't the first two."[14] Yet, at the end of the novel, he performs a penance—fraught with insinuations of judgment—by blinding himself to see more clearly, by walking on crushed stones, and by wearing a circle of barbed wire around his chest.

On another, more subtle level O'Connor seems to push her reluctant characters and equally diffident readers beyond the panoramic vision to what I would call an internally transformed vision. In this second aspect of apocalyptic vision, which one may helpfully associate with Kierkegaard's concept of a forward-moving repetition in which all that has existed in the past takes on new meaning in the present, the sense of opposition or tension characteristic of the panoramic gives way ultimately to a unified life or perception in which the "split of subject and object no longer limit[s] our vision."[15]

What occupies our attention, then, in this chapter is specifically *how* O'Connor artistically brings about collisions inherent in a panoramic vision of the world and, in so doing, encourages a more fundamental, yet subtle, internal apocalypse through laughter or aesthetic experience. When O'Connor's characters or readers cannot laugh it is because they are committed, even in defiance, to panoramic visions of unending categories and separation. Laughter leads to a transformed, unified vision, "which begins in the reader's mind as soon as he has finished reading, a vision that passes through the legalized vision of ordeals and trials and comes out into a second life. In this second life the creator-creature, divine-human antithetical tension has ceased to exist."[16]

Nevertheless, as in the short stories, the agents evoking laughter and possible transformation are the tricksters. O'Connor intermingles tricksters with prophets more complexly in the novels than in the short stories in part because she prefigures her contemporary tales about Hazel and Tarwater in ancient ones in which prophets were mouthpieces for God. Haunted by the sins of their people, Hebrew prophets each experienced an all-consuming divine call to communicate the will of God. These prophets conveyed their messages in "lyrical fragments, prose narratives, in parable or direct speech, curt oracular style . . . or exhortation, diatribe, sermon, proverb, formal psalms, love songs, satire, funeral lament, etc."[17] In their efforts, however, to escape the weight of the sins passed to them from their forebears, Hazel and Tarwater resist the call to prophesy, thereby becoming vulnerable to self-deception and trickery. Although not as respectable as or accepted as widely as prophecy, trickery also figured in biblical literature. "Successful trickery is also a form of wisdom, requiring forethought, planning, cleverness; it too is an attempt to achieve temporary control of one's environment. But tricksters are more quixotic than wisdom heroes; like humor, trickster narratives rely on surprise to be effective, on doubt to encourage changed perception."[18] Through all these intertextual devices O'Connor moves us closer to that living mystery she intended to reveal—the mystery of the Incarnation.

All this preliminary discussion about apocalypse and laughter leads into the examination of the similarities, first in narrative shape, between O'Connor's novels and the Bible. Itself record and mythology of repeated collisions and revelation, the Bible assumes the shape of a divine comedy, which Dante and countless others have recognized.

O'Connor's knowledge of the Bible and of comedy is reflected in the shape of her narratives and implies her artistic ambition to threaten a radical transformation through laughter. Although other critics have noted a three-part structure in O'Connor's novels,[19] especially *The Violent Bear It Away*, few to my knowledge have coherently linked *Wise Blood* to *The Violent Bear It Away* through their narrative shape or investigated the similarities both novels together bear to the biblical narratives. Originating from within the novels themselves, such investigation reveals the source of her artistic power and the role narrative and the imagination play in the endless struggle for freedom.

Being roughly U-shaped, standard comedy begins with "apostasy . . . followed by a descent into disaster and bondage . . . followed by repentance [and] then by a rise through deliverance to a point more or less on the level from which the descent began."[20] These phases occur to many individuals and are repeated in a variety of circumstances in the Bible, either foreshadowing future or fulfilling past transitions through apostasy, disaster, and restoration. An inverted U (n), which Frye suggests as a diagram for tragedy, "rises to a point of 'peripety' or reversal of action and then plunges downward to 'catastrophe.'"[21]

It is important for this study of O'Connor that the Bible "does not . . . think of this movement as tragic but simply as ironic."[22] Because tragedy and comedy in the Bible seem held together within a kind of magnetic field, the center of which we will call God, the circle formed by an inverted U on top of a U is more appropriate for our analytic purposes than simply the U-shape of comedy. The movement of the trickster, as we have seen in preceding chapters, is a center-peripheral movement in which the tragic and the comic cohere within one whole circle. Sometimes originating in the center of his society (as did Jacob) or coming from the outside (as did Satan to God for permission to torment Job), the trickster moves—or is forced by a series of mistakes, disasters, adventures, or prideful acts—to the fringes, thereby producing tension or collision from the centrifugal pull of his outward stretch. From his position on the edges, his action transforms the hearer of his tale, "restoring" or turning both trickster and listener back to the center of the society or community but with a radically altered vision. Because of the penchant for comic and ironic repetition in both the trickster and the Bible, we may not be surprised to find O'Connor's two novels displaying a narrative shape similar to the one identified with biblical narratives.

Each of the novels begins with loss or apostasy. Both young men are on their way to the city, a geopolitical center. In *Wise Blood*, Hazel Motes, returning from the army, possesses only the skeleton of his former life: a chifforobe bequeathed to him and his mother's glasses. Abandoned himself, he tries to abandon the outlines of religious faith, which formerly anchored him to a place and people, and "to be converted to nothing instead of evil." The misery he feels as he rides anonymously on the train he describes simply as a longing for home having "nothing to do with Jesus."[23] Francis Tarwater's great-uncle Mason Tarwater dies at the breakfast table in the opening pages of *The Violent Bear It Away*, leaving Tarwater alone to bury the old man and to fulfill the religious mission to baptize Bishop, Rayber's idiot son. Denouncing his uncle's hunger for the bread of life, young Tarwater likewise heads to the city inwardly pursued by some presentiment that such hunger for the bread of life might be passed through the blood but outwardly rejecting the mission assigned to him by his now dead uncle.

The second parts of both novels episodically work out the rebellion of Hazel and Tarwater and the accompanying disasters that beset them. When Hazel arrives in the city of Taulkinham (a name which Richard Giannone explicates from its Greek parts to mean "home of the small cross"),[24] looking for a home, he goes first to the house of Leora Watts to gain sexual experience as initiation for his prophetic ministry—to preach the church without Christ. On the way he refutes the taxi driver who identifies him as a preacher. To the prostitute he announces that he has come for the usual business and that he is "no goddam preacher." Hazel completes his inverted annunciation (a denunciation) when he boasts to Enoch, in the hearing of Asa and Sabbath, "What do I need with Jesus? I got Leora Watts."[25] After such preparation, he bounces his prophecy against other charlatans like Asa Hawks, Hoover Shoats, and Solace Layfield, through whom he gradually discloses his own deception. He converts a rat-colored Essex into a salvific mobile home, repudiates Enoch Emery's offer of friendship and a new, mummified jesus, exposes Hawks's phony blindness, and becomes victim of the law when an officer pushes his Essex off a hill to destruction. Thus the novel turns toward its third part.

Young Tarwater similarly expresses his defiance in the city home of his deaf psychologist uncle who works to save the misguided young man through appeals to reason. Rejecting a too constricting home, Tarwater paces rebellious as a caged animal between the voices of the past that summon him to accept his call to prophesy and Rayber's aggressive educational reconstruction efforts. Tarwater seems pulled toward Bishop and yet resists him. Through his night flight from Rayber's home to the tabernacle, from the zoo fountain to the lake where Tarwater finally baptizes Bishop as he drowns him, precipitating the novel's shift toward the third part, Tarwater alternately fights and flees the mysterious hold on his life passed through generations.

The low point in each novel—Haze's murder of Solace Layfield and the loss of his car and Tarwater's dreadful ability to baptize Bishop—leaves each young man isolated from all community, however chimeric or corrupt. It also marks the upward turn toward some kind of enigmatic restoration or acceptance. The restoration in these two novels is ironic and therefore puzzling, for neither young man's consciousness seems altered in psychologically, or even religiously, conventional ways. Yet each rests in a new "home" or on transformed old ground as a changed being: Haze has returned "home" to Mrs. Flood's house in death; Tarwater has returned to Powderhead with a new vision burned into his eyes.

Through Haze's "coming home" into death, O'Connor repeats the annunciation or promise of the Word made flesh, in which God entered time and space to save the world through a redemptive death, and implies the eternal movement back and forth between annunciation and apocalypse. For Francis Tarwater, returned to the smoldering center of his universe at the conclusion of *The Violent Bear It Away,* there is no longer a tension between the temporal-material and the eternal-spiritual worlds, between the ancient voices and his own affirmation of vocation. All his ordeals, his confrontations with evil, and his resistance have been consumed by the hunger he resisted earlier and are purified by "the fire that had encircled Daniel, that had raised Elijah from the earth, that had spoken to Moses and would in an instant speak to him."[26]

The great invasion,[27] then, which O'Connor announces in *Wise Blood,* which she embodied in many of her short stories, and which she enigmatically reveals in the apocalyptic *The Violent Bear It Away,* is the collision of mystery and twentieth-century realities, of far and near things, of the centers and peripheries perpetually seeking to escape and replace the Center. This announcement is an antitype, a concept to be discussed in detail later, or fulfillment of the original invasion of the ineffable in human form into the material world.

The biblical allusions, made not only through the shape of the novels but also through the names O'Connor gives her characters and through the comparisons she implies between biblical figures or events and the people and events in her modern narratives, underscore the origins which the present narratives are apparently designed to repeat through parody. Such resonances carried in names and actions is often dense, as we observe in the case of Hazel Motes. Giannone suggests that his name, which in Hebrew means *God sees*, recalls King Hazael of 1 and 2 Kings, a king of Damascus who battled against God and God's people.[28] Hazel's denunciatory search for a new jesus reminds one of King Herod's similar preoccupation with finding a new baby. This young man, who is often referred to as Haze, who is obsessed with Asa Hawks's blindness, and who finally blinds himself, has also been given a surname drawn from the biblical parable about motes in the eyes (Matthew 7:3–5). Giannone makes additional associations of Hazel with St. Paul and St. Francis whose works "lead to their climax in the voluntary sacrifice of their individual lives."[29]

In Enoch Emery's name and his claims of wise blood we hear echoes of the biblical Enoch, father of Methusaleh, who walked faithfully with God for three hundred years (Genesis 18–24) and was rewarded by being taken up to God. Yet this Enoch who follows Hazel first as a spectator then becomes himself a spectacle (what Giannone, following O'Connor, calls a moronic spectacle)[30] by delivering a mummy to be Hazel's new jesus and by donning an ape suit, which symbolically confirms his bestiality. Leora Watts, the well-seasoned prostitute to whom Hazel makes his annunciation, who calls herself momma when she assures him, "Momma don't mind if you ain't a preacher,"[31] and who mockingly dons his preacher hat, inverts the biblical virgin in and through whom the flesh and spirit united. Although both Leora and Enoch seem moronically locked into fleshly existence without recognition of the spiritual, they are paradoxically agents who conduct Hazel on his resistant way toward spiritual redemption.

But O'Connor does not limit herself to embodying only biblical allusions. Haze's self-blinding recalls the Greek legends of Oedipus as well, and Enoch's impassioned attachment to the A-rab mummy suggests yet other cultural expressions of the human preoccupation with purpose and meaning. The frequent comparisons of people to animals in *Wise Blood*—the references to owls, crows, parrots, a hawk with a partially missing tail, and a thin one-eyed bear—bring to mind a primeval garden in which some hierarchical differentiation between animals and humans has not been firmly established.

The entire landscape of *Wise Blood,* from references to Jonah to signs painted on roadside boulders proclaiming "Jesus saves" and "Jesus Died for YOU," imitates a biblical landscape reminiscent in tone of John the Baptist's pronouncements about the one whose coming was announced. The contrary drives of Hazel and Enoch—one compelled by the spirit even in defiance, the other by primordial matter— are mirrored in the landscape. The city is filled with all manner of distorted images of human beings associated with animals and machines. Above the forbiddingly dark view of the city arches "the black sky . . . underpinned with long silver streaks that looked like scaffolding and depth on depth behind it were thousands of stars that all seemed to be moving very slowly as if they were about some vast construction work that involved the whole order of the universe and would take all time to complete." O'Connor emphasizes the separation of earth and sky, matter and spirit, for the people of Taulkinham with the narrator's report that "No one was paying any attention to the sky."[32]

O'Connor encourages reading the novel as a trope of biblical texts through such prefigurements of characters and events and through images of nature that direct our attention to ancient stories similarly filled with contradictions, ambivalence, and strange natural phenomena. For example, in the middle of the novel O'Connor again juxtaposes earth and sky, this time through a large white cloud that arches over Hazel's car trouble in the country and finally turns into a bird "disappearing in the opposite direction."[33] For Giannone, the theophany of chapter 7 mirrors Exodus 34:30: "Splendor in the exact center of *Wise Blood* limns the vast perspective of sacred history from which the entire action is to be viewed . . . [and] the cloud-bird manifests the total perfection in which creation participates and against which Hazel wages war. The cloud sails in one direction: the way of holiness and true blamelessness. Hazel races in another direction: the way of denial and increasing wrath. Sacred history assimilates all ways."[34]

In *The Violent Bear It Away,* similar references to Jonah, Ezekiel, Elijah-Elisha, and Daniel as well as to metaphors like bread, fish, blood, water, and seeds alert one to the religious preoccupations of the author. Francis Marion Tarwater's given name means the "old swamp fox" of the Revolutionary War. Tarwater was also a discredited folk cure-all.[35] Just as the Hebrew Bible richly combines a variety of literary forms and figures from oral history and folklore, so O'Connor mixes biblical allusions with, in this case, American folklore signaling, however puzzlingly, her artistic-religious process of amendment.

The central point structurally and the pivotal moment in *The Violent Bear It Away* occur in chapter 6 in the park scene and illustrate further O'Connor's amendment process. Through the stone lion O'Connor links her novel with Hebrew and Christian texts, for "the sculpted lion stands as a monument to God's bold presence and in that service marks a vantage from which the reader can see all three sojourners through the park in relation to their ultimate need. It points toward the source of love that could strengthen Rayber to care for Bishop and that also watches over the defenseless idiot child under all conditions. For Tarwater, who is ordained by Mason to witness for God in a daring way, the stone lion signals the divine readiness to help him through the trials of prophecy."[36] All varieties of revelation that lead to and follow Rayber, Bishop, and Tarwater through the park on the way to the natural history museum and toward baptism are focused under the gaze of this stone lion, which recalls two biblical passages, one in Revelation 5:5 and the other in Daniel 6:16–23.

Giannone explicates the relation of these two passages to O'Connor's story by suggesting that the lion recalls the condition of Daniel cast into the lions' den for refusing to worship a Babylonian king as a god. Daniel maintains his faith in Yahweh, and his faith is rewarded by an angel who shuts the lions' mouths. The lion represents power acquired "both by belligerence and submission," argues Giannone, because

> it forces change according to the needs of faith. At one time the violent lion bears witness to the kingdom. Matthew (11:12) reminds us of such a time in the epigraph to *The Violent Bear It Away*. After John the Baptist, of course, meekness carries the power of faith. The new dispensation of the cross makes the Messiah the Lion of the tribe of Judah. "'Weep not,'" consoles one of the elders, "'lo, the Lion of the tribe of Judah, the Root of David, has conquered, so that he can open the scroll and its seven seals'" (Revelation 5:5). The seer of Revelation expects the lion to disclose the fixed purposes of God that are sealed in the scroll, but the creature that appears to the seer is "a Lamb standing, as though it had been slain" (Revelation 5:6). O'Connor's revelation in the park draws upon both images. There is the lion and there is Bishop who will be slain.[37]

Just as in *Wise Blood*, the resonances of other texts suggested through characters and analogous or inverted situations are also mirrored in the natural landscape of clouds, sun, and water in *The Violent Bear It Away*. In chapter 8 as Tarwater, Rayber, and Bishop move deeper into the park, O'Connor alerts us to Tarwater's sensitivity to mystery through the movement of the sun "tacking from cloud to cloud" until it comes to rest above the fountain sending a "blinding brightness . . . on the lion's tangled marble head and . . . the stream of water rushing from his mouth. Then the light, falling more gently, rested like a hand on the child's white head."[38] Just before Bishop sets his foot over the edge into the pool, Rayber snatches him away. But the power of this moment has not been lost on Tarwater, who has been moving forward toward the pool himself as if drawn by a magnetic force to Bishop. Looking into the water he sees a face who warns him as it confirms the path that lies ahead, "Well, that's your sign . . . the sun coming out from under a cloud and falling on the head of a dimwit. Something that could happen fifty times a day without no one being the wiser. And it took that schoolteacher to save you and just in time. Left to yourself you would already have done it and been lost forever. . . . you have to quit confusing a madness with a mission. You can't spend your life fooling yourself this way. You have to take hold and put temptation behind you. If you baptize once, you'll be doing it the rest of your life."[39]

The themes of O'Connor's novels insinuate themselves from these allusions of mixed origins. Although the themes are focused in the light of each novel, they also progress from the first to the second work. The overlaying of allusions from Hebrew, Greek, Christian, and American folklore sources contribute to the ironic treatment which sacred themes (promise, redemption, and resurrection) seem subject to in these two novels. Into *Wise Blood* O'Connor weaves the exodus, salvation, and death themes. *The Violent Bear It Away*, seeming loosely to pick up where *Wise Blood* ends, opens with death and fire, this time accompanies exodus with pursuit, and concludes with an apocalyptic resurrection out of ashes that leads to vocation foretold in *Wise Blood*. Although these themes occur in texts of the Jewish and Christian religious traditions, O'Connor juxtaposes them with similar themes from other cultural traditions and inverts them for a world she believed no longer familiar with living mystery.

These traditional religious themes achieve their vitality within the narratives through the metaphors to which they give rise or by which they are carried. Both novels depict the ordeals of a *malgré lui*. Although O'Connor directed her readers to think of Hazel Motes as one driven by something over which he apparently has no control, Francis Tarwater is also similarly driven. Both young men are inwardly pursued by shadows or voices, and both outwardly pursue something inexplicable as well. O'Connor describes their pursuits with inverted quest or exodus metaphors.

From the beginning of *Wise Blood,* Hazel is on a journey implying flight as much as search. First he goes to the city of Taulkinham, then through the city streets searching for Asa Hawks, then from theater to theater street-preaching, and finally, despite his intention to travel to another geopolitical center, to death. Because Haze's story is picked up when he is already in transit and clearly has neither people nor place to call home, one thinks of his journey principally as his soul's sojourn in a Dantean purgatory for his own and his father's sins of looking at a naked woman in a coffin. However, in Haze's defiant denunciation of Christ, his journey bears inverted outlines of a biblical wilderness experience as well. Whereas Abraham and Moses left their land and kinsmen to travel into unknown land undergirded by God's promise of a new land and freedom, Hazel travels alone proclaiming faith in nothing and enslaved to his denial. Robert Fitzgerald interprets Hazel's bondage to nothing as O'Connor's parody of the existentialist point of view. "We can all hear our own disbelief in Hazel Motes's" denial of the Fall and Judgment and in his assertion, "Nothing matters but Jesus was a liar."[40] What Fitzgerald does not acknowledge is that Haze's position is as old as Moses, who also called God a liar.[41] Thus, what appears to be rejection through an inversion of an ancient faithful sojourn in the wilderness is actually a repetition, a modern incarnation of the human longing for and ambivalence toward freedom.

Francis Tarwater's journey from his wilderness home at Powderhead to the city seems even more inwardly and mysteriously motivated than Hazel Motes's. From the time he sets off, almost unconsciously, for the city with his dead great-uncle's warnings about Rayber echoing in his memory, through his flights of attempted escape down city streets, until his hitched return ride over the highways and his violation in the woods, the lines between consciousness and unconsciousness are often blurred. What is inside and what is outside Tarwater's head complicate the journey, making it ambiguous for him and readers alike. O'Connor seems to have intended the journey to be understood both as outward and inward, however, for she uses road images to describe the stories that old Mason repeatedly forced his nephew to travel: "The story always had to be taken to completion. It was like a road that the boy had traveled on so often that half the time he didn't look where they were going."[42] Tarwater's journey coming full circle, beginning and ending in Powderhead, dramatizes his inability to escape his call; that he listens to stories that likewise seem to come full circle again and again suggests the necessity for human beings to "repeat" the quest and tales that free them from chaos, chance, and nothingness.

Related metaphors—home and family—frame both novels and suggest the purposes of each journey or quest. Kathleen Feeley first noted the recurring references to home in *Wise Blood*,[43] a metaphor May extensively examines in his own work. When the novel opens on the train, Mrs. Wally Bee Hitchcock comments to Hazel, "I guess you're going home."[44] At the end of the novel Mrs. Flood observes to her tenant, whom she does not yet recognize as dead, "Well, Mr. Motes, I see you've come home!"[45] May points out "three additional early references to home, one in each of the three chapters following the first, that keep the novel's interpretive language in plain view. Each is a parody of the ultimate affirmation that the novel makes about home."[46] Mrs. Leora Watts tells Haze to "Make yourself at home." The peeler salesman asks, "Whyn't you take one of these home to yer wife?" And Haze confides to the car salesman and his son, "I wanted this car mostly to be a house for me. I ain't got any place to be."[47] Through Haze's loss of home, his search for replacements, and his ironic coming home into the dark of death, O'Connor poses a question about human origins. To whom do human beings belong and in what ground are their roots?

The Violent Bear It Away is framed by distorted familial relationships. At the beginning Mason and Francis live as father and son, indeed joined out of necessity through the disasters that beset young Tarwater's mother and father. At the end, Tarwater's revelation and acceptance of his vocation come through a perverted "familial" relationship, the homosexual's violation of him. Reinforcing these two relationships are the additional family ties between Rayber and Tarwater and between Tarwater and Bishop. O'Connor further underscores the family connections through physical likenesses. As Tarwater stood on his doorstep the first night, Rayber realized "that his nephew looked enough like him to be his son."[48] The voices of old Mason—living both in Rayber's and Tarwater's unconscious—as well as the more ambiguous voices of Tarwater himself, of the copper flue salesman

Meeks, and of the truck driver all force the questions: Who is the true
father (authority)? Whom will I obey? Even the charge to baptize
becomes a familial one not simply directed by Mason; through silver
eyes it metaphorically links one generation with another, as father to
son, and violently repeats an ancient religious rite that transformed an
Old Covenant of law into a New Covenant of sacrifice and mercy. "At
the moment of his death, the old man's 'silver protruding eyes . . .
looked like two fish straining to get out of a net of red threads.' And
Bishop, whose name appropriately means 'overseer,' who 'had pale
silver eyes like the old man's except that they were clear and empty,
looked like the old man grown backwards to the lowest form of innocence.'"[49]

Blood—with its magical and taboo connotations of so-called primitive religions and its redemptive Christian associations—is another
dominant metaphor in both novels that reinforces the family ties in
The Violent Bear It Away, extending them to include humankind; its
associations with wisdom in *Wise Blood* provoke questions about how
community is established and violated; and it is also a vehicle for being
called or having a vocation with which both Hazel Motes and Francis
Tarwater are rebelliously obsessed. It is Enoch Emery in *Wise Blood*
who announces that he possesses his father's "wise blood" and offers
himself as friend and officiant to Haze as Haze makes his way in the
city-wilderness proclaiming his church without Christ and Jesus as "a
trick on niggers."

In offering friendship to Haze, Enoch reminds one of the wise
woman in Proverbs 9 who extends community to passersby by sharing
bread and wine with them. Ironically, however, Enoch's ultimate token
of community is a "stolen" jesus, which connects him with the foolish
woman in the same biblical text who says to passersby that "stolen
water is sweet, and bread eaten in secret is pleasant."[50] Using noisy
language that reveals her anxiety, prejudice, and allows her rationalizations, the foolish woman separates herself from community. By
confusing what is wise and what is foolish in *Wise Blood*, O'Connor
explores a more fundamental truth about community, language, and
transformation which her novels address. Things stolen or possessed
in secret (used only by oneself alone) violate community. Words, like
bread and *wine* or *truth*, are to be shared as vehicles of transformation
and community. The wisdom of Enoch's blood, attracting him to relics
of the past like the mummy and Gonga, pulls him backward to earlier
forms of civilization and stages of evolution and threatens to isolate

him; yet simultaneously and paradoxically these relics help Hazel learn that sin and guilt are communal, not purely individual, matters. Haze, pulling forward through denial of any communal truth, is finally ambiguously rescued by his "wise blood" that drives him to seek God even while fleeing him.

O'Connor develops this pursuit theme more fully in *The Violent Bear It Away* through blood that also connects but in a forward and redemptive more than backward and talismanic manner. The words that haunt Rayber and Tarwater are like "seeds in the blood." In Rayber these seeds produced an irrational love that came "rushing from some inexplicable part of himself"[51] and which he associates with a loss of control. The sudden, overpowering urge to love his child "was only a touch of the curse that lay in his blood. . . . He always felt it with a rush of longing to have the old man's eyes . . . turned on him once again. The longing was like an undertow in his blood dragging him backwards to what he knew to be madness. The affliction was in the family. It lay hidden in the line of blood that touched them, flowing from some ancient source, some desert prophet or polesitter, until, its power unabated, it appeared in the old man and him and, he surmised, in the boy."[52] Through blood O'Connor underscores the inescapability of the human quest—however erratic or misguided—for freedom in vocation.

In both novels, the blood of one or more characters propels him to the city park where there is a zoo in which a forewarning of dramatic collision occurs. Enoch ritualistically takes Haze past the bear cages, the birds, the monkeys, and the hoot owl on the way to the museum in which the mummy is lodged. For Enoch, the trip around the outer edges of the zoo to its center is fraught with mystery he cannot articulate and which Haze defies through words. Enoch unconsciously prepares for something his blood tells him will be special; he starts saving his money, cleaning his room, and even painting gilt gold the inside of the tabernacle-like cabinet, which he considers the most important item in the room. When he hears Haze preaching about a new jesus, Enoch recognizes what has been rising in his blood, "Listenhere, I got him! I mean I can get him! You know! Him! Him I shown you to. You seen him yourself!"[53] This halting annunciation once again inverts the annunciation of Christ made by the angel. It is ironically fulfilled when Sabbath Lily stands with the shriveled mummy in her arms and, as mother of this grotesque Holy Family, says to Hazel, "Call me Momma now. . . . Ask your daddy yonder where he was running off to—sick as he is?"[54] Through a stuffed mummy O'Connor ironically repeats the coming of Christ in uncomely form and embodies the collisional power of that event in the life of Haze whose flight now is turned toward confrontation and murder of a false prophet, who reflects Hazel himself, toward penance, and eventually toward an ambiguous self-sacrifice.

On the trip to the natural history museum in *The Violent Bear It Away,* a similar coalescence of blood-forces occurs and foreshadows the subsequent collision between the mysterious pursuant lodged in the center of Tarwater's psyche and the edges represented by Rayber's scientific rationalism. Rayber's decision to acquaint his nephew with his ancestor the fish—to whom O'Connor has connected him through the eyes of old Mason—in the natural history museum recalls Enoch's leading Haze to the mummy in *Wise Blood.* To get to the museum they must cross the city park in the center of which lies a small zoo. And at the center of the zoo is a fountain and pool that immediately capture Bishop's interest.

As we have already noted, when Bishop wanders into the water, young Tarwater is drawn so irresistibly toward him that he has to exert equal counteractive pressure to restrain himself from going in after him. Witnessing the magnetic attraction of Tarwater for Bishop, Rayber sees that "the skin on the boy's [Tarwater's] face appeared to stretch tighter and tighter. Rayber had the sense that he was moving blindly, that where Bishop was he saw only a spot of light. He felt that something was being enacted before him and that if he could understand it, he would have the key to the boy's future."[55] Although Tarwater's intention toward Bishop is unclear in chapter 6, Rayber realizes that Tarwater is moving to baptize Bishop and rushes to rescue him from the pool. Later, "torn between Mason's order to baptize Bishop and the Devil's behest to kill him,"[56] Tarwater does baptize Bishop as he drowns him. Rayber's own efforts to drown his son and his Satan-like resistance to Mason's faith make possible the fusion of baptism and murder. This puzzling fusion of baptism with murder amends as it distorts the analogical relation between the biblical story about Daniel's preservation from the lion and Tarwater's struggle with the stone lion that becomes an anagogical anchor at the center of *The Violent Bear It Away.*

O'Connor depicts the effects of Tarwater's act of baptizing as a struggle between life and death; "as he struggled to extricate himself from a monstrous enclosing darkness . . . he grappled with the air as if he had been flung like a fish on the shores of the dead without lungs to breathe there."[57] His baptism of Bishop moves him toward another baptism, this time by fire, that will further weaken the barriers between the past and the present, the sacred and the profane, good and evil. After the annunciation of *Wise Blood*, O'Connor fashions an apocalypse in *The Violent Bear It Away* that violently undermines modern theological, psychological, and sociological categories by obfuscating boundaries between the spiritual and the material, the conscious and the unconscious, the call of God and the voice of the devil, and between generations.

In both novels, O'Connor signals the parabolic and repetitive quality of these works through familiar metaphors of eyes (vision) and ears (hearing) that link them with the Christian Bible. She gives contemporary form to Christ's perplexing warning to his disciples about the leaven in the Pharisees, as they lamented having no bread: "'Take heed, beware of the leaven of the Pharisees and the leaven of Herod.' And they discussed it with one another saying, 'We have no bread.' And being aware of it Jesus said to them, 'Why do you discuss the fact that you have no bread? Do you not yet perceive or understand? Are your hearts hardened? Having eyes do you see, and having ears do you not hear?'"[58]

Notes in the Oxford Bible suggest that leaven here probably refers to settled convictions that affect all of life as leaven raises dough. Asa Hawks, Enoch Emery, and Hazel Motes all demonstrate in different ways that they cannot *see* God with the sense of sight alone. In fact, Hazel's final act implies that blindness may yield more "sight" than seeing. Relying on vision metaphors that support observation and speculation, *Wise Blood* prepares for *The Violent Bear It Away* in which the characters are pulled closer to confrontation with the terrifying holy through the metaphor of hearing. Between her first and second novels, O'Connor's central characters turn from trying to see through a glass darkly as spectators to being obsessed with voices that transform them into spectacles forced to *listen* inwardly for God often in silence. Through these carefully crafted metaphors O'Connor stirs up our settled convictions about the nature of reality, God, reason, and madness.

When we look compositely at the metaphors through which O'Connor discloses the themes of these two novels, we note again how they contribute to structures that vibrate with tension between centers and peripheries. At the center of *Wise Blood* stands Christ, embodied here in Haze's imagination as "a trick on niggers," a non-Christ. Hazel claims his church without Christ will give freedom, a longing of all people throughout history. But, as O'Connor pointed out in the author's note to the second edition of *Wise Blood,* "freedom cannot be conceived simply . . . free will does not mean one will, but many wills conflicting in one man."[59]

One way human beings deal with this conflict of wills, or their ambivalence toward freedom, is to create anxiety structures on the peripheries to be a temporary stay against centrifugal disintegration.[60] O'Connor reflects twentieth-century human beings' ambivalence toward freedom on the peripheries of *Wise Blood.* In prostitute houses like Leora Watts's, in charlatanism of an Asa Hawks or religious entrepreneurship of a Hoover Shoats, in idolaters like Enoch Emery, and in the law, people seek refuge from freedom. On these fringes, Hazel Motes, a *malgré lui,* confronts and is transfigured by a dark, mysterious action—perhaps the God assumed dead in the twentieth century.

In *The Violent Bear It Away,* less episodic as a work, O'Connor centers the novel around the call of God planted as seeds in Mason Tarwater's nephews. Rayber, who has received but rejects the seed, pulls centrifugally toward modern peripheries, which O'Connor characterizes as his commitment to sociological rationalism. Young Tarwater also resists the seeds in the blood and flees to the periphery where he confronts an idiot child, voices of his unconscious, the copper flue salesman, the truck driver, and a homosexual assault. O'Connor captures the tension of this centrifugal-centripetal motion in a description of one of Rayber's dreams: "[Rayber] had waked up after a wild dream in which he chased Tarwater through an interminable alley that twisted suddenly back on itself and reversed the roles of pursuer and pursued."[61]

Together *Wise Blood* and *The Violent Bear It Away* announce and unveil the continuing invasion of the divine (mystery) into human affairs (reality) through metaphors about faith and apostasy transplanted and sometimes inverted from ancient texts into the twentieth-century soil of rational skepticism. The revolutionary aspect of the Christian religion is that God, the great mystery, the Word, made "himself" known in the flesh and continues to do so through words and through flesh, even of those who resist and pull toward the peripheries to establish alternative "centers" of influence and authority, if not truth. The ambiguity with which these themes are presented comes through the linguistic devices the author used to make mystery real to skeptical audiences.

Flannery O'Connor effectively used three linguistic devices, which also influence the narrative structures, to render living mystery palpable to those she believed blinded by distorted visions and deafened by their commitment to partial truth and to modern jargons that could not forge communal connections, let alone ones with the invisible. Though these three devices—the flashback, the tale-within-the-tale, and her juxtaposition of metaphoric and metonymic or descriptive language—do not exhaust her technical resources,[62] they are the principal devices through which she attempts to connect her religious preoccupations and her artistic ambitions. By joining these devices with others, like her shifting narrative voice, previously examined, she brought the mythic to bear on the apparently material-mechanical. Although we will examine examples of these devices independently, they obviously operate together, contributing to the density of O'Connor's fiction. Differing from the paucity with which one associates biblical narratives,[63] this density is a modern, if uneven and sometimes exaggerated, manifestation of that earlier impulse to make mystery transparent. As in the preceding analysis of the short fiction, we understand how these devices operate best by examining passages in which they function.

The interplay of these three linguistic devices is more accessible in *Wise Blood* than in *The Violent Bear It Away*. This accessibility occurs because even though O'Connor externalizes the inward obsessions of the characters more in *The Violent Bear It Away*, she obscures the boundaries between inward and outward, past and present, and differing perceptions in the unifying interest, I will argue subsequently, of telescoping the whole Christian creation-death-resurrection myth into one apocalyptic novel. Consequently, by examining first O'Connor's use of these devices in *Wise Blood*, we may better analyze their more complex operation in *The Violent Bear It Away*.

The flashback as a repetitive motion of the mind turns present attention to past events, thereby bringing them anew into the present. Such turning, previously associated in this study with the trickster's actions, is also an essential element in tale telling. Thus, in *Wise Blood* and in *The Violent Bear It Away*, tales within the larger narratives are usually precipitated by the flashback.

The long flashback in the opening chapter of *Wise Blood* begins when Hazel, settled on his berth in the train, falls into a half-sleep. The narrator then reports the movement of Haze's semiconscious thoughts. The narrowness, darkness, and compactness of the berth remind Haze of a coffin. From this single image, Haze recalls his grandfather's coffin and his two younger brothers' coffins; finally, in full sleep, he dreams that he is at his father's burying. During the sleep and half-waking states, the narrator moves the reader back and forth among generations—Haze's, his grandfather's, and his father's. Around the bizarre and often humorous outlines of dreaming and the jolting of the train, which half awakens Haze, the narrator weaves important details: there are no more Moteses in Eastrod; Haze's grandfather was a circuit preacher who traveled the countryside in a Ford, often preaching from its nose; Haze believes that Jesus is soul hungry; Haze went into the army sporadically reading the Bible with the aid of his mother's glasses, but he came out converted to nothing; Haze's activities of the past two days since his release from the army led him back to the remaining skeleton of his home place. The flashback section ends with another dream of a burial—his mother's when he was sixteen. He wakes from the dream startled by the feeling that the coffin lid is closing on him.

Two things characterize the flashback in O'Connor's novels. The first is that an omniscient narrator reports what is stirring in the memory of a character. O'Connor's narrator displays the workings of the human mind, how it moves often randomly over events or leaps large spaces and time periods. Through an omniscient narrator, who utilizes the capacity not so much to see everything at once as to enter serially the minds of individual characters, the flashback gives the reader simultaneously the sense of being drawn in closer to the mind or soul of a particular character *and* of being kept at a distance by the narrator's reportorial style. This tension reflects the tension the mind itself exhibits. One notes, for example, how Haze's reverie begins with his grandfather's coffin, skips a generation forward to his brothers' deaths, then turns back only one generation to his father's burying, and ends with a profound identification of himself with his mother's death. This backward-forward motion of the flashback is evident in a larger way in the novel as a whole. After finishing the novel, the reader realizes that the first flashback of *Wise Blood* foreshadows (again the backward-forward movement) Haze's future and inverted circuit ministry.

The second distinguishing characteristic is that the flashback often gives rise to or fills out a smaller tale within the large narrative. In the flashback under discussion here, for example, Haze's memory and dreams are the catalysts by which the narrator fills in the tale of Hazel Motes's early life and the seeds of his obsession. In another flashback, which O'Connor places in the midst of Haze's second visit to Mrs. Watts, we can see yet more clearly the link between a flashback and a tale-within-the-tale. As Haze flips off the electric light to undress, the narrator turns the reader backward to an earlier sexual experience. Not precipitated by the movement of Haze's mind, this insertion stands like an aside of the narrator. The tale recalls Haze's experience watching a squirming naked woman in a coffin at the carnival in Melsy. After ten-year-old Haze discovered his father in the crowd of excited witnesses, Haze crept out of the tent and home to his mother. As self-inflicted punishment for his sin, the next day he walked in the woods with small stones and rocks inside his Sunday shoes. Once again this tale, rooted in a past experience, also forces the story forward by foreshadowing Haze's final acts of penance.

Other tales-within-the-tale of *Wise Blood* have no direct connection with Haze's past life and are therefore not actual flashbacks. For example, the description of the plot of the movie *Lonnie Comes Home* prepares the reader for Enoch's rising attraction for the gorilla and for his eventual exchange of clothes, ironically symbolizing a change of being. The movie title also ironically underscores Haze's search for a home. In fact, all the episodes about Enoch, which interrupt and humorously complicate the simple story line of Haze's revolt against Christ, form a coherent, if reversed, tale-within-the-tale. As Haze pulls farther away from Christ, Enoch attempts to pull him backward toward some aboriginal security. The tales about Asa Hawks included in the early part of the novel also ironically forecast what lies ahead for Haze and join Haze's past and his present together.

O'Connor's use of the flashback and the tale-within-the-tale structurally signals what the themes also reveal: she wanted to show the continuing, mysterious operations of God's grace. Through these two devices, which are integrally linked to the present action of the story, she demonstrates her ability to bring the past and present together in one person's life, to let the actions of one character mirror or distort another's, or to connect seemingly unrelated episodes in two characters' lives.

Yet, in order to bring two experiences or realities together, O'Connor needed still another device, one that may disconcert modern literary, psychological, and sociological sensibilities. To bring the ancient biblical myth to bear on the lives of twentieth-century readers she juxtaposed metaphoric with descriptive language. Thus, in the following narrative passage, readers, expecting the transparency of speech that is descriptively faithful to an objective natural reality outside themselves as well as the character, falter. "Later [Hazel] saw Jesus move from tree to tree in the back of his mind, a wild ragged figure motioning him to turn around and come off into the dark where he was not sure of his footing, where he might be walking on the water and not know it and then suddenly know it and drown."[64] This passage reveals not simply the power of Haze's imagination, what psychologically astute twentieth-century readers might describe more or less scientifically as his hallucinatory tendencies and his obsessive character, but implies in the last part a consequence of separating subject and object. When Haze doesn't *know* he is walking on water (i.e., separates himself from the water), he thinks he will stay afloat; when he knows it, he will sink and drown. Although this is a negative, superstitious expression, the passage does treat the subject of faith or calling metaphorically. By placing Jesus inside Haze's mind and empowering, or threatening, him to walk on the water, O'Connor tries to express the inescapable connection between the seen and the unseen.

As noted earlier, she uses the sky metaphorically to reinforce this inextricable link between what seems like the objective world to her modern audience and the inner, subjective states of her characters. In chapter three, O'Connor joins Haze's quest in Taulkinham with a radical reconstruction of the universe through the natural phenomena of sky and shadows. "The black sky was underpinned with long silver streaks that looked like scaffolding and depth on depth behind it were thousands of stars that all seemed to be moving very slowly as if they were about some vast construction work that involved the whole order of the universe and would take all time to complete. No one was paying any attention to the sky. . . . Haze's shadow was now behind him and now before him and now and then broken up by the people's shadows, but when it was by itself, stretching behind him, it was a thin nervous shadow walking backwards."[65] What goes on mysteriously and continuously all around the people of Taulkinham and of the universe, no one pays any attention to. Through this metaphor, however, O'Connor forces that which human beings generally regard as outside themselves—the natural universe—into relationship with the subjective or inner realities of human life.

Using the vehicles of scaffolding and the construction project, O'Connor depicts the sky—the eternal universe—as mirror of the endless, human construction project occurring within Haze. As one unaware of the connections between his own inner construction project and the universe's and as one attempting to separate from the mysterious, Haze wanders as a shadow, sometimes broken by other people's shadows. The direction of the shadow's movement, however, is backward, anticipating the final, centripetal motion of the narrative.

O'Connor's association of biblical characters or biblical stories with her modern characters is another way in which she juxtaposes one kind of language or perception with another. This device is virtually lost to those untuned to biblical overtones. For example, O'Connor's subtle line put in the mouth of a bystander when she sees Hazel and Solace Layfield working the same territory, "I never seen no twins that hunted each other down,"[66] not only portends Haze's eventual murder of the false prophet but also suggests a variation on the biblical story of Cain and Abel. Enoch's name and Hazel's last name have already been discussed and also serve linguistically to bring the old myth into collision with the modern human struggle.

O'Connor fulfills her intentions to show how former, mythic realities continue to exist in the present and, at the same time, to demonstrate the mental resistance in modern sojourners like Hazel Motes to the dynamic power of language that connects subject and object more closely through the language play of the text. After Asa charges Haze with fornication and blasphemy, Haze responds, "They ain't nothing but words. If I was in sin I was in it before I ever committed any. . . . I don't believe in sin."[67] Displaying an attitude toward language characteristic of the descriptive period, Hazel concludes that words and actions have separate domains; words have no power over or imaginative connection with the objective world of outward actions. Yet, in the same speech, Haze acknowledges the possibility that, though he doesn't believe in sin, he may have been in it before he ever committed any. Within three sentences, O'Connor dramatically expresses modern ambivalence toward realities that may supersede sense experience.

Haze wants to deny all connections between the present and the past and between himself and others; he wants to reject the possibility that there is any unifying truth and that words have any power to unfold the truth. Ironically, he expresses his defiance through innuendo as much as direct rejection; his speech is laden with metaphoric suggestions about a church, truth, lies, a promised land, or perhaps an afterlife: "I preach there are all kinds of truth, your truth and somebody else's, but behind all of them, there's only one truth and that is that there's no truth. No truth behind all truths is what I and this church preach! Where you come from is gone, where you thought you were going to never was there, and where you are is no good unless you can get away from it. Where is there a place for you to be? No place."[68] O'Connor underscores Haze's defiance expressed in rhetoric of distortion and obfuscation through gestures and notions that imply the signifying of the trickster. The quickness of his car that "had a tendency to develop a tic by nightfall. It would go forward about six inches and then back about four"[69] doesn't merely describe Hazel's car. Its forward and backward movement also reflects O'Connor's subtle juxtaposition of metaphoric and descriptive language that fills *Wise Blood*, and really all her fiction, with echoes that haunt the blood and sinews of her readers.

O'Connor brings this overlapping of language tendencies—that is, her ability to speak metaphorically in a highly descriptive age—to a peak of subtlety in *The Violent Bear It Away*. Despite Shloss's criticism that "myth, which deals with the miraculous, and realism, which deals with the probable, are extremes of a progression of literary form, and fiction that seeks to encompass them both *will* inevitably achieve an uneasy focus,"[70] O'Connor demonstrates what it means to have words opening as silent seeds in the blood. By the end of *The Violent Bear It Away*, one realizes that for O'Connor "the word is both structure and meaning."[71]

The very function of narrative—and the smallest unit of narrative, the word—is to build an order out of disorder, or sometimes to disturb a distorted order, so that a path into the unknown or a connection between people, generations, realism, or extremes might be established. The essential structure of *The Violent Bear It Away* is determined by words dropped as seeds in the blood from one generation to another.

In her second novel, O'Connor departs somewhat from the episodic treatment that flashbacks and tales-within-the-tale produced in *Wise Blood*. Instead, her use of metaphoric language increases; the voices within Tarwater that converse and argue with him, the psychological ratiocinations of Rayber, and the haunting memory of old Mason Tarwater's prophecy give a compressed and sometimes confused immediacy to the flashback. O'Connor's most remarkable, if imperfect, achievement in *The Violent Bear It Away* is that she succeeds in overlaying two complete histories: "The history of the world, beginning with Adam, and the history of the schoolteacher, beginning with his [Rayber's] mother, old Tarwater's one and only sister who had run away from Powderhead when she was eighteen years old and had

become—the old man said he would mince no words, even with a
child—a whore, until she found a man by the name of Rayber who
was willing to marry one."[72] The result is a modern incarnation or
repetition, albeit ironically inverted, of the Christian myth.

The passages containing references to hunger and the images of
over-leavened bread and of seeds in the blood illustrate O'Connor's
use of metaphoric language at the most inward and personal level of
the novel. Although not until late in the novel does O'Connor actually
use the metaphor of the seed, one recognizes its implicit presence in
Mason's conviction that "Jesus is the bread of life,"[73] who produces
hunger in the blood. Old Mason had apparently received an unduly
large portion of such hunger, for in characteristic humor, the narrator
describes him—trying out his coffin before his death—as "over-
leavened bread."[74] Young Tarwater's early fear, and eventual experience, is that such hunger may be passed through the blood from one
generation to another. Both Rayber and young Tarwater flee this im-
pending hunger for the bread of life, the Word made flesh, in different ways; yet both charge each other with its presence. Coming to
the end of his patience for Tarwater's reconstruction-salvation, Rayber
says, "The old man still has you in his grip. Don't think he hasn't." To
which Tarwater retorts, "It's you the seed fell in. . . . It ain't a thing
you can do about it. It fell on bad ground but it fell in deep. With
me . . . it fell on rock and the wind carried it away."[75]

Rayber's and Tarwater's responses to the seed that has been deposited in their blood through the words of their one-notioned
uncle influences the structure of the novel, here dependent on flashbacks and tales-within-tales, which embody voices or psychological
states more often than describe external events. The reader encounters young Tarwater's response first because the scene opens in
Powderhead on the day of old Mason's death. First Tarwater observes
a tremor like a quake pulse through Mason as he died; then he "felt
the tremor transfer itself and run lightly over him,"[76] like Elisha
receiving the mantle from Elijah. As he contemplates what he needs to
do, Tarwater receives the first of many instructions from a mysterious
stranger's voice. This voice and other manifestations of it throughout
the novel give counsel to Tarwater, rebuke him, challenge him, link him
with others who have heard voices, and finally—after the highly ambiguous and unsettling incarnation of the voice in the homosexual—
befriend him, ushering him to a promised land.

The voice constantly provides an enigmatic inner dimension to the narrative. Sometimes its admonitions or questions stimulate a flashback; sometimes they interrupt one of Tarwater's reveries or elaborate a short tale within the long narrative. For instance, as young Tarwater digs the grave for his uncle's body, he debates with the voice about Rayber's actions; this precipitates a flashback to the occasion of Tarwater's first trip to the city with his old uncle. As in *Wise Blood*, this flashback is also directly linked to the present action, for it outlines the conflicts between Rayber and Mason and foreshadows Tarwater's imminent trip, which will pick up those long-standing differences.

Rayber is not prone to hearing voices, perhaps because, as O'Connor amusingly implies, his head depends on batteries for hearing and on psychological theories for understanding. However, these modern dependencies also contribute to the contracted structure by prompting flashbacks or smaller tales from another angle within the narrative. Sometimes Rayber's modern perceptions or explanations call forth remembered events that, when brought into mental focus, not only compress this man's present with his past, but also produce extreme agitation in him. For example, when Rayber chases the fleeing Tarwater through the night streets and finds himself listening to the child evangelist Lucette Carmody through an open window, he rationalizes his furor as concern about exploited children. Then the narrator tells the reader, "It was the thought of a child's mind warped, of a child led away from reality that always enraged him, bringing back to him his own childhood's seduction."[77]

What follows then in the narrative is an extended tale about Rayber's kidnapping told from Rayber's point of view. As an educated adult, he is still also his uncle's child. Despite all his personal efforts to extricate himself from the bonds of Mason, by objectifying people and existence, Rayber remains enmeshed. The reader discerns the extent of his captivity most visibly on those occasions when an inexplicable love—usually for Bishop—experienced as a chill or uncontrollable shudder, passes over him. At those moments his "rigid ascetic discipline"—to keep "himself upright on a very narrow line between madness and emptiness" and when necessary to "lose his balance . . . to lurch toward emptiness"—is unsuccessful.[78] Thus, we know that both Tarwater and Rayber have the seeds of hunger deposited in their blood.

The two characters' responses to those seeds, however, move them in apparently contrary directions, creating an Ezekiel-like wheels-within-wheels gyration in the narrative. If we imagine the narrative as a web or a wheel, old Mason and Powderhead lie at its center. Rayber's earlier intellectual rejection of that seemingly dying world has led him far from it, to the edges of the web or circle where he lives in anxious rebellion. When young Tarwater leaves Powderhead upon his uncle's death, he, too, moves outward toward the fringes where Rayber welcomes him and undertakes to conduct him, through a series of trials and disasters, to freedom through psychological enlightenment. Rayber believes he has successfully severed all strands that would hold him to Powderhead. When Tarwater arrives, carrying voices as well as physical resemblances to Mason within him, Rayber's repressions begin to falter. The inner voices that influence Tarwater on his flight from Powderhead eventually move outside his head and finally become incarnated in the homosexual. Rayber, who generally repudiates guidance by inner voices but instead uses words to rationalize and to control, gradually becomes helpless against what he views as Tarwater's compulsions or obsessions. So, ironically, the agent who would offer Tarwater freedom from his past is himself pulled backward and unconsciously conducts Tarwater in the same direction.

One sees evidence of this backward pull in Rayber's desire to take Tarwater to the museum to see his ancestor the fish, which the narrator associates with Mason and Bishop through their eyes. His subsequent decision that a fishing outing would be useful also implies a mysterious pull—both metaphorically and personally—toward a rejected center. Metaphorically, the fishing trip brings to mind biblical references to Christ as fish and to disciples as fishermen. The outing is personally useful for Rayber who recalls once again his own attempt at a distant ocean to drown Bishop; it is also useful for the reader who is forewarned about Tarwater's eventual action. Finally, when Rayber makes the trip to Powderhead *alone*—a trip on which he had intended to force Tarwater to face his guilt about burning his uncle and his foolish devotion to the past—the reader realizes that Rayber, even in his defiance, has been reweaving strands backward to the center of the web.

Because Tarwater carries voices in his head, he is attached, through spider-like verbal filaments, to Powderhead even as he stretches them outward from that center. During most of the narrative Tarwater and Rayber pass each other moving on their strands in opposite directions; but they are inextricably, if tenuously, held together at several points through their dead uncle and through Bishop who "looked like the old man grown backwards to the lowest form of innocence."[79] After the drowning-baptism, Tarwater begins his own return to Powderhead and to freedom, which, O'Connor seems to say, lies in fulfilling one's vocation. Rayber, on the other hand, "Stood waiting for the raging pain, the intolerable hurt that was his due, to begin, so that he could ignore it, but he continued to feel nothing."[80] He has, as he intended, fallen on the side of emptiness.

O'Connor configures the contrary motion produced by the individual verbal resistances of Tarwater and Rayber from a much larger narrative motion. This is the grand, metaphoric motion created, experienced, and foretold between the beginning and the end of time throughout the Bible. One may, of course, read the novel as a bizarre, though compassionately funny, tale of religious fanaticism or psychological obsession. In so doing, one then probably passes over the allusions to biblical prophets like Moses or Jonah or Ezekiel or Elijah, regarding them as excessive externalizations of an author who wanted to supply adequate props for fanaticism. One then must also ignore that O'Connor compresses a span of three generations' history into seven days, beginning not with creation but with death and ending where the narrative began but with a promise of God's eternal mercy. When one, however, observes these elements and how O'Connor lays them into the life fabric of the Tarwaters, she dares to think that the author has kaleidoscopically reset parts of the whole Jewish-Christian myth in an inverted paradise—Powderhead—at some apocalyptic end time when old Mason, returned from wandering in the woods, "would look as if he had been wrestling a wildcat, as if his head were still full of the visions he had seen in its eyes, wheels of light and strange beasts with giant wings of fire and four heads turned to the four points of the universe."[81]

Both Rayber and his nephew spring from Mason Tarwater's line, which through direct statement and metaphors (and many of her own earlier stories) O'Connor connects with another age and space, with "Abel and Enoch and Noah and Job, Abraham and Moses, King David and Solomon, and all the prophets, from Elijah who escaped death, to John whose severed head struck terror from a dish."[82] In his resistance to his call to prophesy and to baptize, young Tarwater is like Jonah; in his fiery vision and protection from the fire that consumes Powderhead, he brings Daniel to mind. Thus, Powderhead becomes metaphorically the center of all creation, the explosive paradise, from which human beings evicted themselves in their quest for knowledge and power and to which biblical patriarchs and prophets have attempted to recall the wayward and the lost.

Perhaps signaling her artistic intention to overlay a modern story about origins and vocation on an ancient one, O'Connor links the biblical account of creation with the Tarwater story and with a mysterious, continuing story of creation through snake images. Soon after Tarwater arrives in the city, expelled from his burned wilderness-garden, he observes his shadow in a store window, "transparent as a snakeskin [which] moved beside him like some violent ghost who had already crossed over and was reproaching him from the other side."[83] The snake metaphor occurs again, though in a much more encompassing way, as Tarwater and Bishop walk toward the dock and the fateful baptism. "The sky was a bright pink, casting such a weird light that every color was intensified. Each weed that grew out of the gravel looked like a live green nerve. *The world might have been shedding its skin*" (emphasis added).[84] Now it appears to Rayber, who watches the two move away into the evening, "that it was Bishop who was doing the leading, that the child had made the capture."[85]

In this partially inverted creation story, there are unmistakable undertones of the "peaceable kingdom" prophesied in Isaiah 11. When knowledge of God reigns, peace or integrity is restored; then the wolf lies down with the lamb, the calf and the lion cub feed together, and a little child leads them. In O'Connor's narrative, ironically, Rayber's idiot child, "the lowest form of innocence," leads Tarwater closer to his integration through the child's own death.

At the end of the novel there is apparently no more resistance in Tarwater. However enigmatic or sinister seeming to post-Christian twentieth-century readers, for whom Rayber's understanding of freedom is more familiar, Tarwater has experienced an integration within himself between the words dropped in his blood as seeds and refuting ones offered by Rayber and other voices. Beyond this integration, O'Connor implies a macrocosmic one by linking him metaphorically with the human narrative told and retold by the hungry. Tarwater "felt his hunger no longer as a pain but as a tide. He felt it rising in himself through time and darkness, rising through the centuries, and he knew that it rose in a line of men whose lives were chosen to sustain it, who would wander in the world, strangers from that violent country where the silence is never broken except to shout the truth."[86] The hunger of this *malgré lui* may be interpreted as the ageless longing for freedom that appears to come, paradoxically, only from being anchored in the true country, a country that encompasses time, physical realities, and boundaries as well as eternity and endless mystery.

Writing in metaphoric language in an age accustomed to description and building stories through flashbacks and tales-within-tales that resemble shed snakeskins or archaeological sites disclosing earlier civilizations and various human adaptations to freedom, Flannery O'Connor finally, in both novels, brings her main characters to silence. Such silence implies the limits of language through which both Haze and Tarwater have resisted and now face the ineffable. For Hazel Motes, silence comes as fulfillment of denunciation that leads ironically to an inverted repetition of the annunciation that proclaimed the incarnation, suffering, and sacrificial death of God's son. The silence at the conclusion of *The Violent Bear It Away* is the silence of resurrection and apocalypse—the promise that God, through the risen Christ, will provide manna in the desert and will be with human beings always. Tarwater and Rayber experience and humorously resist this reality for all who find such a possibility incomprehensible.

We come, finally, to consider the role of O'Connor's prophets with the persistent question: How is one to interpret these verbal backwoods prophets whose rebellion against many religious shibboleths and sacraments ends not in clear conversion but in apparent acquiescence to an overpowering mystery? Those who proclaim the opposite of what haunts them become claimed by the very voices or history they would refuse. By understanding how these prophets function in the specific narratives as well as in relation to the larger narrative O'Connor seems insistently to repeat, we achieve the clearest sense of O'Connor's incarnational art.

The critical dispute over the functions of such characters does not shed much light on the question at hand. Stanley Hyman interprets Satan in all the voices, including Meeks, the truck driver, and the homosexual, that argue with and cajole Tarwater, and he considers Rayber a monk of Satan. Clinton Trowbridge suggests that old Mason and the three drivers should be understood as guides to Tarwater and only the inner voices as Satan's. If we follow this approach, how do we handle the changes in that voice, from stranger to friend, as Tarwater moves closer to what seems to be acceptance of his vocation? Shloss's analysis, especially of old Mason's and young Tarwater's relationship, pays closest attention to the biblical prototype of these two characters. Although they are associated with other biblical figures, particularly prophets, throughout the novel, at the beginning and at the end O'Connor compares them to Elijah and Elisha. Writing about the Elijah-Elisha allusion, Shloss says, "Even if the implications of the allusion are not understood, it is clear that young Tarwater's life is prefigured in the life of his dead uncle."[87] O'Connor's artistic action of prefiguring her modern characters in ancient ones reveals not simply how individual characters function, but more profoundly, if perplexingly, how essential the prophet-trickster and the act of signifying may be to the human imagination in every age and in various religions and literatures.

One of the temptations O'Connor's fiction, particularly the novels, presents is to read the prefigurement to which Shloss refers as merely allegory or analogy rather than anagogy. However, the fact that O'Connor puts wayward or obsessive southern fundamentalists in roles mistakenly associated with characters of assumed divine stature thwarts that temptation as it also unsettles readers who like neat categories of sin and salvation, obedience and faithlessness, inspiration and madness, reality and fantasy. Mason Tarwater and his nephew are not reproductions of Elijah and Elisha; they are antitypes of the Old Testament prophets. Tarwater's flight from and return to Powderhead—a most unlikely holy center—fulfill a biblical notion that "the diffusion of Christianity is symbolically connected with the progress of man back to the garden of Eden and the wandering but guided pastoral world of the twenty-third Psalm, and its type is the figure, frequent in the Psalms, of referring to the temple as the 'tabernacle,' the portable temple of the wilderness."[88] Consequently, Powderhead is not the garden of Eden but a modern antitype of the wilderness that is the unexpected and movable center of all creation and all generations.

An antitype, in the form of a person or event, generally fulfills a type that has been prepared for or has gone before. The Bible presents an extended saga of antitypes culminating in the life of Jesus who is the antitype of the prophets, particularly Moses and Elijah. In the Bible, we find the antitypes participating in and revealing an "upward metamorphosis, of the alienated relation of man to nature transformed into a spontaneous and effortless life—not effortless in the sense of being lazy or passive, but in the sense of being energy without alienation."[89] Because one associates this upward metamorphosis with revelation, it is easier to see how biblical characters or events become antitypes of one another than how O'Connor's one-notioned fundamentalists might be fulfillments of sacred myth. There is, however, another side of the antitype; it may be an opposite expression of an original type as well as a fulfillment. This double possibility contributes to the trickster-like quality of antitypes and makes the interpretation of O'Connor's antitypes easier and consistent with her dependence on irony.

One begins to see how O'Connor, who felt forced "to take ever more violent means to get [her] vision across to [a] hostile audience,"[90] could have shaped from a biblical antitype its modern "opposite." She appears to have used this means with her character, Enoch Emery, whose devotion to the shriveled mummy inverts the biblical Enoch's faithfulness to God. Likewise, if one interprets Rayber as an enlightened, scientific guide for his nephew, he appears to be an opposite antitype of the guiding God in biblical narrative. If, however, one sees him as Satan's agent, he is an antitype that fulfills Satan's role in the modern age. Through the murders they commit, Hazel and Tarwater become fulfilling antitypes for Cain who slayed his brother Abel and for all those who overturn and undermine established orders or codes.

In his defiance of Christ throughout most of *Wise Blood*, Hazel seems to be an antitype set in violent opposition to all the prophets who proclaimed the coming of Christ. Yet, at the end of the novel, in his suffering, which he has taken on himself for the sins of his grandfather, his father, and himself, he moves closer to an ironic fulfillment of Christ. As a voice of God with a strong vengeance drive; with a violent, if accurate, display of marksmanship that keeps Rayber off his property; with an obsession for proper burial rites; and with extraordinary manipulative power, old Mason seems like an opposite, an inversion of the God for whom he supposedly speaks in *The Violent Bear It Away*.

In their resistance to the prophetic seeds dropped in their blood, Rayber and Tarwater fulfill the reluctance of their forebears like Moses or Jonah. Perhaps the violent fluctuation, between fulfillment and its opposite, in antitypes is most evident in the voices that are both inside and outside young Tarwater's head. As words that ridicule and rebuke him for his call to prophesy, they seem to be unmistakable fulfillments of Satan. But when those voices become mysteriously incarnated in the homosexual who abuses Tarwater but leaves him, when he awakes, convinced of his vocation, one gasps at the inversion. Using again the ambiguity of sexuality traditionally associated with tricksters, O'Connor makes the homosexual—one whose sexual orientation is non-procreative and who in this case violates Tarwater— the agent who facilitates his recognition of and assent toward the holy Other who generates new life.

What is perhaps most disturbing about O'Connor's artistic manipulation of antitypes is her use of frail, distorted, theologically narrow, even physically or psychologically grotesque human characters who stand in place sometimes for God and sometimes for God's advocates or messengers. These characters—acquainted with boundaries and living on peripheries, frequently despised or rejected—are yet often enigmatically anchored in a mysterious center which they may or may not fully apprehend and which they may distort. In this position they are akin to the trickster, the go-between who, in reluctance, defiance, or ignorance, shows us our own images and, ironically, pushes others toward dialogue with God, thereby restoring community.

Through her tricksteresque play with words, through a bizarre progression of inverted and fulfilling characters, and through biblical stories of promise and revelation compressed into two fantastic tales of psychological obsession, O'Connor almost imperceptibly turns us through analogies toward anagogical vision. In so doing, she repeats the story of how life is prefigured in death. Freedom for Haze, for Tarwater, as for the prophets before them, and for a hostile modern audience defying death through material consumption and arsenals of weapons ironically intended to secure life, O'Connor believes is prefigured in the incarnation and death of God through Christ. Life reunited with death undermines dependencies on laws, boundaries, conventions, and categories; it gives human beings the overwhelming, mysterious freedom of the "portable temple of the wilderness," the garden wherever the invisible world becomes the medium by which the world becomes visible.[91] Building fiction on anagogical vision and the principles governing light, which remind us that when we see light it is actually in the past, O'Connor is, indeed, a "realist of distances."[92]

O'Connor's trickster-like narratives repeatedly give flesh to words, bring to silence (humble) those who are wise and proud in their own eyes, and reveal the state of apostasy in which both God and human beings dwell when human beings refuse free and full encounter with mystery/God. Creating analogies between ancient stories and modern figures engaged in perennial struggles of longing and resistance, O'Connor then amends and distorts the analogical relationship through techniques associated with signifying. In Ricoeur's terms, O'Connor's narrative configurations, as analogues of historical-mythical events, also intersect with the actual world of the reader. By inverting the analogical relationship between ancient texts and modern life, however, this artist's work explodes our settled notions of literal, objective reality. Gradually she delivers us the disturbing anagogical insight that the phenomenological world we see and know may be a mere approximation of a reality far more mysterious, surprising, and intricately complex. As repetitions of older narratives, O'Connor's fictions attempt to bring characters and readers closer to their true vocations: to be themselves free articulators of truth and citizens of their true country. This goal she accomplishes by producing a confrontation with apocalyptic proportions between "the fictive world of the text and the real world of the reader."[93] With her narrative strategies through which she configures these novels, which are themselves refigurations of history and earlier narratives, O'Connor invites the reader onto the metaphysical ground of Incarnation there to refigure the world of time in relation to the eternal.

Human anxiety about and resistance to this mysterious freedom to live in the phenomenological world while acknowledging the cosmological, however, keep pulling people off center into ego-infected action, dependence on conventions, and mindless allegiance to doctrines and institutions. Such self-destructive defenses "prevent [them] from seeing what kind of world [they] are really in. The real world is beyond time but can be reached only by a process that goes on in time. . . . The Christian Bible is a written book that points to a speaking presence in history, the presence identified as Christ in the New Testament."[94] The possibility for anxieties, resistance, self-inflation, or destruction always accompanies freedom. Such possibility is a reality biblical *mythoi* depict as irony and not tragedy. The imaginations that told, retold, transcribed, and finally collected biblical narratives may be closer to the trickster than the priest or scholar, for the trickster understands that there are no pure motives or pure categories, that good and evil or freedom and slavery are simply two aspects of a seamless, invisible reality. Without the trickster, O'Connor's stories are subject to literary and religious critical demands that have more in common with Plato's concept of *anamnesis* or recollection than with Kierkegaard's idea of repetition.[95] Also, without the trickster, the mythological foundation of western cultures remains closeted in the unconscious, relegated to the "lowest form of innocence," while isolated individuals on the extreme edges of reality substitute discrete knowledge, private experiences, and boundaries for a center that no longer seems to hold.

Reading O'Connor's works as "repetitions" created through trickster antics associated with signification helps to avoid reductionist interpretations that focus on theological doctrine or philosophy of history. Such reading also discourages a too simple conclusion that this erudite author is mocking her fundamentalist characters. O'Connor's repetition of the Christian myth pokes fun compassionately at *all* forms of religious narrowness, whether theologically erudite or fundamentally simple. Her stories challenge doctrine by reminding those who defend it inflexibly that its roots are in the concrete wildernesses of human life, in the life and death struggle, which is self-recreating, for and against freedom or evil. And, at its heart, O'Connor's fiction embodies profound mystery by revealing the inescapable connection between God, who extends freedom to human beings, and those same human beings, whose rejection of that freedom clouds or distorts the perception of God's power, grace, and mercy in proportion to that denial or rejection.

Young Tarwater's struggle to stay "outside" everyone's head, while he is "found" through voices *in* his own head and blood, illustrates this perplexing mystery. O'Connor's artistic triumph is that she exposes this baffling reality by the two ways she uses language. First, in Hazel's and Tarwater's defiant verbal denials that any words connect them to the past, to some collective truth, or to some invisible reality, O'Connor shows a modern audience the state of its own language and the effect on the imagination blocked from renewing movement of a go-between Spirit or of religious sources,[96] which she embeds in modern psyches. Second, through parabolic narratives that juxtapose two different planes of experience, the tangible and the intangible, O'Connor opens the constricted modern consciousness to the unconscious or intuitive in which myth, mystery, and the actions of the Spirit may still operate.

Through the language of the trickster shaping and reshaping narratives, O'Connor reveals how the past continually becomes or is made new. Kierkegaard's concept of repetition as an action of the mind— particularly evident in the trickster—makes meaning and community possible through indirection. Repetition is not designed merely to recall a past experience but rather to bring that past into the present, and through its articulation, to transform the speaker and the hearer in the present. The vehicle of repetition is human language, which constructs or destroys the communal, both between people and between visible and invisible reality.

Language cut off from its mythic, metaphoric sources deprives human beings of self-recreative possibilities that are pointed to in the Bible; without such possibilities, community is undermined. If language is held too rigidly, possessed within narrow boundaries, or used to defend the fearful, it deteriorates into jargons, prejudices, and rationalizations, all of which imprison the imagination, separate and isolate human beings, and impede the flow of the Spirit. Through language, Flannery O'Connor performs a repetition by challenging all categories and conventions that protect her modern readers from mystery. The secret her fiction discloses, however enigmatically, is that modern humanity, while pursuing freedom on all frontiers except the interior one, while expressing its disbelief and defiance with Hazel or Rayber, and while rejecting a Second Coming, may still slouch toward Bethlehem for a "second life," for even defiance is but an inversion of recognition and affirmation and is held within the whole of life.

5

The Artist As Trickster

Tell all the Truth but tell it slant—
Success in Circuit lies
Too bright for our infirm Delight
The Truth's superb surprise
As Lightning to the children eased
With explanation kind
The Truth must dazzle gradually
Or every man be blind—
—Emily Dickinson

The spectacular array of literary devices that animate the structures of Flannery O'Connor's narratives has led us to the trickster whose activities across time and space and in the imagination not only link O'Connor's stories with diverse literatures but also open a discourse between twentieth-century material-rationalist interpretations of reality and ancient folklore and myth. Coming to the end of the examination of her structures and techniques, we ask about the aesthetic and religious implications of these narratives so governed by a primitive presence and assess the artist's integrity of creation. Although a comprehensive description of the trickster's form and function in diverse cultures lies beyond the scope of this book, particular characteristics attributed to him reveal the trickster's utility for O'Connor's artistic and religious purposes and for contemporary literature and postmodern cultures more generally.[1]

As an artist, O'Connor's foremost interest in symbolic forms that might express an experience of Being reminds us that the human ability to create and to use symbols requires a look at the ability to negate. Though some of O'Connor's characters seem not to understand, we know that the word, the metaphor, or the symbol is *not* the thing; they are not literally true. This ability to negate, asserts Barbara Babcock-Abrahams, has not been examined sufficiently in studies of social and artistic metaphors.[2] The capacity for negation is important to O'Connor's works because that capacity makes it possible to "see through," to move beyond the surfaces and closer to the essences of objects and experiences. The capacity to negate permits one to imagine the *what is not* through the *what is* or to recognize in the *what is not* some new or hidden aspect of the *what is*.

The most common and most easily understood form of this capacity to negate is the symbolic inversion that one can observe in " 'rituals of rebellion,' in role reversals, and institutionalized clowning."[3]

> Since the early Renaissance at least, the word "inversion" has been used to mean "a turning upside down" and "a reversal of position, order, sequence, or relation." More specifically, it was used as a synonym for the rhetorical and grammatical figures of metaphor, *anastrophe* (the reversal of the order of words), and *antistrophe* (the turning of an opponent's argument against itself). . . . The concept . . . is even older than the word; the topos of the world upside down, *mundus inversus*, which grows out of stringing together *impossibilia*, is as old as Greek parody of the Homeric journey to Hades.[4]

As an aesthetic negation, a symbolic inversion allows the testing of limits of absolutes, of negative injunctions within any social or cultural system. Broadly defined, the symbolic inversion is "any act of expressive behavior which inverts, contradicts, abrogates, or in some fashion presents an alternative to commonly held cultural codes, values, and norms be they linguistic, literary or artistic, religious, or social and political."[5] In short, the symbolic inversion pushes the boundaries of a culture, enriches the culture "with the subject-matter without which it could not work efficiently, and enables itself to speak about itself."[6]

The ability to speak, to order and reorder, and imaginatively to invert are capacities central to the trickster who is himself a maker of language and literature.[7] As the image of "man individually and communally seizing the fragments of his experience and *discovering* in them an order sacred by its very wholeness,"[8] the trickster reflects operations inherent in the human mind and encountered in the world when one perceives it as an active subject rather than mere object. The image of the trickster springs from the imaginative processes of the human mind that is "itself radically ambiguous, essentially anomalous, inescapably multivalent . . . linking above and below, animal-like and god-like, social cog and individual solitude, shaped and shaping, part of all that is."[9]

Throughout O'Connor's narratives, we note that the language of the trickster, both in word and gesture, is irony. "The one language befitting this image of the imagination in dialogue with all being is the language of irony."[10] The imagination's fundamental task of imagining the real,[11] or as O'Connor might have said, "to embody mystery through manners,"[12] means giving "body to the human relationship to the ultimately real."[13] The ironic imagination, the imagination with its eye Janus-like between mystery (the sacred or transcendental) and matter (daily life), dissolves the division commonly accepted between these two aspects of reality. Such dissolution is achieved through "*the unusual quality of irony* [that] *is the unexpected coexistence,* to the point of identity, of certain contraries."[14] Elaborating on William Lynch's description of irony, Robert Pelton concludes:

> Irony . . . lies in yoking together in a single figure the "most widely separated" opposites in such a way that they are seen to belong together, without losing their contrariness, in a dialectic expressing what is really so and capable of a transformation of the real, which is its fuller embodiment. Of course Lynch is finally thinking of Christ, but Socrates is also such a figure. . . . And in the world of myth we have the figure of the trickster, in whom the anomalous and the ordered, the sacred and the profane, the absurd and the meaningful are joined to create, not merely an ironic symbol, but an image of irony and of the working of the ironic imagination itself.[15]

In the various forms tricksters have taken throughout history we find both a manifest and latent capacity for going-between two groups or two realms or for joining contradictions. In his explication of the ancient Greek figure of Hermes, William Doty highlights six characteristics of Hermes that have also appeared in some of O'Connor's tricksters: "(1) his marginality and paradoxical qualities; (2) his erotic and relational aspects; (3) his functions as a creator and restorer; (4) his deceitful thievery; (5) his comedy and wit; and (6) the role ascribed to him in hermeneutics, the art of interpretation whose name is said to be derived from his."[16] In his ceremonial ministry, Hermes can lead people through rites from one form of experience to another level of

awareness; as a bard or "expert sound-maker," he carries within himself a capacity to interpret the mysterious. The name *Hermes* probably
comes from the Greek word for "stone heap" and underscores
Hermes' ability to move between two points. "The stone heaps were a
primitive sort of boundary-stone, marking a point of communication
between strangers. . . . In primitive Greece, as in other cultures,
where the basic unit of society is not the individual but the family or
clan, religious and social institutions were strongly affected by distrust
of the stranger, the member of an alien family group."[17]

Henry Louis Gates, Jr., connects the trickster figures of the Yoruba
god Esu with Hermes because all these figures, as aspects of Esu, are
primarily mediators and interpreters. Like Hermes, "Esu is guardian
of the crossroads, master of style and the stylus, phallic god of generation and fecundity, master of the mystical barrier that separates the
divine from the profane worlds. He is known as the divine linguist, the
keeper of the *ase (logos)* with which Olodumare created the universe."[18] The function of going between insiders and outsiders or
between realms reminds one of the biblical prophets' role as interpreter of the "inside" message for those still choosing to remain
"outside." This emphasis on elect and alien groups highlights the
social function of a trickster or a prophet; and to the extent that the
herald-trickster permits communication and knowledge to pass between two groups or two realms, his service is beneficent.

The total cultural significance of the classical trickster, including his
social, religious, and psychological roles, is important to understanding Flannery O'Connor's narrative secret. Her desire to embody, in
the concrete lives and language of her twentieth-century southern
fundamentalists, the mystery she found in the midst of contradictions
and violence led her to create variants of trickster figures. Through
the verbal and nonverbal expression of these figures we may find clues
to the origins, the boundaries, and the values of a given community,
society, or culture. Beneath the manifest levels of her narratives we
discover a latent level charged with the residues of folklore and myth
in which tricksters have traditionally operated.

O'Connor's narratives embody secrecy through her method of indirect communication precisely because she wanted to arouse her readers' inward reflection and evoke their dormant ethical capacities. She
understood that direct or ordinary communication could not confront
unbelieving readers with mystery nor deliver them to themselves.
Rather, through artistic configurations that present puzzling, often

grotesque, possibilities to be considered, O'Connor reveals that "the truth which is subjectivity . . . is appropriated in inwardness, in secret, standing alone" often on the margins of society or of religious convention. Disclosed through the activities of the trickster, the secret in O'Connor's narratives is "to prepare oneself for [their] special workings, [their] twofold strategy of divesting us of our publicly shared expectations and roles and compelling us toward our private and primitive selves."[19]

As we allow ourselves to encounter the trickster, we abandon the assumed certainty of inviolate categories and prepare for a contest between good and evil, clarity and obscurity, truth and deception, and the high God and the trickster. We discover in contradictions and fragments of experience an order that is sacred, despite its ambiguity, because of its wholeness. We may be surprised to locate, in the web of the wild and the multidimensional, a world that binds together human and nonhuman, the personal and the cosmic, and the past within the present. When we encounter the tricksters we begin "to ask about animal characters and ritual transformations, the bipolarity of sacred reality, the function of jokes in shaping a culture, the mythicization of the human condition, and the power of divination to find doors in seemingly blank walls."[20]

Our assessment of O'Connor's artistic achievement must be guided by appreciation for the significance of negation and reversals in all symbolic works. O'Connor aids us by the note added to the second edition of *Wise Blood*. In it she poses a question and her response to which all her works bear testimony and by which readers and critics can assess not only her achievement of her artistic intentions but also the implications of that achievement. "Does one's integrity ever lie in what he is not able to do? I think that it usually does."[21] For O'Connor, Hazel Motes's integrity lies in his not being able "to get rid of the ragged figure who moves from tree to tree in the back of his mind."[22] O'Connor's integrity as an artist—one who confessed herself "congenitally innocent of theory" yet who attentively followed preoccupations akin to Hazel's—lies in her use of language to bring us, through fiction, to the common ground literature and religion share: an interest in truth "both in matter and mode," not as an abstraction or in some propositional sense. "The person who aims after art in his work aims after truth, in an imaginative sense, no more and no less," O'Connor asserted.[23] In her aim for truth, she not only engages in contemporary cultural critique through the dissonant and contradictory dialogues of signification established in her narratives; she also provocatively spans vast spatial and temporal distances through an extra-textual dialogue between biblical and medieval conceptions of order and value, on the one hand, and the modern imagination, on the other, as she leads her readers, if not always her characters, to the subjective experience of truth.

O'Connor's interest in truth, expressed repeatedly as an intention to incarnate mystery for an audience and a historical period scornful of mystery, means that the critic must be as concerned with the imagination's role in the interchange between art and mystery as with the technical aspects of her fiction. Indeed, perhaps O'Connor's greatest achievement is the artistic ability she demonstrates to disclose the nature and source of the imagination through the dusty, humble materials of fiction. When O'Connor talks about the matter and mode of truth, she is talking about *imago* and *imitor* from which the word *imagination* comes. *Imago* means a representation or imitation, and *imitor* means to imitate or reproduce. "The imagination imitates the exemplary models—the Images—reproduces, reactualises and repeats them without end. To have imagination is to be able to see the world in its totality, for the power and the mission of Images is to *show* all that remains refractory to the concept."[24] Matter, then, for O'Connor, is the ground from which all images rise, and the mode is the means by which these images are reproduced.

Through words—behind which stands the Image of the Word— O'Connor seeks to *show* us mystery. Although she did not want to talk *about* the ineffable,[25] she recognized that "in the world of time, . . . the way to deal with the ineffable is to speak. Often one proceeds by using language against itself, making it aware of its boundaries, spinning paradoxes and metaphors and myths, setting images before or between mirrors, trying to get the words to see past themselves or the listener to join their battle on that level until he or she can jump levels . . . and see the world correctly."[26] Thus, O'Connor's estranged and haunted characters—from old Gabriel to Mrs. Turpin, from Hazel Motes to Francis Tarwater—*talk* almost obsessively about an old wild cat coming out of the dark, about niggers and a wart hog from hell, about a Christ-less church, or about baptizing an idiot child. Through metaphors like glasses and eyes, fish and seeds, blood and fire spoken by narrator and characters alike, O'Connor exposes the inner states of her characters and presses readers-listeners, through such metaphors, to a level of Being.

O'Connor's efforts to push out the boundaries of the effable toward the ineffable resemble Ricoeur's explication of the problem of time and eternity or the duality of the phenomenological and the cosmological in narratives. Through imaginary variations of temporality or limit-experiences "fiction multiplies our experiences of eternity," he asserts. "By staking out the borderlines of eternity, the limit-experiences depicted by fiction also explore another boundary, that of the borderline between story and myth."[27] In this liminal territory between time and eternity, between story and myth, O'Connor's characters and their circumstances present limit-experiences in the forms of collisions, bizarre fusions, and confrontations that, through irony, turn our attention toward the resonances of myth and eternity.

For O'Connor, to know the world correctly means to recognize the divine (or mystery) at work in the most profane (material); to see the reciprocity of God and human beings; to entertain the possibility of transcending pragmatic history through spiritual history.[28] Therefore, using the metaphors, symbols, and myths associated with the Word becoming flesh, O'Connor turns the prototypic *logos* event upside down. In so doing, she shows her readers the essential meaning of *logos,* a meaning Martin Heidegger charges has been covered up by such interpretations as reason, judgment, concept, definition, ground, relationship, assertion.[29] *Logos* meaning *discourse* restores the connection between Saying and Being, for both words come from the same root. "The word's rule springs to light as that which makes the thing be a thing. . . . The oldest word for the rule of the word . . . , for Saying, is *logos:* Saying which, in showing, lets beings appear in their 'it is.' The same word, however, the word for Saying, is also the word for Being, that is, for the presencing of beings. Saying and Being, word and thing, belong to each other in a veiled way, a way which has hardly been thought and is not to be thought out to the end."[30] In the *logos* event proclaimed in the Bible, God as the pure ground of Being became flesh in order to walk and *talk* among human beings; God (the ineffable) became human (effable) in order to have dialogue or discourse. In O'Connor's fictional world, she begins with "fallen" language and blaspheming people, pushes them to expose—often through grotesqueness—their affiliations with Being, and thereby uses them to disclose mystery.

Through language O'Connor challenges conclusions like Henri Bergson's that there are two profoundly different and separate ways of knowing. The first implies that we move round the object; the second that we enter into it. "The first depends on the point of view at which we are placed and on the symbols by which we express ourselves. The second neither depends on a point of view nor relies on any symbol. The first kind of knowledge may be said to stop at the relative; the second, in those cases where it is possible, to attain the *absolute*."[31] Slowly, almost imperceptibly like a trickster, O'Connor starts around the edges of a technologically infatuated society and with unlikely southern fundamentalist fanatics; she depicts their egotism, satirizes their optimism, ridicules their idols, and uncovers their capacity for evil. Through such depiction and ridicule she exposes the capacity of the mind to relate, to classify, to categorize, and to remember. Her interest, however, lingers only momentarily with such mimesis. Finding appropriate metaphors and symbols, she turns these twentieth-century characters toward biblical antitypes and their conditions to historical-mythological ones. Thus she leads her readers, if not always her characters, beyond relative knowledge toward dialogue in a "space between"—the interstices—where readers and characters alike may encounter the mystery that by being related to each other through speech or manners, they manifest Being.

The connection of Saying and Being is most apparent through the workings of the imagination, which make us aware of our existence in a "space between" and "present us with a vision, not of the personal greatness of the poet, but of something personal and far greater: the vision of a decisive act of spiritual freedom, the vision of the recreation of man."[32] Imprinted in the Image of the Word made flesh is the vision of the decisive spiritual act of freedom which the artist O'Connor cannot resist. The Image of the Word incarnated expresses God's desire for discourse with the created. The narratives, history, and poetry of the Hebrew scriptures declare this longing for conversation. The central incarnational event of Christian belief—the birth, life, death, and resurrection of Jesus Christ—confirmed the hope of many that God would speak in some unmistakable way. But others, who were looking for a more magnificent event, for a king and not a peasant child born on the fringes and for a leader who would decisively trample evil instead of die himself for it, missed or ignored the event. The parables of the rabbi Jesus carry within them the imprint of the Word made flesh, for they simultaneously appear to disclose—to bring hearers close to—the majesty and presence of the Creator and to hide that presence in riddles or secrecy that confound our expectations of a God longing for discourse.

Flannery O'Connor uses the elements of the original event—the Word becoming flesh—as matter and mode for her twentieth-century stories. Indeed, "the 'form' of a parable (that which can be analyzed in terms of internal synchronic relations) is what ensures the survival of meaning after the disappearance of the original historical setting; and that meaning arises from a kind of conversation between the interpreter and the text."[33] Thus, O'Connor imaginatively reinterprets the original Image by embodying the desire for discourse, the tendency toward hiddenness, the peripheral nature of the Christ event, and the almost endless inversions of human expectation which dialogue between the spiritual and the material causes through the devices of humor and deception inherent in tale-making.

In the activities, proclamations, and profanations of the trickster's presence, O'Connor's fiction leads us finally to understand language—the indispensable tool of the trickster—as a game that helps us see into and past illusions. According to Roger D. Abrahams, this game of signifying "refers to the trickster's ability to talk with great innuendo, to carp, cajole, needle, and lie. It can mean in other instances the propensity to talk around a subject, never quite coming to the point. It can mean making fun of a person or situation. Also it can denote speaking with the hands and eyes, and in this respect encompasses a whole complex of expressions and gestures."[34] Through words uttered by characters or by the narrator, the trickster unveils the grand illusion with which most human beings secure themselves: the assumption that we—our earthly places, our possessions, our prejudices, even our principles, and all the activities with which we justify our existence—form the sum of reality.

Functioning within the limited system of the fictional world, living on boundaries, yet appearing to mediate between a finite reality and a limitless, unified one, the trickster pushes O'Connor's narratives, prefigured in ancient ones and in the desire for discourse between consciousness and the unconscious, toward an enlarged and more complex consciousness. As both creator and subverter of limited systems like language, the trickster knows that language cannot contain what Bruce Kawin calls "the timeless essence" but that it "can create the conditions for the timeless to manifest itself."[35] As "spoken" vehicles dependent on irony, the classical goal of which was to return the hearer to the gods, these narratives are a means of discourse between Saying and Being, between the effable and the ineffable.

We conclude from the foregoing analyses of O'Connor's fiction that she creates a special world, one that ironically discloses another dimension through the limits of prevailing twentieth-century secularism and one that mirrors the wonderful game she witnessed in the universe. She demonstrates through her works that "fiction is a system within the system of the human mind, and . . . the human mind either is within or often likes to see itself as being within a larger system that can be explored transcendentally."[36] For O'Connor there is no doubt that the human mind and all that it can imagine or create belongs to a larger system, a unitive sacral reality. In this respect she departs decisively from positivists, rationalists, or existentialists. Because she understands both the grandeur of the human mind and its tendencies toward distortion and deception, she uses its double capacity (as storytellers of diverse ages and traditions have done) to create a closed system through which to open paths to complexity and ambiguity. By limiting her world to southern Baptists and other fundamentalists and by showing characters who are locked into fixed, albeit haunted, minds and embattled by their prejudices or partial visions, she calls attention to those limits and suggests "that there is something more outside the system."[37]

In these narratives, the trickster's role, played sometimes by one or more characters or dispersed as a presence through the narrator's shifting voice, makes visible the limitations and artifice of all closed systems, for which fiction is but a metaphor. By pushing the boundaries of the fictional world toward a "space between," by defying all manner of human conventions, the trickster encourages the reader to suspend belief—not disbelief—in limited perceptions like positivism, fundamentalism, or secularism. Hence, in O'Connor's fictional world, the trickster undertakes to make the reader distrust the absolute authority of the temporal-material world: either by drugs, "overload[ing] the perceptual centers, unfocusing the eyes," or by presenting "reason with something paradoxical and incontestable."[38]

O'Connor uses all these ways. When Haze first puts on his mother's glasses and finally blinds himself, thereby unfocusing his vision; when the homosexual intoxicates Tarwater, thereby stopping his internal dialogue; or when Rayber, a satanic figure, is paradoxically and incontestably pulled back to Powderhead, the reader realizes that the mind can do more than interpret surfaces and that a comprehensive, though mysterious, realm of experience exists. If the trickster succeeds in getting a character or an audience to suspend belief in a particular fictional system of illusions, he makes possible "a void that can be occupied by another category of perception."[39] Ironically, the beliefs O'Connor's tricksters urge us to suspend, through God-intoxicated southerners, are traditional religious notions and conventions, which we say we no longer believe anyway and characterize as "superstition or psychological aberration."[40] These religious notions—warped for generations because people have used them to cloak themselves in self-righteousness, to oppose outsiders, to preserve illusory kingdoms and power, to justify wars rationalized as keeping peace, to domesticate evil, rather than to open themselves to mystery—paradoxically reflect and contribute to the desacralization of the world. Through the funny religious delusions and psychological obsessions of her characters, whom she places against a backdrop of myth and grafts onto biblical antitypes, through personified evil and satanic figures, who operate at the center of her fictional world as often as God, O'Connor's fiction leads us to a silence deeper than all professions or denial of faith, more profound than narrow moralism, and larger than the individual mind.

O'Connor's desire to incarnate mystery puts her texts under pressure, which accrues from trying to show the ineffable through the effable. Though inadequate, one way to deal with such pressure is through "sheer rhetorical excess,"[41] a complaint Shloss levels against *The Violent Bear It Away*.[42] A more successful way to handle such pressure, and the reason the identification of a trickster element in O'Connor's fiction is significant, is for the fiction to become aware of itself as a text—not as an isolated, self-conscious text but as one belonging to the whole tradition of text-making necessitated by the relationship between Saying and Being. For a work to become aware of itself as a text does not necessarily require the self-consciousness of the characters; indeed, the self-consciousness of O'Connor's texts arises from the interplay of narrative techniques we have already examined in her works, on the prefiguring of her narratives in older ones, and on the readers' willing suspension of belief that the limited world of the story, or any closed system, contains the ultimate revelations of life. To the extent that characters or readers do become conscious, however, through O'Connor's texts, that they themselves are "texts" bearing witness—even in folly and violence—to something larger than themselves, they may be saved from estrangement.

Nevertheless, most of O'Connor's adult characters cannot recognize that, though they are part of the phenomenal universe, their beings and the entire universe exist in eternity and participate in the ground of Being or the cosmological. They fail to see their lives as "an integrated series of illusions perpetuated by laziness and ignorance" or fear of freedom;[43] instead, they elevate their limited visions and systems to the level of absolute. Through devices that force us to distance or separate from a character or event portrayed, O'Connor signals her readers that such vision is inevitably partial and hence distorted. We have observed that one way O'Connor creates such distance is by framing many of her stories or telling smaller tales within larger ones. This technique places a character or an event farther from the readers but paradoxically brings us closer to it through our altered view of the circumstances. Her ultimate framing technique, of course, is to set her narratives against or within the biblical saga of the God-human relationship, which makes them seem simultaneously foreign and familiar.

As we have seen, O'Connor's framing technique plus the shifting voice of the narrator define the structure of the stories. The "living" quality of these structures, which points beyond the stories, arises from the trickster who perpetually moves between peripheries and a center. O'Connor reinforces the sense of movement, established in the structure through the tension between fringes and centers and emphasized by the changing narrative voice, by additionally creating a dissonant dialogue between at least two characters with different views of the same situation. One recalls, for example, how Mrs. Shortley and Mrs. McIntyre react to Mr. Guizac, how Mary Fortune Pitts and her grandfather view the woods, how Julian and his mother respond to rising people, how Rayber and Francis regard Mason Tarwater, and how Hazel seeks to be rid of Jesus as Enoch looks in another direction for a new jesus.

Sometimes O'Connor's doubled characters not only show different ways of seeing but also incarnate shadows, which operate in the unconscious and prevent integration (wholeness) within an individual. Additionally, through Protestant fundamentalists, nihilists, and ruthless agents of evil, O'Connor reveals that disintegration may as easily be a collective condition. The capacity for evil and the need for deception increase in proportion to the inability of religious groups, regions, political parties, social classes, or nations to confront collective shadows. Ignoring shared shadows inevitably leads to distorted views of reality, which must be buttressed by intricate webs of illusion.

The trickster-like manipulation of all these devices not only distances readers from the text and helps us perceive its limitations; it also indirectly engages our subjective reflection on ourselves through the stories. Through the differing angles of vision provided by the narrative voice, the author implies that the world of the text itself is not the sum of reality. By showing an unacknowledged subterranean field of activity or lost or forgotten images of an individual or a community, the author makes the text ironically self-conscious. Through all its orifices it says: I am not only what I seem to be. The self-consciousness toward which O'Connor's texts point suggests that there can be no private *self*-consciousness. In orthodox Christian terms this realization constitutes redemption. Full self-consciousness depends on acknowledging and restoring the true condition of humanity.

Flannery O'Connor's artistic ambition to make from the effable a text that would push toward the ineffable seems unmistakable in *The Violent Bear It Away*. By metaphorically linking the road of Tarwater's physical journey away from Powderhead to the tale over which he traveled repeatedly with his great uncle and by juxtaposing Rayber's success in making old Mason "a textbook case" with young Tarwater's efforts not to become a text himself, O'Connor discloses the inevitable struggle between language (Saying) and mystery (Being). Because Rayber like Mrs. Cope, Hulga, Mrs. Hope, Sheppard—all textbook cases themselves in their elevated, hence partial, views of themselves—does not recognize the limits of his sociological rationalism, he also misses the possibility that a text may point to a silence beyond itself. On the other hand, Tarwater instinctively, if fearfully, resists becoming a text. He escapes not through rational argument or by asserting his independent will but because O'Connor links him, through the metaphor of seeds in the blood, with a much larger and mysterious text: the ground of Being from which the prophets before him also sprang.

By joining Saying to Being through metaphoric language drawn heavily from the Bible, by prefiguring her works in former narratives and her prophet-tricksters in biblical prophets, O'Connor creates a repetition of ancient texts, which themselves approached mystery through time, space, and manners. O'Connor's fiction demonstrates that the structure and task of metaphor are to open both readers' minds and texts "for the timeless to manifest itself."[44]

In weaving all these technical threads into narrative webs as dense and paradoxical as O'Connor's, the artist herself functions as a trickster. Although O'Connor never called herself a trickster, she compared the artist to the prophet "when she said that the Lord doesn't speak to the novelist as he did to his servant, Moses, mouth to mouth. Rather, 'he speaks to him as he did to those two complainers, Aaron and Aaron's sister Mary: through dreams and visions, in fits and starts, and by all the lesser and limited ways of the imagination.'"[45] The distinction between the prophet and the trickster is crucial to our understanding of O'Connor's incarnational art. Prophets always live in tension with a community; they are social figures recalling those who wander faithlessly toward the peripheries of heresy back to the center of authority. Their urge is always toward restoration, retrenchment—in the excision of excesses—and stasis. Although the trickster also mediates between realms or between centers and fringes, his impulse is more psychological, dynamic, and subversive than is the prophet's. Under the direction of the trickster, all the narrative devices O'Connor employs contravene many of the conventions that sustain first order ways of knowing such as theological proposition and realistic fiction. Such contraventions yield ambiguity, multiplicity of vision and voice, indirection, and irony. Repeatedly through his antics and reversibility he reminds us that he is not, nor are we, the ultimate image. By spreading strife and undermining everything with which we may try to defend ourselves, he calls us and our sacred institutions and image to *become*—by being reinformed by the numinous—and enter again.

Through the imagination, the artist tries to show that "the roots of every [person's] personality extend beyond the historical area of his factual existence into the world of the numinosum."[46] Eric Neumann, whose works O'Connor knew, described in psychological terms what O'Connor knew as a spiritual problem: that the numinosum, or mystery, can be concealed from the effable by cultural efforts, such as "the advance of specialization and differentiation,"[47] to restrict the intervention of the unpredictable numinous forces and by the tendency to confuse limited systems with the timeless. Thus, the artist, whether as seer, prophet, mystic, or trickster, necessarily mediates between civilization's boundaries, categories, and conventions, on the one hand, and the eternal center that is everywhere, on the other.

What O'Connor embodies in her fiction is the artist's "trick," which reflects in a glass darkly God's "trick." In the Incarnation, God put "himself" under pressure of human limitations by entering time and history in order to point to a center of Being beyond time. In contrast, by calling attention to the artifice and illusions of the fictional world and by prefiguring God-intoxicated backwoods prophets in ancient ones, this artist puts the text (the tale, characters, and readers) under the pressure of eternity. The secret of O'Connor's narratives is that these tricks are mutually dependent, inseparable, and continuous and that without Saying or narration (texts) the presence of Being or Incarnation (mystery) cannot become manifest.

Through fiction that is self-conscious about its own limits and yet strives to communicate the unspeakable, O'Connor gives her readers an opportunity to recognize the limits of egoism. Her works illustrate that "no art is sunk in the self, but rather in art the self becomes self-forgetful in order to meet the demands of the thing seen and the thing being made."[48] Such self-forgetfulness is not the same as self-annihilation, which results from a dualistic outlook that provides no mediation between the spirit and the flesh.[49] Rather, self-forgetfulness, which arises from a vision of one's whole condition, pushes toward fuller consciousness—a rebirth of mystery—where, as Gertrude Stein states in "Henry James," "I am I not any longer when I see."[50]

If such a radical reorientation of vision occurs from O'Connor's works, it does so through the trickster, who not only weaves the narrative but also mediates between the text and reader's minds. Because what a good writer makes "will have its source in a realm much larger than that which his conscious mind can encompass and will always be a greater surprise to him than it can ever be to his reader,"[51] the artist herself performs operations akin to the tricksters. As she configures her texts from rich but forgotten sacred oral traditions, O'Connor offers us a renewed old way to think about narratives and the raconteur. The artist herself becomes a storytelling mediator, offering readers access to past ages and myths or to hidden truths through metaphors and symbols simultaneously drawn from the concrete present and attached to older stories. By so doing she shows us the image of the Word seeking discourse imprinted on our beings and reflected in all our words, even those of denial and defiance. She reminds us that the narrative is a metaphoric kingdom in which contradictions—greed and generosity, good and evil, lust and love, certainty and ambiguity, God and Satan, Misfits and grandmothers—coexist, where the imagination can rearrange the psyche, and where the seen and the unseen play at hiding but are never separated.

To the artist's mediation we must add the reader with whom O'Connor was so preoccupied. To make the eternal "speak" is only one half of Incarnation, as the Magnificat of Luke's gospel illustrates. Without hearing or reading there would be no incarnation, no in-dwelling of the infinite in the finite. In the final analysis, the reader's reading (or hearer's hearing) mediates between the world of the text, under the influence of the trickster, and her own world. By performing mutually dependent operations of imagination, artist and reader open pathways or dialogue between the limits of the text and the informing presence that animates all texts. Such mediation not only gives the literary work its significance but also renders a transformation of vision or refiguration possible.[52]

In the end, we judge Flannery O'Connor's artistic achievement by her own estimation of integrity: "Does one's integrity ever lie in what one is not able to do?" She concluded it does. But unless we understand the significance of the trickster elements in O'Connor's fiction, we will, I think, misjudge both her artistic achievement and her integrity. Through the trickster, who inhabits inner and outer limens with us, O'Connor restores relationship between imagination and reason in an effort to bring us closer to mystery. O'Connor recognized that when reason and imagination are separated, art—and I would add mystery—dies. She witnessed the consequences of this death not merely in atheism, existentialism, or secularism of the twentieth century but also in shallow optimism, self-righteousness, and the widespread "fatuous belief in a highly technological society."[53] She depicts the effects of this separation in her tales about haunted prophets, fundamentalist fanatics, cliché-stuffed matrons, philosophers, and social scientists. Because these characters' minds are filled with distorted self-images, abstractions, or material pursuits, there can be no conversation between reason and the imagination, between the conscious and the unconscious, nor discourse with God. For O'Connor's grotesque representations of the modern human being, God is simply dead, a stumbling block, or an inarticulate ragged figure.

Without perceiving the trickster in O'Connor's stories, readers are prone to condemn her southern fundamentalists for their theological narrowness and lack of sophistication without recognizing the ironic catholicity in all manner of fundamentalisms that legalistically obstruct the transforming winds of the Spirit. Furthermore, without recognizing the trickster's role in these stories, readers may leave them concluding either that they are dark comedies or that O'Connor's Christian vision—because it appears to project suffering and self-annihilation as the only paths to relationship with the divine—is really an existentialist one. Such conclusions (inasmuch as they isolate humor from pain, the unseemly from the beautiful, ignorance from insight, and life from death) reflect the separation of reason and imagination, thereby perpetuating the central problem, egocentrism, that plagues O'Connor's characters and our century.

The trickster, however, elicits from our pretenses and deceits, from the personal unconscious, and from our collective history and myth those shadows deeply repressed and long forgotten through the ascent of rationalism. Through the trickster's capacity to go between realms or levels of perception, O'Connor brings her characters and readers to the stumbling block, which bears suggestive resemblances to the stone heaps that "were a primitive sort of boundary-stone marking a point of communication between strangers" for ancient Greeks.[54] The encounter with the stumbling-block God told in these tales overwhelms most of O'Connor's characters who, as modern human beings, exhibit no integrated reason and imagination to enter into dialogue. But these encounters may remind readers that apocalypse—the confrontation or in-breaking of the holy into the partial—and sacrifice are continuous occurrences without which a sacramental vision of the world is impossible. The sacrifice required is not self-annihilation, for without the self there can be no discourse; it is rather the sacrifice of self-forgetfulness to which we come, sometimes through great pain and loss or through laughter, when we recognize the true range of our history and varieties of our image.

Flannery O'Connor's integrity and her contribution to literature lie in her inability to shake the image of the Word made flesh from her creative being. Through the imprint of this image, itself filled with paradox and irony, O'Connor repeats the Incarnation event that once turned and repeatedly turns the world upside down and may still turn us toward mystery. Through the actions of the trickster, O'Connor reveals to us that nobility and folly share the same space and that freedom lies in being bonded to our true image. By bringing us to a "space between," O'Connor restores conversation between our imagination and our reason and shows us who we are reflected in what we have been and who we may become.

Notes

Introduction

1. Writing about the role of the freak as a hero in an essay "On Her Own Work," Flannery O'Connor concluded that "he is not simply showing us what we are, but what we have been and what we could become." *Mystery and Manners: Occasional Prose,* ed. Sally and Robert Fitzgerald (1957; rpt. New York: Farrar, Straus & Giroux, 1979), 118.

2. Frederick Crews, "The Power of Flannery O'Connor," *New York Review of Books,* 26 April 1990, 49–55.

3. John R. May, "The Methodological Limits of Flannery O'Connor's Critics," *Flannery O'Connor Bulletin* 15 (1986): 16–28.

4. Marion Montgomery, *Why Flannery O'Connor Stayed Home* (LaSalle, Ill.: Sherwood Sugden, 1981).

5. Readers interested in other recent critical works on diverse aspects of Flannery O'Connor's fiction must include in their examination: Jill P. Baumgaertner, *Flannery O'Connor: A Proper Scaring* (Wheaton, Ill.: Harold Shaw Publishers, 1988); John F. Desmond, *Risen Sons: Flannery O'Connor's Vision of History* (Athens: University of Georgia Press, 1987); Stephen G. Driggers and Robert J. Dunn, with Sarah Gordon, *The Manuscripts of Flannery O'Connor at Georgia College* (Athens: University of Georgia Press, 1989); Richard Giannone, *Flannery O'Connor and the Mystery of Love* (Urbana: University of Illinois Press, 1989); Rosemary M. Magee, ed., *Conversations with Flannery O'Connor* (Jackson: University Press of Mississippi, 1987).

6. Robert Coles, *Flannery O'Connor's South* (Baton Rouge: Louisiana State University Press, 1980).

7. In addition to his *Structural Anthropology* cited in note 13, see Claude Lévi-Strauss, *Anthropology and Myth: Lectures 1951–1982* (Oxford: Blackwell, 1982). See also Roland Barthes *et al.,*

Structural Analysis and Biblical Exegesis Interpretational Essays, trans. Aldred M. Johnson, Jr. (Pittsburgh, Pa.: Pickwick Press, 1974); Roland Barthes, *The Rustle of Language,* trans. Richard Howard (New York: Hill & Wang, 1986); Gérard Genette, *Narrative Discourse: An Essay in Method,* trans. Jane E. Lewin (Ithaca: Cornell University Press, 1980); J. Frank Kermode, *The Sense of An Ending: Studies in the Theory of Fiction* (New York: Oxford University Press, 1967); J. Frank Kermode, *The Genesis of Secrecy: On the Interpretation of Narrative* (Cambridge: Harvard University Press, 1979).

8. Susan Sniader Lanser, *The Narrative Act: Point of View in Prose Fiction* (Princeton: Princeton University Press, 1981).

9. May Sarton, *Journal of a Solitude* (New York: W. W. Norton, 1973), 112.

10. Flannery O'Connor, *Mystery and Manners,* 41–42. O'Connor's use of *his* in this quotation, and at numerous other places, reflects the tradition of using masculine terms to refer to both genders. In direct quotations by her and other authors, I have not reformulated the authors' language. However, I prefer making gender-inclusive usage standard in all other places.

11. Frederick Asals, *Flannery O'Connor: The Imagination of Extremity* (Athens: University of Georgia Press, 1982).

12. Marshall Bruce Gentry, *Flannery O'Connor's Religion of the Grotesque* (Jackson: University Press of Mississippi, 1986), and Robert H. Brinkmeyer, Jr., *The Art and Vision of Flannery O'Connor* (Baton Rouge: Louisiana State University Press, 1989).

13. Claude Lévi-Strauss, *Structural Anthropology,* trans. Claire Jacobson and Brooke Grundfest Schoepf (Garden City, N.Y.: Basic Books, 1963).

14. Victor Turner, *The Ritual Process: Structure and Anti-Structure* (Ithaca: Cornell University Press, 1969).

15. Genette, *Narrative Discourse,* 25–32.

16. Paul Ricoeur, *The Rule of Metaphor: Multi-Disciplinary Studies· of the Creation of Meaning in Language* (Toronto: University of Toronto Press, 1977).

17. Henry Louis Gates, Jr., *Figures in Black: Words, Signs, and the "Racial" Self* (New York: Oxford University Press, 1987), and *The Signifying Monkey: A Theory of Afro-American Literary Criticism* (New York: Oxford University Press, 1988).

18. William J. Hynes and William G. Doty, eds., *Mythical Trickster Figures: Contours, Contexts, and Criticisms* (Tuscaloosa: University of Alabama Press, 1993).

19. Russell A. Lockhart, *Psyche Speaks* (Wilmette, Ill.: Chiron Publishers, 1987).

20. Flannery O'Connor acknowledged that elements may arise in a story that are not placed there by an author's conscious intention. "If a writer is any good, what he makes will have its source in a realm much larger than that which his conscious mind can encompass and will always be a greater surprise to him than it can ever be to his reader" (*Mystery and Manners,* 83).

21. Warwick Wadlington, *The Confidence Game in American Literature* (Princeton: Princeton University Press, 1975), 5.

22. C. G. Jung, "On the Psychology of the Trickster-Figure," in *Four Archetypes,* trans. R. F. C. Hull, Bollingen Series (Princeton: Princeton University Press, 1959), 135.

23. See René Girard's *Violence and the Sacred,* trans. Patrick Gregory (Baltimore: Johns Hopkins University Press, 1977), for full explanation of the role of the scapegoat or surrogate victim in rituals of sacrifice.

24. C. Ross Mullins, Jr., "Flannery O'Connor: An Interview," *Jubilee* 11 (June 1963): 32–35, quoted in Magee, *Conversations,* 103.

25. Zhong Ming, "Designed Shock and Grotesquerie: The Form of O'Connor's Fiction," *Flannery O'Connor Bulletin* 17 (1988): 51–61, discusses O'Connor's use of the repetitive form within her own stories that, through restatement and emphasis, contributes to the coherence of her works. In this study I examine how O'Connor's fiction extends this principle of repetition beyond her works.

1. *The Regionless Region*

1. Flannery O'Connor, *Mystery and Manners: Occasional Prose,* ed. Sally and Robert Fitzgerald (1957; rpt. New York: Farrar, Straus & Giroux, 1979), 129.

2. Giles Gunn, ed., *Literature and Religion* (New York: Harper & Row, 1971), 28.

3. Flannery O'Connor, "The Nature and Aim of Fiction," in *Mystery and Manners,* 73.

4. Robert Young, "Post-Structuralism: An Introduction," in *Untying the Text: A Post-Structuralist Reader,* ed. Robert Young (Boston: Routledge and Kegan Paul, 1981), 14.

5. In his "Return of the Poetician," Roland Barthes suggests that Aristotle's *Poetics* "provides the first structured analysis of the levels and the parts of the tragic oeuvre, Valéry . . . insisted that literature be established as an object of language, [and] Jakobson . . . calls *poetic* any message which emphasizes its own verbal signifier." For Genette, "figures are . . . logical forms, manners of discourse, whose field is not only a little group of words but the structure of the text in its entirety; . . . what belongs to the Figure is not only the poetic image but also . . . the form of the narrative, present object of narratology." Roland Barthes, *The Rustle of Language,* trans. Richard Howard (New York: Hill & Wang, 1986), 172. See also Shoshana Felman, "Turning the Screw of Interpretation," *Yale French Studies* 55/56 (1977): 94–207.

6. Robert Alter, *The Art of Biblical Narrative* (New York: Basic Books, 1981), 188.

7. J. Frank Kermode, *The Genesis of Secrecy: On the Interpretation of Narrative* (Cambridge: Harvard University Press, 1979), 23 and 47.

8. Alter, *Art of Biblical Narrative,* 176.

9. Claudio Guillen, "On the Concept and Metaphor of Perspective," in *Literature as System: Essays toward the Theory of Literary History* (Princeton: Princeton University Press, 1971), 310.

10. Flannery O'Connor, "The Grotesque in Southern Fiction," *Mystery and Manners,* 48.

11. Marion Montgomery, "The Prophetic Poet and the Loss of Middle Earth," *Georgia Review* 33 (1979): 66–83. Montgomery argues that Middle Earth was the region where the poet could "sojourn more or less comfortably with his elected audience. . . . [It was] an undoubted country . . . in which mind and heart, reason and feeling, were companionable—a country existing somewhere between the ineffable transcendent and that natural world which the senses constantly speak" (69).

12. Flannery O'Connor, "Novelist and Believer," *Mystery and Manners,* 161.

13. Ellen Reisman Babby, *The Play of Language and Spectacle: A Structural Reading of Selected Texts by Gabrielle Roy* (Toronto: ECW Press, 1985), 5–6.

14. Dan O. Via, Jr., ed., in the Foreword to Daniel Patte, *What is Structural Exegesis?* (Philadelphia: Fortress, 1976), iv.

15. Flannery O'Connor, "Writing Short Stories," *Mystery and Manners,* 93.

16. For fuller discussion of indirect communication see James D. Whitehill, "The Indirect Communication: Kierkegaard and Beckett," in *Art and Religion as Communication,* ed. James Waddell and F. W. Dillistone (Atlanta: John Knox Press, 1974), 79–93. Drawing on Kierkegaard's *Point of View for My Work as an Author: Report to History and Related Writings,* trans. Walter Lowrie, ed. Benjamin Nelson (New York: Harper, 1962), Whitehill claims that the goal of indirect communication is "disabusing men of the illusion that they were Christians and of leading them, hence, to Christianity. . . . The intention of an indirect communication consists, then, in the existential activation of the receiver by presenting him with a possibility that he may choose to incarnate in his existence as he comes to terms with it subjectively" (81).

17. Whitehill, "The Indirect Communication," 82.

18. Ibid., 83.

19. Louise Westling, *Sacred Groves and Ravaged Gardens: The Fiction of Eudora Welty, Carson McCullers, and Flannery O'Connor* (Athens: University of Georgia Press, 1985), 7.

20. Whitehill, "The Indirect Communication," 84.

21. Frederick Asals, *Flannery O'Connor: The Imagination of Extremity* (Athens: University of Georgia Press, 1982), 65–94.

22. Westling, *Sacred Groves and Ravaged Gardens,* 155. See also 157 and 165 for comment upon the problems caused by such inversion.

23. Flannery O'Connor, "A Temple of the Holy Ghost," in *Flannery O'Connor: Collected Works* (New York: Library of America, 1988), 209.

24. Flannery O'Connor, "On Her Own Work," in *Mystery and Manners,* 111.

25. M. Conrad Hyers, "The Dialectic of the Sacred and the Comic," in *Holy Laughter: Essays on Religion in the Comic Perspective*, ed. M. Conrad Hyers (New York: Seabury Press, 1969), 224.

26. Westling formulates a similar idea in her chapter 6, arguing that although O'Connor's landscape and characters could occur nowhere else besides Georgia, by coupling them "with her sacramental view of the natural world as bristling with spiritual meaning" (133), she makes the settings universal.

27. Harvey Breit, Interview with Flannery O'Connor, *Galley Proof*, WRCA TV, New York, May 1955.

28. Flannery O'Connor, "Recollections on My Future Childhood," unpublished essay, File folder 2, Flannery O'Connor Collection, Georgia College, Milledgeville, Georgia.

29. Flannery O'Connor, "The Turkey," in *Collected Works*, 747.

30. In an article entitled "Southern Writers are Stuck with the South," appearing in *Atlanta Magazine* 3 (August 1963) and included in Rosemary M. Magee's *Conversations with Flannery O'Connor* (Jackson: University Press of Mississippi, 1987), the writer reports that O'Connor's "magnificent demon-ridden prophets, raving in an Old Testament world devoid of Grace, 'are images of man forced out to meet the extremes of his own nature'" (110).

31. Westling argues persuasively for her purposes that "A Temple of the Holy Ghost" illustrates O'Connor's ambivalence about sexuality. She cites a letter which O'Connor wrote to A in which she says, "What you say about there being two [sexes] now brings it home to me. I've always believed there were two but generally acted as if there were only one." In this study, the girl child's preoccupation with sexuality and the hermaphrodite recalls the trickster who, in his ability to change sexes, mediates between opposites or between realms.

32. Flannery O'Connor, "Wildcat," in *Collected Works*, 725, 729.

33. O'Connor, "The Turkey," 742, 745.

34. O'Connor, "A Temple of the Holy Ghost," 203, 207.

35. O'Connor, "The Turkey," 741.

36. Ibid., 744.

37. O'Connor, "A Temple of the Holy Ghost," 203.

38. Ibid., 205, 206.

39. The *as if* territory is the province of the trickster. Chapter 2 in Ruthann Knechel Johansen, "The Narrative Secret of Flannery O'Connor: The Trickster As Interpreter" (diss., Drew University, 1983), describes at length the nature of the trickster and the character of the territory over which he presides. Edward Kessler, *Flannery O'Connor and the Language of Apocalypse* (Princeton: Princeton University Press, 1986), subsequently discusses O'Connor's use of *as if* in "The Virtue in *As If*." Readers interested in the philosophical and linguistic subtleties of the *as if (als ob)* construction should see H. Vaihinger, *The Philosophy of 'As if': A System of the Theoretical, Practical and*

Religious Fictions of Mankind, trans. C. K. Ogden (London: Routledge & Kegan Paul, 1924), to which both the present author and Kessler are indebted.

40. Robert D. Pelton, *The Trickster in West Africa: A Study of Mythic Irony and Sacred Delight* (Berkeley: University of California Press, 1980), 258.

41. Søren Kierkegaard, *The Concept of Irony,* trans. Lee M. Capel (Bloomington: Indiana University Press, 1965), 32.

42. Ibid., 268.

43. In "The Nature and Aim of Fiction," O'Connor discusses a writer's need for anagogical vision, which is "the kind of vision that is able to see different levels of reality in one image or one situation" (O'Connor, *Mystery and Manners,* 72).

44. In a little-known essay entitled *Repetition,* Søren Kierkegaard distinguishes between the notion of recollection and his own ideas about repetition, asserting that "when the Greeks said that all knowledge is recollection they affirmed that all that is has been; [however], when one says that life is repetition one affirms that existence which has been now becomes. When one does not possess the categories of recollection or of repetition the whole of life is resolved into a void and empty noise" (*Repetition: An Essay in Experimental Psychology* [1941; rpt. New York: Harper Torchbooks, 1964], 52–53).

45. J. Louis Martyn, "From Paul to Flannery O'Connor with the Power of Grace," *Katallegate* (Winter 1981): 12.

46. Borrowing the term from Arnold van Gennep's concept of *rites de passage,* Victor Turner describes liminality as a process involving separation from the prevailing social structure, experiencing a period of time "on the margins" in which one may be transformed or prepared for another situation or position. In the liminal state one belongs neither here nor there; one is literally "on the edge" or "in transition" between his former status or wisdom and new insight or spiritual power which is yet to come. See especially chapter 3, "Liminality and Communitas," in Victor Turner, *The Ritual Process: Structure and Anti-Structure* (Ithaca: Cornell University Press, 1969), 94–130.

47. Pelton, *The Trickster in West Africa,* 259.

48. Ibid., 258.

49. William Lynch, *Images of Faith: An Exploration of the Ironic Imagination* (Notre Dame: University of Notre Dame Press, 1973), 63.

50. O'Connor, *Mystery and Manners,* 124.

51. Mircea Eliade, *Patterns in Comparative Religion,* trans. Rosemary Sheed (New York: World Publishing, 1963), and *Images and Symbols,* trans. Philip Mairet (New York: Sheed & Ward, 1961), describe magico-religious experience and its relation to symbol making.

52. Pelton, *The Trickster in West Africa,* 262–63.

53. Barbara Babcock-Abrahams, "Liberty's a Whore: Inversions, Marginalia and Picaresque Narratives," in *The Reversible World: Symbolic Inversion in Art and Society,* ed. Barbara Babcock-Abrahams (Ithaca: Cornell University Press, 1978), 14.

54. Several forms of the trickster, and sources in which the reader may learn more about each form, bear mention: Egyptian Seth Typhon as evil contrast to Osiris (D. J. Gifford, "Iconographical Notes Toward a Definition of Medieval Fool," in *The Fool and the Trickster: Studies in Honour of Enid Welsford,* ed. Paul V. A. Williams [Cambridge: D. S. Brewer, 1979]; Hermes as a magician and messenger (Norman O. Brown, *Hermes the Thief: The Evolution of a Myth* [1947; rpt. New York: Vintage, 1969]); Marcolf, a friend and rival of King Solomon (E. G. Duff, *The Dialogue or Communing Between the Wise King Solomon and Marcolphus* [London: Lawrence & Bullen, 1892]); the court or domestic fool, the buffoon, and the disputer fool in both East and West (Enid Welsford, *The Fool: His Social and Literary History* [London: Faber and Faber, 1935]); Wakdujunkaga of the Winnebago Indians (Paul Radin, *The Trickster: A Study in American Indian Mythology* [New York: Philosophical Library, 1956]); Brer Rabbit and other wily creatures (Joel Chandler Harris, *The Complete Tales of Uncle Remus* [Boston: Houghton Mifflin, 1955]); Ananse of Ashanti, Legba of the Fan, Eshu of the Yoruba, and Ogo-Yurugu of the Dogon (Pelton, *The Trickster in West Africa*); Mike Fink or Davy Crockett (Lawrence W. Levine, "'Some Go Up and Some Go Down': The Meaning of the Slave Trickster," in *Hofstadter Aegis: A Memorial,* ed. Stanley Elkins and Eric McKitrick [New York: Alfred A. Knopf, 1974]).

55. Robert H. Brinkmeyer, Jr., *The Art and Vision of Flannery O'Connor* (Baton Rouge: Louisiana State University Press, 1989), 30–34.

56. Richard Pearce, quoting Welsford, *Stages of the Clown* (Carbondale: Southern Illinois University Press, 1970), 3–4.

57. Brinkmeyer, *Art and Vision of Flannery O'Connor,* 14–15.

58. See, for example, "The Tar Baby" (#75) and "Rabbit Deceives the Other Animals" (#76) in *Shem, Ham, and Japheth: The Papers of W. O. Tuggle,* ed. Eugene Current-Garcia and Dorothy B. Hatfield (Athens: University of Georgia Press, 1973), 314–17, versions of which also appear in Harris, *The Complete Tales of Uncle Remus.*

59. Pearce, *Stages of the Clown,* 3–4.

60. Pelton, *The Trickster in West Africa,* 30–31. For the actual *anansem,* see R. S. Rattray, *Akan-Ashanti Folk-Tales* (Oxford: Clarendon Press, 1930).

61. Pelton, *The Trickster in West Africa,* 56–57.

62. Welsford, *The Fool,* 76.

63. Brown, *Hermes the Thief,* 25.

2. *Episodic Tales of Sin*

1. Flannery O'Connor, *The Habit of Being: Letters of Flannery O'Connor,* ed. Sally Fitzgerald (New York: Vintage Books, 1979), 74.

2. See O'Connor's Letters to Robert Giroux dated March 29, 1954; September 3, 1954; November 15 and 30, 1954; December 6 and 11, 1954; February 26, 1955; and March 7, 1955 in *The Habit of Being,* 71–75.

3. Martha Stephens, *The Question of Flannery O'Connor* (Baton Rouge: Louisiana State University Press, 1973), 18. Religious scholars like Preston M. Browning, Jr., *Flannery O'Connor* (Carbondale: Southern Illinois University Press, 1974) and Nathan Scott, "Flannery O'Connor's Testimony: The Pressure of Glory" in *The Added Dimension: The Art and Mind of Flannery O'Connor,* ed. Melvin J. Friedman and Louis A. Lawson (New York: Fordham University Press, 1966, 1977), also pay too little attention to O'Connor's defiance of sacred and secular conventions through humor.

4. Sarah Gordon, "Flannery O'Connor and the Common Reader," *Flannery O'Connor Bulletin* 10 (1981): 44.

5. Ibid.

6. Flannery O'Connor, *Mystery and Manners: Occasional Prose,* ed. Sally and Robert Fitzgerald (1957; rpt. New York: Farrar, Straus & Giroux, 1979), 199.

7. Joel Wells, "Off the Cuff," *Critic* 21 (August–September 1962): 4–5, 71–72; Louis D. Rubin, Jr., moderator, "Recent Southern Fiction: A Panel Discussion," *Bulletin of Wesleyan College* 41 (January 1961); Granville Hicks, "A Writer at Home with Her Heritage," *Saturday Review* 45 (May 12, 1962): 22–23, included in Rosemary M. Magee, ed., *Conversations with Flannery O'Connor* (Jackson: University Press of Mississippi, 1987), 87, 71, and 83.

8. Flannery O'Connor, "A Good Man Is Hard to Find," in *Flannery O'Connor: Collected Works* (New York: Library of America, 1988), 137.

9. Ibid., 138.

10. Ibid., 148.

11. Ibid., 148–49.

12. Ibid., 149.

13. Ibid., 151.

14. Ibid.

15. Mark Sexton, "Flannery O'Connor's Presentation of Vernacular Religion in 'The River,'" *Flannery O'Connor Bulletin* 18 (1989): 3, 10–11.

16. Flannery O'Connor, "The River," in *Collected Works,* 163.

17. Ibid., 165.

18. John R. May, *The Pruning Word: The Parables of Flannery O'Connor* (Notre Dame: University of Notre Dame Press, 1976), 65.

19. O'Connor, "The River," 171.

20. Ibid., 173.

21. Ibid.

22. Katherine Furgin, Faye Rivard, and Margaret Sieh, "An Interview with Flannery O'Connor," *Censer* (Fall 1960): 28–30, included in Magee, *Conversations with Flannery O'Connor,* 58.

23. Flannery O'Connor, "A Late Encounter with the Enemy," in *Collected Works,* 253, 258.

24. Ibid., 253–54.

25. Ibid., 252–53.

26. Rebecca Butler, "What's So Funny About Flannery O'Connor?" *Flannery O'Connor Bulletin* 9 (1980): 37. Butler draws this idea from Louis D. Rubin, ed., *The Comic Imagination in Literature* (New Brunswick: Rutgers University Press, 1973), who explains that in all American comic writing there is an incompatibility of the vulgar and the refined that reflects American attraction to noble ideals but resistance to institutions that embody those ideals.

27. O'Connor, *Mystery and Manners*, 92, 101.

28. Victor Shklovsky, "Art as Technique," *Russian Formalist Criticism: Four Essays*, trans. and ed. Lee L. Lemon and Marion Reis. Cited in Zhong Ming, "Designed Shock and Grotesquerie: The Form of O'Connor's Fiction," *Flannery O'Connor Bulletin* 17 (1988): 56.

29. May, *The Pruning Word*, 194.

30. O'Connor, "A Stroke of Good Fortune," in *Collected Works*, 190.

31. Ibid.

32. Ibid., 186.

33. Ibid., 193.

34. Flannery O'Connor, "A Circle in the Fire," in *Collected Works*, 232–33.

35. Ibid., 233.

36. Ibid., 234.

37. Ibid., 243.

38. Ibid., 250.

39. O'Connor, Letter to Robert Giroux, February 26, 1955, in *The Habit of Being*, 75.

40. Flannery O'Connor, "Good Country People," in *Collected Works*, 264.

41. Ibid., 270–71.

42. Ibid., 271.

43. Ibid.

44. Ibid., 268.

45. Rose Bowen, O.P., "Baptism by Inversion," *Flannery O'Connor Bulletin* 14 (1985): 96.

46. O'Connor, "Good Country People," 281.

47. Ibid., 282.

48. O'Connor, "The River," 161.

49. Ibid., 171.

50. Louise Westling, *Sacred Groves and Ravaged Gardens: The Fiction of Eudora Welty, Carson McCullers, and Flannery O'Connor* (Athens: University of Georgia Press, 1985), 147.

51. Flannery O'Connor, "The Life You Save May Be Your Own," in *Collected Works*, 174.

52. Ibid., 177.

53. Ibid., 181.

54. Ibid., 179.

55. Ibid.

56. O'Connor, "Good Country People," 263.

57. Ibid., 268.

58. Ibid., 267.

59. Ibid., 275.

60. Westling, *Sacred Groves and Ravaged Gardens*, 3, 158, and 174.

61. O'Connor, Letter to "A," February 4, 1961, in *The Habit of Being*, 430.

62. O'Connor, Letter to Janet McKane, February 25, 1963, in *The Habit of Being*, 509.

63. Flannery O'Connor, "The Displaced Person," in *Collected Works*, 290–91.

64. Ibid., 285.

65. Ibid., 288.

66. Ibid., 295.

67. Ibid., 301.

68. Ibid., 305.

69. Job 1:21, *The Jerusalem Bible*.

70. O'Connor, "The Displaced Person," 315.

71. Ibid., 322.

72. Ibid., 318.

73. Ibid., 326.

74. Ibid., 327.

75. O'Connor, "A Circle in the Fire," 232.

76. Ibid., 234.

77. Ibid., 235–36.

78. Ibid.

79. Ibid., 238.

80. Westling, *Sacred Groves and Ravaged Gardens*, 167.

81. O'Connor, "A Circle in the Fire," 241.

82. Ibid., 248.

83. Ibid., 249, 251.

84. May, *The Pruning Word*, 77.

85. Ibid.

86. Flannery O'Connor, "The Artificial Nigger," in *Collected Works*, 210.

87. Ibid., 230.

88. Ibid., 212.

89. Ibid., 230.

90. Ibid., 219, 220–21.

91. Ibid., 228.

92. Ibid., 220.

93. Ibid., 211.

94. Ibid., 225.

95. O'Connor, Letter to "A," August 2, 1955, in *The Habit of Being*, 92.

96. Sarah Gordon, "The News From Afar: A Note on Structure in O'Connor's Narratives," *Flannery O'Connor Bulletin* 14 (1985): 81.

97. Westling labels Tom Shiftlet and Manley Pointer "Christlike" seducers. Because O'Connor subverts our expectations that this will be another story with a "typical . . . come-uppance for a miserly widowed farm owner" which "instead turns into an indictment of the hypocritical robber bridegroom Tom L. Shiftlet and an exposure of misogyny," I think rather that both Shiftlet and Pointer function as trickster figures, imposters of Christ (153).

98. O'Connor, "The Life You Save May Be Your Own," 183.

99. Loxley Nichols, "Shady Folk and Shifty Things," *Flannery O'Connor Bulletin* 14 (1985): 55.

100. O'Connor, "The Displaced Person," 300.

101. Ibid., 315.

102. Ibid., 312.

103. O'Connor, "A Good Man Is Hard to Find," 150.

104. O'Connor, "A Late Encounter with the Enemy," 253.

105. Marion Montgomery, "Grace: A Tricky Fictional Agent," *Flannery O'Connor Bulletin* 9 (1980): 26.

106. Robert H. Brinkmeyer, Jr., *The Art and Vision of Flannery O'Connor* (Baton Rouge: Louisiana State University Press, 1989), 44.

107. Ibid., 51.

108. Ibid.

109. Melody Graulich, "'They Ain't Nothing but Words': Flannery O'Connor's *Wise Blood*," *Flannery O'Connor Bulletin* 7 (1978): 65.

110. Whitehill, "The Indirect Communication," 85.

111. Ibid., 84.

112. Northrop Frye, *Anatomy of Criticism* (Princeton: Princeton University Press, 1957), 140.

113. Carol H. Shloss, *Flannery O'Connor's Dark Comedies* (Baton Rouge: Louisiana State University Press, 1980), 48.

114. Ibid.

115. Ibid.

116. Barbara Herrnstein Smith, *Poetic Closure: A Study of How Poems End* (Chicago: University of Chicago Press, 1968), viii.

117. Paul Ricoeur, *Time and Narrative*, vol. 2, trans. Kathleen McLaughlin and David Pellauer (Chicago: University of Chicago Press, 1985), 20.

3. *A Story Cycle of Communitas*

1. For a theoretical discussion of the relationship among *story, narrative,* and *narrating* see Gérard Genette, *Narrative Discourse: An Essay in Method,* trans. Jane E. Lewin (Ithaca: Cornell University Press, 1980).

2. Carol H. Shloss, *Flannery O'Connor's Dark Comedies* (Baton Rouge: Louisiana State University Press, 1980), 32.

3. Flannery O'Connor, *Mystery and Manners: Occasional Prose,* ed. Sally and Robert Fitzgerald (1957; rpt. New York: Farrar, Straus & Giroux, 1979), 172.

4. Unpublished manuscript of speech by Flannery O'Connor, Georgia College for Women, January 7, 1960; quoted by Kathleen Feeley, *Flannery O'Connor: Voice of the Peacock* (New Brunswick: Rutgers University Press, 1972), 45.

5. Tzvetan Todorov, "Les Catégories du récit littéraire," *Communications* 8 (1966), identifies these devices of narration as tense, aspect, and mood. See also Genette's discussion of Todorov's categories (Genette, *Narrative Discourse,* 29).

6. Nathaniel Hawthorne, *The Complete Works of Nathaniel Hawthorne,* ed. George Parsons Lathrop (Boston: Houghton Mifflin, 1882), III: 13. Shannon Burns describes Flannery O'Connor's indebtedness to Nathaniel Hawthorne in greater detail in "The Literary Theory of Flannery O'Connor and Nathaniel Hawthorne," *Flannery O'Connor Bulletin* 7 (1978): 101–13.

7. Forrest L. Ingram, "O'Connor's Seven Story Cycle," *Flannery O'Connor Bulletin* 2 (1973): 22.

8. Paul Ricoeur, *Time and Narrative,* vol. 2, trans. Kathleen McLaughlin and David Pellauer (Chicago: University of Chicago Press, 1985), 23.

9. Ibid., 25.

10. Ingram's argument that O'Connor's arrangement of stories for *Everything That Rises Must Converge* did not include "Parker's Back" and "Judgment Day" must be revised since the publication of her letters. In several letters to friends and to her editor, Catherine Carver, O'Connor discusses both stories as part of the collection. See particularly Flannery O'Connor, Letter to Catherine Carver, July 15, 1964, *The Habit of Being: Letters of Flannery O'Connor,* ed. Sally Fitzgerald (New York: Vintage Books, 1979), 593.

11. Ingram, "O'Connor's Seven Story Cycle," 20.

12. Ibid., 25.

13. Ibid., 20.

14. O'Connor, *The Habit of Being,* 449.

15. Julian Huxley, "Introduction," in Pierre Teilhard de Chardin, *The Phenomenon of Man,* trans. Bernard Wall (New York: Harper, 1959), 14.

16. Ingram, "O'Connor's Seven Story Cycle," 22.

17. Flannery O'Connor, "A View of the Woods," in *Flannery O'Connor: Collected Works* (New York: Library of America, 1988), 526 and 531.

18. Flannery O'Connor, "The Lame Shall Enter First," in *Collected Works,* 609.

19. Flannery O'Connor, "Revelation," in *Collected Works,* 637.

20. O'Connor, "The Lame Shall Enter First," 617.

21. O'Connor, "Revelation," 644.

22. Robert H. Brinkmeyer, Jr., *The Art and Vision of Flannery O'Connor* (Baton Rouge: Louisiana State University Press, 1989), 64–68.

23. Flannery O'Connor, Author's Note to the Second Edition, *Wise Blood* (1949; New York: Farrar, Straus & Giroux, 1962), n.p.

24. Caroline Gordon, "Rebels and Revolutionaries: The New American Scene," *Flannery O'Connor Bulletin* 3 (1974): 44.

25. Ibid., 48.

26. Ibid., 50.

27. Ibid., 51.

28. Ibid., 52.

29. Frederick Asals, "The Road to *Wise Blood*," *Renascence* 21 (1969): 190.

30. O'Connor, "A View of the Woods," 526.

31. Flannery O'Connor, "Greenleaf," in *Collected Works*, 501.

32. Flannery O'Connor, "Parker's Back," in *Collected Works*, 655.

33. Flannery O'Connor, "Everything That Rises Must Converge," in *Collected Works*, 491.

34. Ibid., 494.

35. Ibid.

36. O'Connor, "Parker's Back," 661.

37. O'Connor, "Everything That Rises Must Converge," 486.

38. Flannery O'Connor, "The Enduring Chill," in *Collected Works*, 571–72.

39. Ibid., 572.

40. O'Connor, "Greenleaf," 501.

41. Shloss, *Flannery O'Connor's Dark Comedies*, 70.

42. O'Connor, "A View of the Woods," 529.

43. Ibid., 542.

44. O'Connor, "Revelation," 638.

45. Ibid., 646.

46. Ibid., 647.

47. Ibid., 652.

48. Flannery O'Connor, "The Comforts of Home," in *Collected Works*, 574–75.

49. O'Connor, "Revelation," 650–51.

50. O'Connor, "The Enduring Chill," 572.

51. O'Connor, "Revelation," 636.

52. O'Connor, "Greenleaf," 522.

53. O'Connor, "Everything That Rises Must Converge," 486.

54. Ibid., 494.

55. O'Connor, "A View of the Woods," 529.

56. O'Connor, "The Enduring Chill," 550.

57. Ibid.

58. O'Connor, "The Lame Shall Enter First," 596.

59. Ibid., 611.

60. Charles Taylor, "Inescapable Frameworks," in *Sources of the Self: The Making of Modern Identity* (Cambridge: Harvard University Press, 1989), 5–24.

61. Ronald Emerick, "Hawthorne and O'Connor: A Literary Kinship," *Flannery O'Connor Bulletin* 18 (1989): 46–54, cites O'Connor's letters to John Hawkes and William Sessions in which she acknowledged her kinship to Haw-

thorne (47). Of special significance to O'Connor's use of tales-within-tales is a statement she made in an interview with Gerald E. Sherry in *Critic* 21 (June–July 1963): "I write 'tales' in the sense Hawthorne wrote tales—though I hope with less reliance on allegory" (quoted in Emerick, 47). Commenting on O'Connor's adaptation of Hawthorne's romance or tale, Emerick confirms what I have been describing as a "space between": "Like Hawthorne, O'Connor conceives of the romance as a borderland between two worlds, the natural and the supernatural, a land suffused with truth and mystery" (49).

62. O'Connor, "The Comforts of Home," 583, 575.

63. Ibid., 575.

64. Robert Giroux expresses this idea in "Introduction," in *The Complete Stories* (New York: Farrar, Straus & Giroux, 1971), xvi.

65. O'Connor, "Parker's Back," 658.

66. Ibid., 659.

67. Ibid., 666.

68. Ibid., 672.

69. Flannery O'Connor, "Judgment Day," in *Collected Works*, 676.

70. John R. May, *The Pruning Word: The Parables of Flannery O'Connor* (Notre Dame: University of Notre Dame Press, 1976), 97.

71. Ibid.

72. O'Connor, "Everything That Rises Must Converge," 500.

73. Ibid., 494.

74. Robert Fitzgerald and Caroline Gordon challenge the prevalent critical notion that O'Connor's understanding of convergence was the same as Teilhard's. Fitzgerald wrote in the preface to *Everything That Rises Must Converge*, p. xxx: "Teilhard's vision of the omega point, virtually at the end of time, or at any rate of a time-span rightly conceivable by the paleontologist alone, has appealed to people to whom it may seem to offer one more path past the Crucifixion. That could be corrected by no sense of life better than O'Connor's. Quite as austere in its way as his, her vision will hold us down to earth where the clashes of blind wills and low dodges of the heart permit any rising or convergence only at the cost of agony. At that cost, yes, a little." Caroline Gordon concluded her lecture, "Rebels and Revolutionaries," subsequently published in *Flannery O'Connor Bulletin* 3 (1974): 40–56, with the following judgment: "I . . . feel sure that Miss O'Connor was fully cognizant of the irony implicit in her title. Everything that rises must converge but everything that converges must have risen" (55).

75. O'Connor, "A View of the Woods," 546.

76. Ibid.

77. C. G. Jung, "On the Psychology of the Trickster-Figure," in *Four Archetypes,* trans. R. F. C. Hull, Bollingen Series (1959; rpt. Princeton: Princeton University Press, 1973).

78. O'Connor, "The Comforts of Home," 575.

79. Ibid., 577.

80. Ibid.

81. May, *The Pruning Word*, 112.

82. O'Connor, "The Lame Shall Enter First," 630.

83. Ibid., 631.

84. Ibid., 632.

85. O'Connor, "Revelation," 645–46.

86. Ibid., 653.

87. Ibid.

88. May, *The Pruning Word*, 120.

89. Flannery O'Connor, "Judgment Day," in *Collected Works*, 681.

90. Ibid., 694; the words quoted here are taken from *The Complete Stories* (New York: Farrar, Straus & Giroux, 1971), 549.

91. Louise Westling, *Sacred Groves and Ravaged Gardens: The Fiction of Eudora Welty, Carson McCullers, and Flannery O'Connor* (Athens: University of Georgia Press, 1985), 164–65.

92. Ibid., 165–66.

93. Ibid., 165.

94. O'Connor, "Greenleaf," 523.

95. O'Connor, "The Enduring Chill," 555.

96. Ibid., 556.

97. Ibid., 572.

98. O'Connor, "Parker's Back," 667.

99. Luke 18:11–12. Revised Standard Version.

100. O'Connor, "A View of the Woods," 526.

101. Anne Doueihi, "Inhabiting the Space Between Discourse and Story in Trickster Narratives," in *Mythical Trickster Figures: Contours, Contexts, and Criticisms,* ed. William J. Hynes and William G. Doty (Tuscaloosa: University of Alabama Press, 1993), 200.

102. See John Hawkes, "Flannery O'Connor's Devil," *Sewanee Review* 70 (Summer 1962): 395–407.

103. O'Connor, "A Good Man Is Hard to Find," 153.

104. Shloss writes that "the calculated absurdity of O'Connor's rendering, the detachment fostered by comic treatment, and the lack of explanations effectively inhibit sympathy or imaginative identification with fictional personality and predicament" (*Flannery O'Connor's Dark Comedies*, 56). Shloss compares *The Violent Bear It Away* to the Old Testament and concludes that O'Connor's narrative is different from the Old Testament because she externalizes everything, even mystery (ibid., 91–93).

105. Edward Kessler, *Flannery O'Connor and the Language of Apocalypse* (Princeton: Princeton University Press, 1986), 62.

106. Thomas Merton, ed., "Gandhi and the One-Eyed Giant," in *Gandhi on Non-Violence* (New York: New Directions, 1964), 12.

107. O'Connor, "Parker's Back," 667.

108. Caroline Gordon, "Heresy in Dixie," *Sewanee Review* 76, no. 2 (1968): 263–97.

109. John F. Desmond, *Risen Sons: Flannery O'Connor's Vision of History* (Athens: University of Georgia Press, 1987).

110. Victor Turner, *The Ritual Process: Structure and Anti-Structure* (Ithaca: Cornell University Press, 1969), 94–130.

4. *The Novels*

1. James G. Murray, "Southland a la Russe," *Critic* 21, no. 6 (June–July 1963): 27.

2. See Judith F. Wynne's, "The Sacramental Irony of Flannery O'Connor," *Southern Literary Journal* 7, no. 2 (Spring 1975): 33–49, for detailed discussion of how this juxtaposition contributes to O'Connor's sophisticated or sacramental irony.

3. Susan Niditch, *Underdogs and Tricksters: A Prelude to Biblical Folklore* (San Francisco: Harper & Row, 1987), xi.

4. Ibid., xiii.

5. For elaboration of the relationship between written songs and remembered ones of oral tradition, see Albert B. Lord, *The Singer of Tales*, Harvard Studies in Comparative Literature, No. 24 (Cambridge: Harvard University Press, 1960; rpt. Atheneum, 1974). Flannery O'Connor not only amended biblical narratives to her stories but also parts from her own earlier work. For example, *Wise Blood* incorporates "The Train," "The Peeler," "The Heart of the Park," and "Enoch and the Gorilla." Her 1955 story, "You Can't Be Any Poorer Than Dead," is worked into *The Violent Bear It Away* in which there are also echoes of "Wildcat" suggested in old Mason's wrestling with a wildcat and in the voices that lurk in young Tarwater's mind and of "The Artificial Nigger" in Mason and Tarwater's visit to the city.

6. The term *intertextuality,* often used to identify sources of a work or to express mere influence of one writer upon another, was originally introduced by Julia Kristeva. "It is defined in *La Révolution du langage poétique* as the transposition of one or more *systems* of signs into another, accompanied by a new articulation of the enunciative and denotative position." Kristeva associates *intertextuality* with *signifying practice,* which she defines as "the establishment and the countervailing of a sign system. Establishing a sign system calls for the identity of a speaking subject within a social framework which he recognizes as a basis for that identity. Countervailing the sign system is done by having the subject undergo an unsettling, questionable process; this indirectly challenges the social framework with which he previously identified." See Julia Kristeva, *Desire in Language: A Semiotic Approach to Literature and Art,* ed. Leon S. Roudiez, trans. Thomas Gora, Alice Jardine, and Leon S. Roudiez (New York: Columbia University Press, 1980), 15, 18.

7. Henry Louis Gates, Jr., *Figures in Black: Words, Signs, and the "Racial" Self* (New York: Oxford University Press, 1987), 49; see also Gates, *The Signifying Monkey: A Theory of Afro-American Literary Criticism* (New York: Oxford University Press, 1988).

8. M. Bernetta Quinn, "Flannery O'Connor, a Realist of Distance," in *The Added Dimension: The Art and Mind of Flannery O'Connor*, ed. Melvin J. Friedman and Lewis A. Lawson (New York: Fordham University Press, 1966, 1977), 181.

9. John R. May, *"The Violent Bear It Away:* The Meaning of the Title," *Flannery O'Connor Bulletin* 2 (Autumn 1973): 86.

10. J. Frank Kermode, *The Genesis of Secrecy: On the Interpretation of Narrative* (Cambridge: Harvard University Press, 1979), 44.

11. Arthur Koestler, "The Jester," in *The Art of Discovery and the Discoveries of Art,* Book I of *The Act of Creation* (New York: Macmillan, 1964), 45.

12. Northrop Frye, *The Great Code: The Bible and Literature* (New York: Harcourt Brace Jovanovich, 1982), 136.

13. Ibid.

14. Flannery O'Connor, *Wise Blood* (1949, 1952; rpt. New York: Farrar, Straus & Giroux, 1962), 105.

15. Frye, *The Great Code,* 137.

16. Ibid.

17. Alexander Jones, ed., "Introduction to the Prophets," *The Jerusalem Bible* (New York: Doubleday & Co., 1966), 1116.

18. Susan Niditch, *Underdogs and Tricksters,* 105–06.

19. Melvin J. Friedman, "Introduction," in *The Added Dimension,* ed. Friedman and Lawson, 12.

20. Frye, *The Great Code,* 169.

21. Ibid., 176.

22. Ibid.

23. O'Connor, *Wise Blood,* 24.

24. Richard Giannone, *Flannery O'Connor and the Mystery of Love* (Urbana: University of Illinois Press, 1989), 38.

25. O'Connor, *Wise Blood,* 56.

26. Flannery O'Connor, *The Violent Bear It Away* (1955; rpt. New York: Farrar, Straus & Giroux, 1979), 242.

27. The reader is referred to J. Louis Martyn, "From Paul to Flannery O'Connor with the Power of Grace," *Katallegate* (Winter 1981): 10–17, previously cited in chapter 1.

28. Giannone, *Flannery O'Connor and the Mystery of Love,* 9.

29. Ibid., 30.

30. Ibid., 19.

31. O'Connor, *Wise Blood,* 34.

32. Ibid., 37.

33. Ibid., 127.

34. Giannone, *Flannery O'Connor and the Mystery of Love,* 24.

35. Stanley Hyman, *Flannery O'Connor,* University of Minnesota Pamphlets on American Writers, No. 54 (Minneapolis: University of Minnesota Press, 1966).

36. Richard Giannone, "The Lion of Judah in the Thought and Design of *The Violent Bear It Away,*" *Flannery O'Connor Bulletin* 14 (1985): 26.

37. Ibid., 30.

38. O'Connor, *The Violent Bear It Away,* 164.

39. Ibid., 165–66.

40. Robert Fitzgerald, "Introduction" to *Everything That Rises Must Converge* (New York: Farrar, Straus & Giroux, 1965), xxvi–xxvii.

41. See Exodus 5:22–23 where Moses charges God with failing to keep his promise.

42. O'Connor, *The Violent Bear It Away,* 65.

43. Kathleen Feeley, *Flannery O'Connor: Voice of the Peacock* (New Brunswick: Rutgers University Press, 1972).

44. O'Connor, *Wise Blood,* 10.

45. Ibid., 231.

46. John R. May, *The Pruning Word: The Parables of Flannery O'Connor* (Notre Dame: University of Notre Dame Press, 1976), 130.

47. O'Connor, *Wise Blood,* 34, 39, 73.

48. O'Connor, *The Violent Bear It Away,* 93.

49. May, *The Pruning Word,* 145.

50. Proverbs 9:17, *The Holy Bible,* Revised Standard Version.

51. O'Connor, *The Violent Bear It Away,* 112.

52. Ibid., 113–14.

53. O'Connor, *Wise Blood,* 141.

54. Ibid., 187.

55. O'Connor, *The Violent Bear It Away,* 145–46.

56. Ibid.

57. Ibid., 216.

58. Mark 8:15–18, *New Oxford Bible.* See both text and notes to Mark 8:14.

59. O'Connor, Author's Note to the Second Edition, *Wise Blood,* n.p.

60. Frye, *The Great Code,* 232.

61. O'Connor, *The Violent Bear It Away,* 139–40.

62. I am indebted to Northrop Frye's descripton of language periods in *The Great Code* (3–30), from which these labels are drawn. Frye turns to Vico who proposes three ages in a cycle of history: a mythical age, a heroic age, and an age of the people, after which there is a return, and the whole process begins again. Each period produces its own kind of language; from Vico's categories Frye develops his: the hieroglyphic (or metaphoric), the hieratic (or metonymic), and the demotic (or descriptive). In the first period, which Frye identifies with most Greek literature before Plato, with the pre-biblical cultures of the Near East, and in much of the Old Testament, "there is relatively little emphasis on a clear separation of subject and object: the

emphasis falls rather on the feeling that subject and object are linked by a common power or energy. . . . Words in such a context are words of power or dynamic forces" (6). In the second period (the hieratic or metonymic), "language is more individualized, and words become primarily the outward expression of inner thoughts or ideas. Subject and object are becoming more consistently separated, and 'reflection,' with its overtones of looking into a mirror, moves into the verbal foreground" (7). The third language period "begins roughly in the sixteenth century. . . . Here we start with a clear separation of subject and object, in which the subject exposes itself, in sense experience, to the impact of an objective world. The objective world is the order of nature; thinking or reflection follows the suggestions of sense experience, and words are the servo-mechanisms of reflection" (13).

63. See Carol H. Shloss's *Flannery O'Connor's Dark Comedies* (Baton Rouge: Louisiana State University Press, 1980) for her argument that O'Connor's stories do not possess the density of biblical narratives (90–92).

64. O'Connor, *Wise Blood*, 22.

65. Ibid., 37.

66. Ibid., 168.

67. Ibid., 53.

68. Ibid., 165.

69. Ibid., 154.

70. Shloss, *Flannery O'Connor's Dark Comedies*, 13.

71. May, *The Pruning Word*, 42.

72. O'Connor, *The Violent Bear It Away*, 57.

73. Ibid., 21.

74. Ibid., 13.

75. Ibid., 192.

76. Ibid., 11.

77. Ibid., 125.

78. Ibid., 115.

79. Ibid., 111.

80. Ibid., 203.

81. Ibid., 8.

82. Ibid., 17.

83. Ibid., 160.

84. Ibid., 197.

85. Ibid.

86. Ibid., 242.

87. Shloss, *Flannery O'Connor's Dark Comedies*, 97.

88. Frye, *The Great Code*, 159.

89. Ibid., 76.

90. Flannery O'Connor, *Mystery and Manners: Occasional Prose*, ed. Sally and Robert Fitzgerald (1957; rpt. New York: Farrar, Straus & Giroux, 1979), 33–34.

91. Frye, *The Great Code*, 124.

92. O'Connor, *Mystery and Manners*, 44.

93. Paul Ricoeur, *Time and Narrative*, vol. 3, trans. Kathleen Blamey and David Pellauer (Chicago: University of Chicago Press, 1988), 159.

94. Frye, *The Great Code*, 76.

95. Based on the principle that all that can be known systematically is the past, *anamnesis* recalls the past in order to understand it; *repetition*, however, is future oriented in that it seeks to give events or experiences from the past reality in the present and thereby to suggest how they may transcend time while experienced anew in different times.

96. John V. Taylor in *The Go-Between God: The Holy Spirit and Christian Mission* (New York: Oxford University Press, 1972), characterizes the Holy Spirit as "going between" God and people and between people, generating awareness and communion.

5. *The Artist As Trickster*

1. For more comprehensive examination of the trickster in various literatures and cultures see "The Universal Trickster" in Ruthann Knechel Johansen, "The Narrative Secret of Flannery O'Connor: The Trickster As Interpreter" (diss., Drew University, 1983). See also other sources cited in bibliography.

2. Barbara Babcock-Abrahams, "Liberty's a Whore: Inversions, Marginalia and Picaresque Narratives," in *The Reversible World: Symbolic Inversion in Art and Society*, ed. Barbara Babcock-Abrahams (Ithaca: Cornell University Press, 1978), 13.

3. Ibid., 14–15.

4. Ibid., 15.

5. Ibid., 14–15.

6. Ibid., 20–21.

7. Robert D. Pelton, *The Trickster in West Africa: A Study of Mythic Irony and Sacred Delight* (Berkeley: University of California Press, 1980), 243.

8. Ibid., 255.

9. Ibid., 258.

10. Ibid., 259.

11. William A. Lynch, *Images of Faith: An Exploration of the Ironic Imagination* (Notre Dame: University of Notre Dame Press, 1973), 63.

12. Flannery O'Connor, *Mystery and Manners: Occasional Prose*, ed. Sally and Robert Fitzgerald (1957; rpt. New York: Farrar, Straus & Giroux, 1979), 124.

13. Pelton, *The Trickster in West Africa*, 258.

14. Lynch, *Images of Faith*, 84–85.

15. Pelton, *The Trickster in West Africa*, 259.

16. William G. Doty, "A Lifetime of Trouble-Making: Hermes As Trickster,"

in *Mythical Trickster Figures: Contours, Contexts, and Criticisms,* ed. William J. Hynes and William G. Doty (Tuscaloosa: University of Alabama Press, 1993), 46.

17. Norman O. Brown, *Hermes the Thief: The Evolution of a Myth* (1947; rpt. New York: Vintage, 1969), 32.

18. Henry Louis Gates, Jr., *Figures in Black: Words, Signs, and the "Racial" Self* (New York: Oxford University Press, 1987), 237.

19. James D. Whitehill, "The Indirect Communication: Kierkegaard and Beckett," in *Art and Religion as Communication,* ed. James Waddell and F. W. Dillistone (Atlanta: John Knox Press, 1974), 85, 90.

20. Pelton, *The Trickster in West Africa,* 259.

21. Flannery O'Connor, Author's Note to the Second Edition, *Wise Blood* (1949, 1952; rpt. New York: Farrar, Straus & Giroux, 1962), n.p.

22. Ibid.

23. O'Connor, *Mystery and Manners,* 65.

24. Mircea Eliade, *Images and Symbols,* trans. Philip Mairet (New York: Sheed & Ward, 1961), 20.

25. *Ineffable* refers to that which cannot be expressed or described in language; hence, that which transcends expression points toward mystery. Throughout this chapter, I use *ineffable* and *mystery* interchangeably in contrast to the *effable,* that which can be uttered and known through language or sense experiences.

26. Bruce Kawin, *The Mind of the Novel: Reflexive Fiction and the Ineffable* (Princeton: Princeton University Press, 1982), 106.

27. Paul Ricoeur, *Time and Narrative,* vol. 3, trans. Kathleen Blamey and David Pellauer (Chicago: University of Chicago Press, 1988), 271.

28. Pragmatic history refers to those external details about a society in the world that can be verified through sciences like anthropology or archaeology; spiritual history refers to a recognition that the world and all societies and individuals participate in a spiritual order of being, which includes but lies beyond pragmatic history and to which human beings and societies may seek to be attuned, even if imperfectly. For fuller understanding of these ideas and his ideas about history as an exodus from civilization, see Eric Voegelin, *Israel and Revelation,* vol. 1 of *Order and History* (Baton Rouge: Louisiana State University Press, 1956).

29. Martin Heidegger, *Being and Time,* trans. John Macquarrie and Edward Robinson (New York: Harper & Row, 1962), 55.

30. Martin Heidegger, "Words," in *On the Way to Language,* trans. Peter D. Hertz (New York: Harper & Row, 1971), 155.

31. Henri Bergson, *An Introduction to Metaphysics,* 2nd ed., trans. T. E. Hulme (Indianapolis: Bobbs-Merrill, Library of Liberal Arts, 1955), 21.

32. Northrop Frye, *Anatomy of Criticism* (Princeton: Princeton University Press, 1957), 94.

33. J. Frank Kermode, *The Genesis of Secrecy: On the Interpretation of Narrative*

(Cambridge: Harvard University Press, 1979), 44, quoting Paul Ricoeur, "Biblical Hermeneutics, *Semeia* 4 (1975): 29–148.

34. Roger D. Abrahams, *Deep Down in the Jungle: Negro Narrative Folklore from the Streets of Philadelphia* (Chicago: Aldine, 1970), 52. For Abrahams's further illustration of the trickster's antics and the "toasts" associated with the signifying monkey, see 113–19, 142–47, and 153–56.

35. Kawin, *The Mind of the Novel*, 137.

36. Ibid., 13.

37. Ibid., 26.

38. Ibid., 86.

39. Ibid., 211.

40. Preston M. Browning, Jr., *Flannery O'Connor* (Carbondale: Southern Illinois University Press, 1974), 9.

41. Kawin, *The Mind of the Novel*, 143.

42. Carol H. Shloss, *Flannery O'Connor's Dark Comedies* (Baton Rouge: Louisiana State University Press, 1980), 91–92.

43. Kawin, *The Mind of the Novel*, 125.

44. Ibid., 137.

45. Charles M. Hegarty, "Prophecy, Mystery, and the Grotesque: Flannery O'Connor's Portrait of the Artist," in *The Word in the World: Essays in Honor of Frederick L. Moriarity,* ed. Richard J. Clifford and George W. MacRae (Cambridge: Weston College Press, 1973), 266–67.

46. Eric Neumann, *Art and the Creative Unconscious,* trans. Ralph Manheim, Bollingen Series 61 (Princeton: Princeton University Press, 1959), 131.

47. Ibid., 97.

48. O'Connor, *Mystery and Manners*, 82.

49. See Frederick Asals, *Flannery O'Connor: The Imagination of Extremity* (Athens: University of Georgia Press, 1982), for a full discussion of O'Connor's dualism.

50. Gertrude Stein, "Henry James," in *Gertrude Stein: Writings and Lectures 1909–1945,* ed. Patricia Meyerowitz (Baltimore: Penguin, 1971), 292.

51. O'Connor, *Mystery and Manners*, 83.

52. For fuller discussion of the mediation of reading see Ricoeur's discussion of mimesis in *Time and Narrative*, vol. 3, especially 241–74.

53. Browning, *Flannery O'Connor*, 14.

54. Brown, *Hermes the Thief,* 32. See also O'Connor's description of God as a stumbling block in *Mystery and Manners*, 161.

Bibliography

Works by Flannery O'Connor

Everything That Rises Must Converge. Intro. Robert Fitzgerald. New York: Farrar, Straus & Giroux, 1965.

Flannery O'Connor: Collected Works. New York: Library of America, 1988.

A Good Man Is Hard to Find and Other Stories. New York: Harcourt, Brace, 1955.

The Habit of Being: Letters of Flannery O'Connor. Ed. Sally Fitzgerald. New York: Vintage Books, 1979.

Mystery and Manners: Occasional Prose. Ed. Sally and Robert Fitzgerald. 1957. Reprint, New York: Farrar, Straus & Giroux, 1979.

"Recollections on My Future Childhood." Unpublished essay, File folder 2, Flannery O'Connor Collection. Georgia College, Milledgeville, Georgia.

The Violent Bear It Away. New York: Farrar, Straus & Giroux, 1960.

Wise Blood. New York: Harcourt, Brace, 1949, 1952. Reprint, Farrar, Straus & Giroux, 1962.

Secondary Sources

Abrahams, Roger D. *Deep Down in the Jungle: Negro Narrative Folklore from the Streets of Philadelphia.* 1st rev. ed. Chicago: Aldine, 1970.

Ahenakew, E. "Cree Trickster Tales." *Journal of American Folklore* 42 (1929): 309–53.

Aichele, George, Jr. *The Limits of Story.* Philadelphia: Fortress Press, 1985.

Alter, Robert. *The Art of Biblical Narrative*. New York: Basic Books, 1981.

Amory, Frederic. *The Entry of the Trickster to the High Cultures of the West*. Folklore Preprint Series, Vol. 5, No. 2. Bloomington: Indiana University Folklore Publications Group, n.d.

Anderson, Bernhard, and Walter Harrelson, eds. *Israel's Prophetic Heritage*. New York: Harper & Brothers, 1962.

Asals, Frederick. "The Double in Flannery O'Connor's Stories." *Flannery O'Connor Bulletin* 9 (1980): 49–84.

———. *Flannery O'Connor: The Imagination of Extremity*. Athens: University of Georgia Press, 1982.

———. "Flannery O'Connor as Novelist: A Defense." *Flannery O'Connor Bulletin* 3 (1974): 23–39.

———. "Hawthorne, Mary Ann, and 'The Lame Shall Enter First.'" *Flannery O'Connor Bulletin* 2 (Autumn 1973): 3–18.

———. "Review of Kathleen Feeley's *Flannery O'Connor: The Voice of the Peacock*." *Flannery O'Connor Bulletin* 1 (1972): 61–65.

———. "The Road to *Wise Blood*." *Renascence* 21, No. 4 (1969): 181–94.

Auerbach, Erich. *Mimesis: The Representation of Reality in Western Literature*. Princeton: Princeton University Press, 1953.

Babby, Ellen Reisman. *The Play of Language and Spectacle: A Structural Reading of Selected Texts by Gabrielle Roy*. Toronto: ECW Press, 1985.

Babcock-Abrahams, Barbara, ed. *The Reversible World: Symbolic Inversion in Art and Society*. Ithaca: Cornell University Press, 1978.

Backus, Emma. "Animal Tales from North Carolina." *Journal of American Folklore* 11 (1898): 284–91.

Bal, Mieke. *Death and Dissymmetry: The Politics of Coherence in the Book of Judges*. Chicago: University of Chicago Press, 1988.

———. *Murder and Difference: Gender, Genre, and Scholarship on Sisera's Death*. Trans. Matthew Gumpert. Bloomington: Indiana University Press, 1988.

———. *On Story-Telling: Essays in Narratology*. Ed. David Jobling. Sonoma, Calif.: Polebridge Press, 1991.

Barthes, Roland. *The Rustle of Language*. Trans. Richard Howard. New York: Hill & Wang, 1986.

———, et al. *Structural Analysis and Biblical Exegesis: Interpretational Essays*. Trans. Alfred M. Johnson, Jr. Pittsburgh: Pickwick Press, 1974.

Baumgaertner, Jill P. *Flannery O'Connor: A Proper Scaring*. Wheaton, Ill.: Harold Shaw Publishers, 1988.

Beidelman, T. O. "The Moral Imagination of the Kaguru: Some Thoughts on Tricksters, Translation, and Comparative Analysis." *American Ethnologist* 7, No. 1 (February 1980): 27–42.

Bergson, Henri. *An Introduction to Metaphysics*. 2nd ed. Trans. T. E. Hulme. Indianapolis: Bobbs-Merrill, Library of Liberal Arts, 1955.

———. *Laughter: An Essay on the Meaning of the Comic*. Trans. Cloudesley Brereton and Fred Rothwell. New York: Macmillan, 1911.

Berlin, Adele. *Poetics and Interpretation of Biblical Narrative.* Sheffield, Eng.: Almond Press, 1983.

Blackwell, Louise. "Flannery O'Connor's Literary Style." *Antigonish Review* 10 (1972): 57–66.

Bloomfield, Leonard. *Menomini Texts.* Publications of the American Ethnological Society, Vol. 12. New York: G. E. Stechert & Co., 1928.

Boas, Franz. *Kwakiutal Culture as Reflected in Mythology.* New York: G. E. Stechert, for the American Folklore Society, 1935.

Botkin, Benjamin A., ed. *Lay My Burden Down: A Folk History of Slavery.* Federal Writers' Project. Chicago: University of Chicago Press, 1945.

Bowen, Rose, O.P. "Baptism by Inversion." *Flannery O'Connor Bulletin* 14 (1985): 94–98.

Breit, Harvey. Interview with Flannery O'Connor. *Galley Proof.* WRCA TV, New York. May 1955.

Brewer, John Mason. *American Negro Folklore.* Chicago: Quadrangle Books, 1972.

Brinkmeyer, Robert H., Jr. *The Art and Vision of Flannery O'Connor.* Baton Rouge: Louisiana State University Press, 1989.

Brooks, Stella Brewer. *Joel Chandler Harris, Folklorist.* Athens: University of Georgia Press, 1950.

Brown, Francis, S. R. Driver, and Charles Briggs, eds. *A Hebrew and English Lexicon of the Old Testament.* Rev. ed. Oxford: Clarendon Press, 1968.

Brown, Norman O. *Hermes the Thief: The Evolution of a Myth.* 1947. Reprint, New York: Vintage, 1969.

Browning, Preston M., Jr. *Flannery O'Connor.* Carbondale: Southern Illinois University Press, 1974.

———. "Flannery O'Connor and the Demonic." *Modern Fiction Studies* 19 (1973): 29–41.

———. "Flannery O'Connor and the Grotesque Recovery of the Holy." In *Adversity and Grace: Studies in Recent American Literature.* Vol. 4 of *Essays in Divinity,* 133–61. Chicago: University of Chicago Press, 1968.

———. "'Parker's Back': Flannery O'Connor's Iconography of Salvation by Profanity." *Studies in Short Fiction* 6 (1969): 525–35.

Burns, Shannon. "The Literary Theory of Flannery O'Connor and Nathaniel Hawthorne." *Flannery O'Connor Bulletin* 7 (1978): 101–13.

Burns, Stuart L. "Flannery O'Connor's *The Violent Bear It Away:* Apotheosis in Failure." *Sewanee Review* 76 (1968): 319–36.

———. "Freaks in a Circus Tent: Flannery O'Connor's Christ-Haunted Characters." *Flannery O'Connor Bulletin* 1 (1972): 1–23.

———. "'Torn By the Lord's Eye': Flannery O'Connor's Use of Sun Imagery." *Twentieth Century Literature* 13 (1967): 154–66.

Buss, Martin J. "The Study of Form." In *Old Testament Form Criticism.* Ed. John H. Hayes, 1–56. San Antonio: Trinity University Press, 1974.

Butler, Rebecca. "What's So Funny About Flannery O'Connor?" *Flannery O'Connor Bulletin* 9 (1980): 30–40.

Campbell, Joseph. *The Hero With a Thousand Faces.* Bollingen Series No. 17. Princeton: Princeton University Press, 1949.

Carroll, Michael P. "Lévi-Strauss, Freud, and the Trickster: A New Perspective Upon an Old Problem." *American Ethnologist* 8, No. 2 (May 1981): 301–13.

Chatman, Seymour, ed. *Approaches to Poetics.* New York: Columbia University Press, 1973.

———. *Literary Style: A Symposium.* New York: Oxford University Press, 1971.

Cheney, Brainard. "Miss O'Connor Creates Unusual Humor Out of Ordinary Sin." *Sewanee Review* 71 (1963): 644–52.

Childs, Brevard S. "Midrash and the Old Testament." In *Understanding the Sacred Text: Essays in Honor of Norton S. Enslin on the Hebrew Bible and Christian Beginnings.* Ed. John Reumann, 45–59. Valley Forge: Judson Press, 1972.

Christensen, Abigail. *Afro-American Folk-Lore.* Boston: J. G. Cupples, 1892.

Clements, Ronald E. *One Hundred Years of Old Testament Interpretation.* Philadelphia: Westminster Press, 1976.

Clinis, David J. A., David M. Gunn, and Alan J. Hauser, eds. *Art and Meaning: Rhetoric in Biblical Literature.* Sheffield: Journal for the Study of the Old Testament Supplement Series 19, 1982.

Coffin, Tristram P., ed. *Indian Tales of North America: An Anthology for the Adult Reader.* Bibliography and Special Series, Vol. 13. Philadelphia: American Folklore Society, 1961.

Coles, Robert. *Flannery O'Connor's South.* Baton Rouge: Louisiana State University Press, 1980.

Crews, Frederick. "The Power of Flannery O'Connor." *New York Review of Books,* 26 April 1990, 49–55.

Culley, Robert C. *Studies in the Structure of Hebrew Narrative.* Philadelphia: Fortress Press, 1976.

———. "Themes and Variations in Three Groups of Old Testament Narratives." *Semeia* 3 (1975): 3–13.

Davis, Jack, and June Davis. "Tarwater and Jonah: Two Reluctant Prophets." *Xavier University Studies* 9, No. 1 (1970): 19–27.

Desmond, John F. *Risen Sons: Flannery O'Connor's Vision of History.* Athens: University of Georgia Press, 1987.

Detweiler, Robert. "The Curse of Christ in Flannery O'Connor's Fiction." *Comparative Literature Studies* 3 (1966): 235–45.

Dixon, Roland B. "Some Coyote Stories from the Maidu Indians of California." *Journal of American Folklore* 13 (1900): 267–70.

Dobie, James Frank, Mody C. Boatright, and Harry H. Ransom, eds. *Coyote Wisdom.* Texas Folklore Society Publications, No. 14. Dallas: Southern Methodist University Press, 1938.

Dorson, Richard M. *American Negro Folktales.* New York: Fawcett, 1967.

Douay-Rheims Version of The Holy Bible. Rockford: Tan Books and Publishers, 1899.

Driggers, Stephen G., and Robert J. Dunn, with Sarah Gordon. *The Manuscripts of Flannery O'Connor at Georgia College.* Athens: University of Georgia Press, 1989.

Driskell, Leon V., and Joan T. Brittain. *The Eternal Crossroads: The Art of Flannery O'Connor.* Lexington: University of Kentucky Press, 1971.

Duff, E. G. *The Dialogue or Communing Between the Wise King Solomon and Marcolphus.* London: Lawrence & Bullen, 1892.

Dundes, Alan. "African Tales Among the North American Indians." *Southern Folklore Quarterly* 29 (1965): 207–19.

Eggenschwiler, David. *The Christian Humanism of Flannery O'Connor.* Detroit: Wayne State University Press, 1972.

———. "Flannery O'Connor's True and False Prophets." *Renascence* 21 (1969): 151–61.

Eliade, Mircea. *Images and Symbols.* Trans. Philip Mairet. New York: Sheed & Ward, 1961.

———. *Patterns in Comparative Religion.* Trans. Rosemary Sheed. New York: World Publishing, 1963.

———. *The Quest: History and Meaning in Religion.* Chicago: University of Chicago Press, 1969.

———. *The Sacred and the Profane: The Nature of Religion.* Trans. Willard R. Trask. New York: Harper Torchbooks, 1961.

Emerick, Ronald. "Hawthorne and O'Connor: A Literary Kinship." *Flannery O'Connor Bulletin* 18 (1989): 46–54.

Espinosa, Aurelio. "Notes on the History of the Tar-Baby." *Journal of American Folklore* 56 (1943): 129–209.

Fahey, William A. "Out of the Eater: Flannery O'Connor's Appetite for Truth." *Renascence* 20 (1967): 22–29.

Farmer, David. *A Descriptive Bibliography of the Works of Flannery O'Connor.* New York: Burt Franklin/Lenox Hill, 1976.

Farmer, Kathleen Anne. "The Trickster Genre in the Old Testament." Diss. Southern Methodist University, 1978.

Farnham, James F. "Disintegration of Myth in the Writings of Flannery O'Connor." *Connecticut Review* 8, No. 1 (1974): 11–19.

———. "Flannery O'Connor and the Incarnation of Mystery." *Cross Currents* 20 (1970): 252–56.

Feeley, Kathleen. *Flannery O'Connor: Voice of the Peacock.* New Brunswick: Rutgers University Press, 1972.

Feldman, Shammai. "Biblical Motives and Sources." *Journal of Near Eastern Studies* 22 (1963): 73–103.

Felman, Shoshana. "Turning the Screw of Interpretation." *Yale French Studies* 55/56 (1977): 94–207.

Fitzgerald, Sally R. "The Country Side and the True Country." *Sewanee Review* 70 (1962): 380–94.

Fowlie, Wallace. *Clowns and Angels.* New York: Sheed & Ward, 1943.

Frazer, James George. *Folklore in the Old Testament: Studies in Comparative Religion, Legend, and Law.* 3 vols. London: Macmillan, 1919.

Freud, Sigmund. *Complete Psychological Works,* Vol. 14. Trans. James Strachey. London: Hogarth Press, 1957.

———. *Wit and Its Relation to the Unconscious.* Book 4 of *The Basic Writings of Sigmund Freud.* Trans. and ed. A. A. Brill. New York: Random House, 1938.

Friedman, Melvin J. "Flannery O'Connor: Another Legend in Southern Fiction." *English Journal* 51 (1962): 233–43.

Friedman, Melvin J., and Lewis A. Lawson, eds. *The Added Dimension: The Art and Mind of Flannery O'Connor.* New York: Fordham University Press, 1966, 1977.

Frye, Northrop. *Anatomy of Criticism.* Princeton: Princeton University Press, 1957.

———. *The Great Code: The Bible and Literature.* New York: Harcourt Brace Jovanovich, 1982.

Furgin, Katherine, Faye Rivard, and Margaret Sieh. "An Interview with Flannery O'Connor." *Censer* (Fall 1960): 28–30; included in Magee, *Conversations with Flannery O'Connor,* 58–60.

Gaster, Theodor H. *Myth, Legend and Custom in the Old Testament: A Comparative Study, with Chapters from Sir James G. Frazer's "Folklore in the Old Testament."* New York: Harper & Row, 1969.

Gates, Henry Louis, Jr. *Figures in Black: Words, Signs, and the "Racial" Self.* New York: Oxford University Press, 1987.

———. *The Signifying Monkey: A Theory of Afro-American Literary Criticism.* New York: Oxford University Press, 1988.

Geertz, Clifford. "Deep Play: Notes on a Balinese Cockfight." *Daedalus* 101 (1972): 1–38.

Genette, Gérard. *Narrative Discourse: An Essay in Method.* Trans. Jane E. Lewin. Ithaca: Cornell University Press, 1980.

Gennep, Arnold van. *Rites of Passage.* Trans. Monika B. Vizedom and Gabrielle L. Caffee. Chicago: University of Chicago Press, 1960.

Gentry, Marshall Bruce. *Flannery O'Connor's Religion of the Grotesque.* Jackson: University Press of Mississippi, 1986.

Getz, Lorine M. *Flannery O'Connor: Her Life, Library and Book Reviews.* Vol. 5 of *Studies in Women and Religion* New York: Edwin Mellen, 1980.

Giannone, Richard. *Flannery O'Connor and the Mystery of Love.* Urbana: University of Illinois Press, 1989.

———. "The Lion of Judah in the Thought and Design of *The Violent Bear It Away.*" *Flannery O'Connor Bulletin* 14 (1985): 25–32.

Girard, René. *Violence and the Sacred.* Trans. Patrick Gregory. Baltimore: Johns Hopkins University Press, 1977.

Giroux, Robert. Introduction. *The Complete Stories,* by Flannery O'Connor, vii–xvii. New York: Farrar, Straus & Giroux, 1971.

Glatzer, Nahum N., ed. *The Dimensions of Job: A Study and Selected Readings.* New York: Schocken Books, 1969.

Golden, Robert E., and Mary C. Sullivan. *Flannery O'Connor and Caroline Gordon: A Reference Guide.* Boston: G. K. Hall, 1977.

Goldziher, Ignaz. *Mythology Among the Hebrews and Its Historical Development.* Trans. Russell Martineau. 1877. Reprint, New York: Cooper Square Publishers, 1967.

Good, Edwin M. *Irony in the New Testament.* Philadelphia: Westminster Press, 1965.

Gordon, Caroline. "Heresy in Dixie." *Sewanee Review* 76, No. 2 (1968): 263–97.

———. "Rebels and Revolutionaries: The New American Scene." *Flannery O'Connor Bulletin* 3 (1974): 40–56.

Gordon, Sarah. "Flannery O'Connor and the Common Reader." *Flannery O'Connor Bulletin* 10 (1981): 38–45.

———. "The News From Afar: A Note on Structure in O'Connor's Narratives." *Flannery O'Connor Bulletin* 14 (1985): 80–87.

Graulich, Melody. "'They Ain't Nothing but Words': Flannery O'Connor's *Wise Blood.*" *Flannery O'Connor Bulletin* 7 (1978): 64–83.

Gray, Louis Herbert, gen. ed. *The Mythology of All Races.* 13 vols. Boston: Marshall Jones Co., 1916–32.

Green, James L. "Enoch Emery and His Biblical Namesakes in *Wise Blood.*" *Studies in Short Fiction* 10 (1973): 417–19.

Gregorius I. *The Dialogues of Gregory the Great,* Book II: *Saint Benedict.* Uhlfelder. Indianapolis: Bobbs-Merrill Co., 1967.

Gregory, Donald. "Enoch Emery: Ironic Doubling in *Wise Blood.*" *Flannery O'Connor Bulletin* 4 (1975): 52–64.

Greisch, J. R. "Violent Shakings of Grace." *Christianity Today,* July 26, 1977, 19–20.

Guardini, Roman. *The Church and the Catholic and the Spirit of the Liturgy.* New York: Sheed & Ward, 1967.

———. *Freedom, Grace, and Destiny.* New York: Pantheon, 1961.

Guillen, Claudio. *Literature as System: Essays Toward the Theory of Literary History.* Princeton: Princeton University Press, 1971.

Gunkel, Hermann. "Jacob." In *What Remains of the Old Testament and Other Essays.* Trans. A. K. Dallas. New York: Macmillan, 1928.

———. *The Legends of Genesis: The Biblical Saga and History.* Trans. W. H. Carruth. New York: Schocken Books, 1964.

Gunn, Giles. *The Interpretation of Otherness: Literature, Religion, and the American Imagination.* New York: Oxford University Press, 1979.

———, ed. *Literature and Religion.* New York: Harper & Row, 1971.

Harris, Joel Chandler. *The Complete Tales of Uncle Remus.* Boston: Houghton Mifflin, 1955.

Harrison, Margaret. "Hazel Motes in Transit: A Comparison of Two Versions of Flannery O'Connor's 'The Train' with Chapter 1 of *Wise Blood.*" *Studies in Short Fiction* 8 (1971): 287–93.

Hawkes, John. "Flannery O'Connor's Devil." *Sewanee Review* 70, No. 3 (Summer 1962): 395–407.

Hegarty, Charles M. "Prophecy, Mystery and the Grotesque: Flannery O'Connor's Portrait of the Artist." In *The Word in the World: Essays in Honor of Frederick Moriarity.* Ed. Richard J. Clifford and George W. MacRae, 257–69. Cambridge: Weston College Press, 1973.

Heidegger, Martin. *Being and Time.* Trans. John Macquarrie and Edward Robinson. New York: Harper & Row, 1962.

———. *On the Way to Language.* Trans. Peter D. Hertz. New York: Harper & Row, 1971.

Hendin, Josephine. "In Search of Flannery O'Connor." *Columbia Forum* 13, No. 1 (1970): 38–41.

———. *The World of Flannery O'Connor.* Bloomington: Indiana University Press, 1970.

Hicks, Granville. "A Writer at Home with Her Heritage." *Saturday Review* 45 (May 12, 1962): 22–23; included in Magee, *Conversations with Flannery O'Connor,* 81–84.

Hieb, Louis. "Meaning and Mismeaning: Toward an Understanding of the Ritual Clown." In *New Perspectives on the Pueblo.* Ed. Alfons Ortiz, 163–96. Albuquerque: University of New Mexico Press, 1972.

Hoffman, Frederick J. *The Art of Southern Fiction: A Study of Some Modern Novelists.* Carbondale: Southern Illinois University Press, 1967.

Hopper, Stanley R. "Irony—the Pathos of the Middle." *Cross Currents* 12, No. 1 (1962): 31–40.

Hudson, Charles. *The Southeastern Indians.* Knoxville: University of Tennessee Press, 1976.

Huelsbeck, Charles J. "Of Fiction, Integrity, and Peacocks." *Catholic World,* December 1969, 128.

Hughes, Langston, and Arna Bontemps. *The Book of Negro Folklore.* New York: Dodd, Mead, 1958.

Huxley, Julian. Introduction. *The Phenomenon of Man,* by Pierre Teilhard de Chardin. Trans. Bernard Wall. New York: Harpers, 1959.

Hyers, M. Conrad, ed. *Holy Laughter: Essays on Religion in the Comic Perspective.* New York: Seabury Press, 1969.

Hyman, Stanley. *Flannery O'Connor.* University of Minnesota Pamphlets on

American Writers, No. 54. Minneapolis: University of Minnesota Press, 1966.

Hynes, William J., and William G. Doty, eds. *Mythical Trickster Figures: Contours, Contexts, and Criticisms.* Tuscaloosa: University of Alabama Press, 1993.

Ingram, Forrest L. "O'Connor's Seven Story Cycle." *Flannery O'Connor Bulletin* 2 (1973): 19–28.

"Introduction to the Prophets." *The Jerusalem Bible.* New York: Doubleday, 1966.

Jaynes, Julian. *The Origin of Consciousness in the Breakdown of the Bicameral Mind.* Boston: Houghton Mifflin, 1976.

Jeremy, Sister. "The Comic Ritual of Flannery O'Connor." *Catholic Library World* 39 (1967): 195–200.

Johansen, Ruthann Knechel. "The Narrative Secret of Flannery O'Connor: The Trickster As Interpreter." Diss. Drew University, 1983.

Jung, C. G. *Answer to Job.* Vol. 11 of *The Collected Works of C. G. Jung.* Bollingen Series. Princeton: Princeton University Press, 1958.

———. "On the Psychology of the Trickster-Figure." In *Four Archetypes.* Trans. R. F. C. Hull. Bollingen Series. 1959. Reprint, Princeton: Princeton University Press, 1973.

———. *Psyche and Symbol.* New York: Doubleday Anchor, 1958.

Kawin, Bruce. *The Mind of the Novel: Reflexive Fiction and the Ineffable.* Princeton: Princeton University Press, 1982.

Kerenyi, Karoly. *Hermes, Guide of Souls: The Mythologem of the Masculine Source of Life.* Zurich: Spring Publications, 1976.

Kermode, J. Frank. *The Genesis of Secrecy: On the Interpretation of Narrative.* Cambridge: Harvard University Press, 1979.

———. *The Sense of an Ending: Studies in the Theory of Fiction.* New York: Oxford University Press, 1967.

Kessler, Edward. *Flannery O'Connor and the Language of Apocalypse.* Princeton: Princeton University Press, 1986.

Kierkegaard, Søren. *The Concept of Irony.* Trans. Lee M. Capel. Bloomington: Indiana University Press, 1965.

———. *Point of View for My Work As an Author: Report to History and Related Writings.* Trans. Walter Lowrie. Ed. Benjamin Nelson. New York: Harper, 1962.

———. *Repetition: An Essay in Experimental Psychology.* Trans. Walter Lowrie. Princeton: Princeton University Press, 1941. Reprint, New York: Harper Torchbooks, 1964.

Kinney, Arthur. *Flannery O'Connor's Library: Resources of Being.* Athens: University of Georgia Press, 1985.

Klapp, Orrin. "The Clever Hero." *Journal of American Folklore* 67 (1954): 21–34.

Koestler, Arthur. "The Jester." In *The Art of Discovery and the Discoveries of Art*. Book I of *The Act of Creation*. New York: Macmillan, 1964.

Kristeva, Julia. *Desire in Language: A Semiotic Approach to Literature and Art*. Ed. Leon S. Roudiez. Trans. Thomas Gora, Alice Jardine, and Leon S. Roudiez. New York: Columbia University Press, 1980.

Lanser, Susan Sniader. *The Narrative Act: Point of View in Prose Fiction*. Princeton: Princeton University Press, 1981.

Lawson, Lewis A. "Flannery O'Connor and the Grotesque: *Wise Blood*." *Renascence* 17 (1965): 137–47, 156.

Leach, Edmund. *Genesis as Myth and Other Essays*. London: Jonathan Cape, 1969.

Levine, Lawrence W. "'Some Go Up and Some Go Down': The Meaning of the Slave Trickster." In *Hofstadter Aegis: A Memorial*. Ed. Stanley Elkins and Eric McKitrick, 94–124. New York: Alfred A. Knopf, 1974.

Lévi-Strauss, Claude. *Anthropology and Myth: Lectures 1951–1982*. Oxford: Blackwell, 1982.

———. *The Savage Mind*. Trans. George Weidenfeld and Nicolson Ltd. The Nature of Human Society Series. Chicago: University of Chicago Press, 1966.

———. *Structural Anthropology*. Trans. Claire Jacobson and Brooke Grundfest Schoepf. Garden City, N.Y.: Basic Books, 1963.

Lewis, R. W. B. *The Picaresque Saint*. Philadelphia: J. B. Lippincott, 1959.

Lockhart, Russell A. *Psyche Speaks*. Wilmette, Ill.: Chiron Publishers, 1987.

Longstreet, Augustus Baldwin. *Georgia Scenes*. New York: Harper & Brothers, 1897.

Lord, Albert B. *The Singer of Tales*. Harvard Studies in Comparative Literature, No. 24. 1960. Reprint, New York: Atheneum, 1974.

Lowie, Robert H. "The Hero-Trickster Discussion." *Journal of American Folklore* 1 (1888): 97–108.

Lynch, William A. *Images of Faith: An Exploration of the Ironic Imagination*. Notre Dame: University of Notre Dame Press, 1973.

McCown, Robert. "Flannery O'Connor and the Reality of Sin." *Catholic World*, January 1959, 285–91.

McDowell, Frederick P. "Toward the Luminous and the Numinous: The Art of Flannery O'Connor." *Southern Review* 9 (1973): 998–1013.

Magee, Rosemary M., ed. *Conversations with Flannery O'Connor*. Jackson: University Press of Mississippi, 1987.

Mano, D. Keith. Review of *Mystery and Manners*. *New York Times Book Review*, May 25, 1969, 6–7, 20.

Martin, Carter W. "Comedy and Humor in Flannery O'Connor's Fiction." *Flannery O'Connor Bulletin* 4 (1974): 1–12.

———. *The True Country: Themes in the Fiction of Flannery O'Connor*. Nashville: Vanderbilt University Press, 1969.

Martyn, J. Louis. "From Paul to Flannery O'Connor with the Power of Grace." *Katallegate* (Winter 1981): 10–17.

May, John R. "Flannery O'Connor and the New Hermeneutic." *Flannery O'Connor Bulletin* 2 (1973): 29–42.

———. "Flannery O'Connor: Critical Consensus and the 'Objective' Interpretation." *Renascence* 27 (1975): 179–92.

———. "Language—Event as Promise: Reflections on Theology Literature." *Canadian Journal of Theology* 16 (1970): 129–39.

———. "The Methodological Limits of Flannery O'Connor Critics." *Flannery O'Connor Bulletin* 15 (1986): 16–28.

———. "Of Huckleberry Bushes and the New Hermeneutic." *Renascence* 24 (1972): 85–95.

———. *The Pruning Word: The Parables of Flannery O'Connor.* Notre Dame: University of Notre Dame Press, 1976.

———. *Toward a New Earth: Apocalypse in the American Novel.* Notre Dame: University of Notre Dame Press, 1972.

———. "*The Violent Bear It Away:* The Meaning of the Title." *Flannery O'Connor Bulletin* 2 (Autumn 1973): 83–86.

Mayer, David R. "*The Violent Bear It Away:* Flannery O'Connor's Shaman." *Southern Literary Journal* 4, No. 2 (1972): 41–54.

Merton, Thomas. *Raids on the Unspeakable.* New York: New Directions, 1966.

———, ed. "Gandhi and the One-Eyed Giant." *Gandhi on Non-Violence: A Selection from the Writings of Mahatma Gandhi.* New York: New Directions, 1964.

Ming, Zhong. "Designed Shock and Grotesquerie: The Form of O'Connor's Fiction." *Flannery O'Connor Bulletin* 17 (1988): 51–61.

Montgomery, Marion. "Flannery O'Connor: Prophetic Poet." *Flannery O'Connor Bulletin* 3 (1974): 79–94.

———. "Flannery O'Connor's Territorial Center." *Critique: Studies in Modern Fiction* 11, No. 3 (1969): 5–10.

———. "Grace: A Tricky Fictional Agent." *Flannery O'Connor Bulletin* 9 (1980): 19–29.

———. "O'Connor and Teilhard de Chardin: The Problem of Evil." *Renascence* 22 (1969): 34–42.

———. "The Prophetic Poet and the Loss of Middle Earth." *Georgia Review* 33 (1979): 66–83.

———. *Why Flannery O'Connor Stayed Home.* LaSalle, Ill.: Sherwood Sugden, 1981.

Mullins, C. Ross, Jr. "Flannery O'Connor: An Interview." *Jubilee* 11 (June 1963): 32–35; included in Magee, *Conversations with Flannery O'Connor,* 103.

Murray, James G. "Southland a la Russe." *Critic* 21, No. 6 (June–July 1963): 26–28.

Napier, Bunyan Davie. *From Faith to Faith: Essays on Old Testament Literature.* New York: Harper & Brothers, 1955.

Neumann, Eric. *Art and the Creative Unconscious.* Trans. Ralph Manheim. Bollingen Series 61. Princeton: Princeton University Press, 1959.

New Oxford Annotated Bible. Ed. Herbert G. May and Bruce M. Metzger. New York: Oxford University Press, 1962.

Nichols, Loxley. "Shady Talk and Shifty Things." *Flannery O'Connor Bulletin* 14 (1985): 44–58.

Niditch, Susan. *Underdogs and Tricksters: A Prelude to Biblical Folklore.* San Francisco: Harper & Row, 1987.

Nouwen, Henri. *Clowning in Rome: Reflections on Solitude, Celibacy, Prayer, and Contemplation.* New York: Image Books of Doubleday, 1979.

Oates, Joyce Carol. "Realism of Distance and Realism of Immediacy." *Southern Review* 7 (1971): 295–313.

———. "The Visionary Art of Flannery O'Connor." *Southern Humanities Review* 7 (1973): 235–46.

Orvell, Miles. *Invisible Parade: The Fiction of Flannery O'Connor.* Philadelphia: Temple University Press, 1972.

Oster, Harry. "Negro Humor: John and Old Marster." *Journal of the Folklore Institute* 5 (1968): 42–57.

Palmer, Parker. "*Lectio Divina:* Another Way to Learn." *Pendle Hill Bulletin,* No. 322, October 1981.

Patte, Daniel. *What Is Structural Exegesis?* Philadelphia: Fortress, 1976.

Pearce, Richard. *Stages of the Clown.* Carbondale: Southern Illinois University Press, 1970.

Pelton, Robert D. *The Trickster in West Africa: A Study of Mythic Irony and Sacred Delight.* Berkeley: University of California Press, 1980.

Petersen, David L. "A Thrice-told Tale: Genre, Theme, and Motif." *Biblical Research* 18 (1973): 30–43.

Poirier, Richard. *The World Elsewhere: The Place of Style in American Literature.* New York: Oxford University Press, 1966.

Radin, Paul. "Religion of the North American Indians." *Journal of American Folklore* 27 (1914): 335–73.

———. *The Trickster: A Study in American Indian Mythology.* New York: Philosophical Library, 1956.

———. *The World of Primitive Man.* New York: Henry Schuman, 1953.

Rappeport, Angelo Solomon. *Myth and Legend of Ancient Israel.* 3 vols. London: Gresham Publishing Co., 1928.

Rattray, R. S. *Akan-Ashanti Folk-Tales.* Oxford: Clarendon Press, 1930.

Regalado, Nancy Freeman. "Tristan and Renart: Two Tricksters." *L'Esprit Créateur* 16, No. 1 (Spring 1976): 30–38.

Reichard, Gladys A. *Navajo Religion: A Study of Symbolism.* 2 vols. Bollingen Series 18. New York: Pantheon Books, 1950.

Ricketts, Mac Linscott. "The North American Indian Trickster." *History of Religions* 5 (1965): 327–50.

———. "The Structure and Religious Significance of the Trickster-Transformer-Culture Hero in the Mythology of the North American Indians." Diss. University of Chicago, 1964.

Ricoeur, Paul. *The Rule of Metaphor: Multi-Disciplinary Studies of the Creation of Meaning in Language.* Toronto: University of Toronto Press, 1977.

———. *Time and Narrative.* Vols. 1–3. Trans. Kathleen McLaughlin and David Pellauer. Chicago: University of Chicago Press, 1984, 1985, 1988.

Rosenthal, Bernard. "Herman Melville's Wandering Jews." In *Puritan Influences in American Literature.* Ed. Emory Elliott. Urbana: University of Illinois Press, 1979.

Rubin, Louis D., Jr., ed. *The Comic Imagination in Literature.* New Brunswick: Rutgers University Press, 1973.

———, moderator. "Recent Southern Fiction: A Panel Discussion." *Bulletin of Wesleyan College* 41 (January 1961); included in Magee, *Conversations with Flannery O'Connor,* 61–78.

Sandmel, Samuel. "The Haggada Within Scripture." *Journal of Biblical Literature* 80 (1961): 105–22.

———. *The Hebrew Scripture: An Introduction to Their Literature and Religious Ideas.* New York: Alfred A. Knopf, 1963.

Sandoz, Ellis. "Eric Voegelin and the Nature of Philosophy." *Modern Age* 13 (Spring 1969): 152–68.

Sarton, May. *Journal of a Solitude.* New York: W. W. Norton, 1973.

Schmerler, Henrietta. "Trickster Marries His Daughter." *Journal of American Folklore* 44 (1931): 196–207.

Scholes, Robert E. *The Fabulators.* New York: Oxford University Press, 1967.

———. *Structuralism in Literature: An Introduction.* New Haven: Yale University Press, 1974.

Scholes, Robert E., and Robert Kellogg. *The Nature of Narrative.* New York: Oxford University Press, 1966.

Scouten, Kenneth. "The Mythological Dimensions of Five of Flannery O'Connor's Works." *Flannery O'Connor Bulletin* 2 (1973): 59–72.

Sexton, Mark. "Flannery O'Connor's Presentation of Vernacular Religion in 'The River.'" *Flannery O'Connor Bulletin* 18 (1989): 1–12.

Shaw, Joy Farmer. "The South in Motley: A Study of the Fool Tradition in Selected Works by Faulkner, McCullers, and O'Connor." Diss. University of Virginia, 1977.

Sherry, Gerald E. "An Interview with Flannery O'Connor." *Critic* 21, No. 6 (June–July 1963): 29–31.

Shklovsky, Victor. "Art as Technique." *Russian Formalist Criticism: Four Essays.* Trans. and ed. Lee L. Lemon and Marion Reis. Lincoln: University of Nebraska Press, 1965.

Shloss, Carol H. *Flannery O'Connor's Dark Comedies.* Baton Rouge: Louisiana State University Press, 1980.

Smith, Barbara Herrnstein. *Poetic Closure: A Study of How Poems End.* Chicago: University of Chicago Press, 1968.

Smitten, Jeffrey R., and Ann Daghistany, eds. *Spatial Form in Narrative.* Ithaca: Cornell University Press, 1981.

Sonnenfeld, Albert. "Flannery O'Connor: The Catholic Writer as Baptist." *Contemporary Literature* 13 (1972): 445–57.

Spivey, Ted R. "Flannery O'Connor's South: Don Quixote Rides Again." *Flannery O'Connor Bulletin* 1 (1972): 46–53.

———. "Flannery O'Connor's View of God and Man." *Studies in Short Fiction* 1 (1964): 200–06.

Stafford, John. "Patterns of Meaning in *Nights With Uncle Remus.*" *American Literature* 18 (1946): 89–108.

Stein, Gertrude. *Gertrude Stein: Writings and Lectures 1909–1945.* Ed. Patricia Meyerowitz. Baltimore: Penguin, 1971.

Stephens, Martha. *The Question of Flannery O'Connor.* Baton Rouge: Louisiana State University Press, 1973.

Sternberg, Meir. *The Poetics of Biblical Narrative: Ideological Literature and the Drama of Reading.* Bloomington: Indiana University Press, 1985.

Swan, Jesse G. "Flannery O'Connor's Silence-Centered World." *Flannery O'Connor Bulletin* 17 (1988): 82–89.

Tate, Allen. "Remarks on the Southern Religion." In *I'll Take My Stand: The South and the Agrarian Tradition.* By Twelve Southerners, 155–75. 1930. Reprint, New York: Harper Torchbooks, 1962.

Taylor, Charles. *Sources of the Self: The Making of the Modern Identity.* Cambridge: Harvard University Press, 1989.

Taylor, John V. *The Go-Between God: The Holy Spirit and the Christian Mission.* New York: Oxford University Press, 1972.

Teilhard de Chardin, Pierre. *The Divine Milieu.* New York: Harper & Brothers, 1960.

———. *The Phenomenon of Man.* Trans. Bernard Wall. Intro. Julian Huxley. New York: Harper, 1959.

Todorov, Tzvetan. "Les Catégories du récit littéraire." *Communications* 8 (1966).

———. *The Fantastic: A Structural Approach to a Literary Genre.* Trans. Richard Howard. Cleveland: Press of Case Western Reserve University, 1973.

———. *Literature and Its Theorists: A Personal View of Twentieth Century Criticism.* Trans. Catherine Porter. Ithaca: Cornell University Press, 1984.

———. *Symbolism and Interpretation.* Trans. Catherine Porter. Ithaca: Cornell University Press, 1982.

Tolomeo, Diane. "Flannery O'Connor's 'Revelation' and the Book of Job." *Renascence* 30 (1978): 78–90.

Trowbridge, Clinton. "The Comic Sense of Flannery O'Connor: Literalist of the Imagination." *Flannery O'Connor Bulletin* 12 (1983): 77–92.

———. "The Symbolic Vision of Flannery O'Connor: Patterns of Imagery in *The Violent Bear It Away.*" *Sewanee Review* 76 (1968): 298–318.

True, Michael D. "Flannery O'Connor: Backwoods Prophet in the Secular City." *Papers on Language and Literature* 5 (1969): 209–23.

Tuggle, W. O. *Shem, Ham and Japheth: The Papers of W. O. Tuggle.* Ed. Eugene Current-Garcia with Dorothy B. Hatfield. Athens: University of Georgia Press, 1973.

Turner, Victor. *The Ritual Process: Structure and Anti-Structure.* Ithaca: Cornell University Press, 1969.

Vaihinger, H. *The Philosophy of 'As if': A System of the Theoretical, Practical and Religious Fictions of Mankind.* Trans. C. K. Ogden. London: Routledge & Kegan Paul, 1924.

Van Seters, John. *Abraham in History and Tradition.* New Haven: Yale University Press, 1975.

Via, Dan O., Jr. *Kerygma and Comedy in the New Testament: A Structuralist Approach to Hermeneutic.* Philadelphia: Fortress Press, 1975.

———. Foreword. *What Is Structural Exegesis?* by Daniel Patte. Philadelphia: Fortress, 1976.

Voegelin, Eric. *Israel and Revelation.* Vol. 1 of *Order and History.* Baton Rouge: Louisiana State University Press, 1956.

———. "Postscript: On Paradise and Revolution." *Southern Review* 7 (1971): 25–48.

Waddell, James, and F. W. Dillistone, eds. *Art and Religion as Communication.* Atlanta: John Knox Press, 1974.

Wadlington, Warwick. *The Confidence Game in American Literature.* Princeton: Princeton University Press, 1975.

Walters, Dorothy. *Flannery O'Connor.* Twayne's United States Authors Series, No. 216. New York: Twayne Publishers, 1973.

Wells, Joel. "Off the Cuff." *Critic* 21 (August–September 1962): 4–5, 71–72; included in Magee, *Conversations with Flannery O'Connor,* 85–90.

Welsford, Enid. *The Fool: His Social and Literary History.* London: Faber and Faber, 1935.

Westling, Louise. *Sacred Groves and Ravaged Gardens: The Fiction of Eudora Welty, Carson McCullers, and Flannery O'Connor.* Athens: University of Georgia Press, 1985.

Wharton, James A. "The Secret of Jahweh: Story and Affirmation in Judges 13–16." *Interpretation* 27 (1973): 48–66.

Whitehill, James D. "The Indirect Communication: Kierkegaard and Beckett." In *Art and Religion as Communication.* Ed. James Waddell and F. W. Dillistone. Atlanta: John Knox Press, 1974.

Willeford, William. *The Fool and His Scepter: A Study in Clowns and Jesters and Their Audience*. Evanston, Ill.: Northwestern University Press, 1969.

Williams, Paul V. A., ed. *The Fool and the Trickster: Studies in Honour of Enid Welsford*. Cambridge: D. S. Brewer, 1979.

Wolfe, Bernard. "Uncle Remus and the Malevolent Rabbit." In *Mother Wit from the Laughing Barrel: Readings in the Interpretation of Afro-American Folklore*. Ed. Alan Dundes, 25–40. Englewood Cliffs: Prentice-Hall, 1973.

Wynne, Judith F. "The Sacramental Irony of Flannery O'Connor." *Southern Literary Journal* 7, No. 2 (Spring 1975): 33–49.

Young, Robert, ed. *Untying the Text: A Post-Structuralist Reader*. Boston: Routledge and Kegan Paul, 1981.

Zuber, Leo J., and Carter W. Martin, eds. *The Presence of Grace and Other Book Reviews*. Athens: University of Georgia Press, 1983.

Index